Greg Raymer

Greg Raymer has enjoyed tremendous success as a poker player, enjoying a winning career both live and online, in cash games and tournaments, that has spanned three decades.

He has career tournament cashes in excess of $8 million, has won a few dozen tournaments, including several major events, and made the final table in numerous other tournaments.

You can follow him online at www.Twitter.com/FossilMan, and contact him at his website, www.FossilManPoker.com.

Praise for *FossilMan's Winning Tournament Strategies* and Greg Raymer

Having played a lot with Greg over the years, I know he plays a great game. Having taught with Greg, I know he's even better at teaching poker. But what really sets Greg apart is his skill at the final table. He has won over 30% of the times he made the final 9, and has won 70% of the times he made the final 3 in a no-limit or pot-limit game! Amazing!

Joe Hachem

Everyone knows Greg won the WSOP in 2004. What you might not know is that he came back the next year and almost won it again! Add in his 4 HPT titles, and Greg has a great all-around tournament track record. Greg takes a logical and mathematical approach to the game and teaches that approach very well. He has taught for the WSOP Academy and held his own boot camps around the country for years helping players improve. This book will help any tournament player to improve their game.

Chris Moneymaker

Greg Raymer came out of nowhere to win the WSOP Main Event. Then he backed it up with two more deep Main Event runs, and impressed me! Greg has continued to impress with many more deep runs and wins.

Phil Hellmuth

FOSSILMAN'S
WINNING
TOURNAMENT
STRATEGIES

GREG RAYMER

POKER

First published in 2019 by D&B Publishing

British Library Cataloguing-in-Publication Data
A catalogue record for this book is available from the British Library.
ISBN: 978 1 912862 01 6

Cover and book design by Horacio Monteverde.
Printed and bound by Versa Press in the US.

All sales enquiries should be directed to D&B Publishing:
info@dandbpoker.com

POKER
www.dandbpoker.com

CONTENTS

ACKNOWLEDGEMENTS

The most important person in my life, and the one I need to thank the most, is my lovely wife Cheryl. She puts up with my stupidity, laziness, and other negative traits, and still sees the best in me. Our daughter Sophie is also important to thank, as my poker career took me away from her so much. Instead of being a 9-5 attorney for a big company, I have been on the road half the time these last 13 plus years. That has been a sacrifice for all of us. This has been the major regret of winning the Main Event, this time away from them. It is hard to balance, as I love them both so much, but also love poker. Thank you, my lovely ladies, for your help in my life, and your sacrifices for me.

Without my parents, where and who would I be? Unfortunately, we lost my dad in 2015, so he did not get to see this book, one of the many reasons I regret not finishing it sooner. But my mom is still with us, is very healthy, and I hope she is happy to see this, even though she doesn't play poker. You can find her in Hendon Mob, however, as she and I cashed in the Jack-and-Jill tournament at WinStar in 2010. She really had no idea how to play, so I just kept an eye on her stack, and gave her a range of hands with which to shove. So, whenever it was her turn, she would either fold, or go all-in, but only doing so if she had a strong enough hand given the size of her stack. It was a lot of fun, and she was very excited to win us some money. They were great parents, giving me love and support, believing in me in all that I did, and teaching me many important life lessons. I owe it all to you, mom and dad!

For the earliest parts of my poker education, I can thank rec.gambling. poker and the RGP newsgroup, as well as the BARGE community. You guys were always fun, and debating strategy with you online helped me become so much better at this game we love. After that, I was a regular poster on the twoplustwo.com poker forums, and learned even more there. It is still today the best place to go online for poker discussions with the world. And there have been so many friends throughout the years, players who discussed and debated strategy with me, growing us both as players. There are so many that I feel like I can't name even one, or 10, of you, as I'm going to forget to mention so many others, and will feel guilty about it. You know who you are!

For this book, I very much want to thank my friends Preston Oade and Peter Priest, for their time and effort in reviewing the rough draft, and all of their great suggestions on how to make it better. Preston in particular prac-tically wrote a couple of chapters himself, with all of his notes, suggestions, and commentary on the text. I also want to mention Marc Reeves and my brother Brian Raymer for their help in the formatting and editing of the book. Thank you all!

And finally, my gratitude to you, the reader, for buying this book and taking the time to read it. I have always loved teaching, and will be thrilled to hear your feedback, even if it is too late to change the book. I would also enjoy hearing your stories, especially if this book improved your game, and helped you achieve some great results on the felt!

PREFACE

Somewhere as a schoolkid, I learned the rules of poker. But to be honest, I have no recollection of when exactly that happened. I do know that by the time I was in college, living in the Kappa Sigma fraternity house at the University of Missouri at Rolla, I did know the basic rules of poker games like seven card stud and 5 card draw. I didn't play much poker in college, just a friendly game maybe 1-3 times per year in somebody's room. We played for very small stakes, literally betting with pocket change, nickels, dimes, and quarters; and we played with very little skill. I'm sure we thought we were real men, playing a real man's game, and that we were good at it, but we were all pretty clueless as to correct winning strategy.

After graduating with my chemistry degree, I moved north to attend graduate school at the University of Minnesota. Even though it was an infrequent activity, I had always enjoyed those poker games at the frat house, and I would invite friends over to my apartment and do the same thing while attending graduate, and later Law school, at the U*. Just like at Rolla, we

---

* Maybe because the state of Minnesota has no other nationally famous colleges or universities, the University of Minnesota is commonly referred to as "the U".

FOSSILMAN'S WINNING TOURNAMENT STRATEGIES

would play crazy games like night baseball, anaconda, and pass-the-trash. We still used coins instead of chips, and still played with very little skill. But it was always a good time, and I won more than I lost. Not that it ever added up to much at those stakes. Not even much by the standards of a poor student.

One Christmas, an aunt gave me an interesting gift, a book titled *The World's Greatest Blackjack Book*[*]. This book taught the rules of blackjack, basic strategy, and a lot about card counting. Using this book and others, I became a winning card counter at the relatively new tribal casinos near the Twin Cities. Instead of waiting tables or some other such typical student job to make extra money, I drove to the casinos and counted cards, winning about $7/hour during those years. Not much, but probably more than I would have made in a more typical job, plus I could set my own hours, and it was fun.

When I finished Law School, and got my first job, I went to work for a big patent litigation firm in Chicago. I was still a card counter, and looking forward to winning even more now that I would be able to maintain a larger bankroll. And though there were no tribal casinos anywhere near me, there were riverboat casinos not too far away, and I expected to spend a good bit of time beating those games on weekends. However, what I soon found out, using some software I had, is that with their 8-deck shoes and player-unfriendly rules, these riverboat games were not very beatable for me. My edge was very small, and I was going to need a huge bankroll to make even $25/hour. At that rate, I was much better off spending my weekends doing legal work and getting bonuses from the law firm. Then a friend mentioned they had seen these temporary casinos that were in and around Chicago, and were completely legal, operating under the Illinois charitable gambling laws. And they had blackjack.

What my friend hadn't known, or hadn't realized would matter to me, is that the Illinois law limited bets to $10 or less for these charity casinos. Thus, even if they let me sit out when the count was negative, and bet the maximum when the count was high, I was still never going to be able to bet enough to yield a worthwhile hourly average. So, I had to give up on these blackjack games also. But before I left, I noticed that they had poker games,

---

[*] Humble, Lance and Cooper, Carl. *The World's Greatest Blackjack Book*. New York: Doubleday, 1980.

primarily $3-$6 limit holdem and limit Omaha hi-lo. Although I didn't really know these "flop" games, I figured it might be fun, like playing with my friends in college. Even though I won that first night, I quickly realized how much I didn't know about poker. And not just the rules of these unfamiliar games. Pot odds? Never heard of that before. But my love of poker had really been ignited, and I decided I was going to learn all I could about poker, and how to beat these games, and see if I could beat them for enough that it was worth my time.

At the next opportunity, I went to a used book store, to see what they had. There were only three poker books available, so I bought them all. Two were enjoyable to read, and of some help to a player like me so lacking in knowledge, but I now know all they taught was weak-tight strategy that would only work against total fish and calling stations. The third book was perfect for me, teaching not a set of strategies, but the general concepts needed to win at poker. And not just one type of poker, but all the different poker games, limit or no-limit, flop games, stud games draw games, all of it. And that is how I still approach poker today. I work in ideas, not rules and charts, to guide my play.

In this book, it is my goal to teach you the concepts you should know, understand, and be able to apply to each decision you face as a poker player. I'm not going to give you a chart to memorize, and tell you that this is how you should play. In fact, you're going to have to do a lot of work to properly integrate and apply the information I provide to your game. You're going to find many situations where some of my advice is pushing you towards one decision, and some of my advice is pushing you the other way. But hopefully I have written this well enough, and you have worked hard enough, that you will be able to discern from all of my advice, and everything else you know about poker, which decision is the best for you make, given the weight of each factor guiding your decision in that hand.

This is not easy to do. You will always find reasons you should fold, reasons you should call, and reasons you should raise. But the more you understand these concepts, and the more information you can glean from your opponents and the situation, the better you can give the proper weight to each reason, and ultimately make the best, most profitable, decision.

While the primary focus of the advice in this book is tournament poker, much of what I've written is applicable to cash games. Similarly, while the focus of this book is on no-limit holdem tournaments, almost all of it is applicable in other tournaments. Certainly, this advice is applicable in other tournaments where no-limit betting is the rule, and mostly applicable in tournaments where pot-limit betting is the rule. Some of it will not apply very well to limit tournaments, which is why I've written special chapters on limit tournament games, as well as pot-limit.

I cannot promise that this book will make you a great player, or even a winning player. I can promise you that what is in this book, combined with a lot of effort, will make you a much better player than you are today. And with enough well-directed effort, everybody is capable of being a strong, winning player.

MY POKER PHILOSOPHY

Every poker player says they're playing to win the money. And with very few exceptions they are all being honest, in the sense that they would pass a lie detector test. But in many cases, they are at least partially fooling themselves. It is very common in poker tournaments to find players who are playing to survive much more than they are playing to maximize the amount of money they could win. In many cases, they think it is a sign of failure if they are eliminated early in the tournament. Once they've played long enough that they no longer feel there is any dishonor in being eliminated, they now realize that the money bubble is getting somewhat close, and thus they continue to play to survive so as to (try to) maximize their chances of making the money.

But all of these goals and concerns are often counter-productive in terms of maximizing their EV*. And really, isn't that what it's all about? If you want to

---

* EV = Expected Value, that is, how much would you expect to win, or lose, on average, in a given situation. For example, if I offer to give you $200 to $100 on the flip of a fair coin, the EV of this bet to you is +$50, as you expect to win $200 for each time you lose $100, for a profit of $100 every 2 flips of the coin. In many (most) poker decisions, you cannot determine the exact EV of each decision you might choose, but by accurately estimating the EV of each decision, you can learn to choose the highest EV decision most of the time.

make the most money, you must make the decisions that will, on average, lead to the most money, even if those same decisions sometimes also increase your chances of being eliminated early, even this very hand.

Now I'm not saying that you cannot have these other goals, or that you can't make decisions that fail to maximize your EV, but instead maximize these other goals (such as making the money, making day 2 of a prestigious tournament, extending your time in the tournament for reasons of pride or further entertainment). What I am saying is that this book is going to completely ignore such things. Even if this is your one and only time that you will get to play in the WSOP Main Event, and it is important to you that the experience lasts as long as possible, I cannot accurately put a value on that experience to you. And even if I could, it would be a different value from one person to another. So, for purposes of this book, all such non-monetary considerations will be ignored. If you wish to consider such things, feel free to do so. Just make sure that you are properly weighing the monetary costs, and that the monetary costs are not too high for what you're getting in return.

There is a hypothetical I like to ask my students that says a lot about how the student thinks about poker and risk, and what things are important to them. Imagine it is the first hand of the Main Event, you have T50,000* and blinds are T75,T150. You are in the big blind, and everyone folds to the small blind. They now announce "All-in." Not only is this a crazy play, but quite unexpected. In fact, you're so surprised, you now ask "All-in?" Unfortunately, the small blind doesn't understand that you've asked a question, and thinks you have stated yourself to also be all-in. As such, believing the action complete, they tables their cards. Of course, you were not actually saying you were all-in, but asking if you heard them correctly, i.e., did they really say all-in? If the dealer and other players confirm that your words were a question, not a statement, the correct ruling is going to be that it is unfortunate for the small blind that they misunderstood, but the decision is still on you, to fold or call, and you now have the advantage of knowing their two cards. So, what do you do?

Obviously, if the small blind has the better hand, you fold. But assuming

---

* Throughout this book I will use the symbols T and $ to distinguish between tournament chips and money. Whenever you see T100, for example, that means 100 tournament chips; whereas $100 means 100 dollars in cash, or cash equivalent. While most players are not terribly familiar with this system, it does serve the purpose of making it easier to distinguish between the two, and thus easier to understand what I'm saying.

you have the better hand, how big of an edge do you require before you will call and risk all your chips on the first hand of the most important tournament of the year? Will you call if you're a small favorite, like 2-2 (52%) vs. A-K (48%)? How about something like A-10 (60%) vs. K-Q (40%)? Do you need more, like J-J (70%) vs. A-10 (30%) or J-J (80%) vs. 5-5 (20%)? Or even more edge, such as rare matchups like K-K (92%) vs. K-5 (8%)?

I've asked this question of thousands of students, and dozens of co-instructors. The range of answers is all over the board, and occasionally I even hear the answer that they would never call preflop, even if a huge favorite, because they are unwilling to risk all of their chips on the first hand. In fact, my question is closely related to a commonly asked question every year as the Main Event approaches. Go to any online poker forum, and somebody will ask if you would (or they should) call an all-in preflop on the first hand if holding pocket aces. Against a random hand, A-A will win about 85% of the time. So in a sense they are asking if 85:15 is enough of an edge to risk it all.

I'm sure you can pretty much guess my answer, given what I've already written in this chapter. If you're an average player in the field, then calling with any edge will make you money. At this very early stage of the tournament, doubling your stack will essentially double your equity in the tournament. That is, T100,000 chips are worth almost exactly double the T50,000 chips you started with. The fact that this is a tournament, and chips are worth more per chip in a short stack than in a big stack (see chapter 3 on ICM for details of this concept) does not really apply yet. That concept doesn't have a noticeable impact until you are in the money, getting very close to the money, or have amassed a truly huge stack at an earlier stage.

An interesting thing to consider, if you are a below average player compared to the field, is the fact that you will increase your EV by calling all-in here even if you are slightly behind. That is, if you know that most of the players are a lot better than you*, you should call here even if you've got the two overcards vs. the opponent's pair. You know you're putting it in slightly behind, but since your opponents are more skillful, this is likely a better spot than what you will find later.

---

* Even if you're average or so for the field as a whole, if you happened to draw a very tough starting table, and most of these players are much better than you, and you know that this table probably won't break for a long time, this concept would apply.

Several years ago, my friend Matt Matros wrote an article for *CardPlayer Magazine* in which he considered this question, that is, at what point should the well above average player still call, and when should they fold, even though they're the favorite when making this call? Most people would agree that a typical player would make more money, on average, by calling any and every time they had even a small edge. The tougher question is how much edge do you need to profitably call if you are a better than average player? Matt did the math assuming the better player was not just a little better, but a lot. In fact, he assumed the hypothetical player was three times better than average. That is, if this superior player folded in this spot, they would still go on to an average result of winning $30,000 in this tournament, for a profit of $20,000, by playing their normal (highly talented) game. Of course, if this great player called and lost, they were out. But if they called and won, they had twice as many chips as anybody else at that time, and still had all of their tremendous skill moving forward.

Now you might guess that if this hypothetical great player is three times better than average, they would need to be at least a 3:1 favorite (i.e., 75% vs. 25%) before they should profitably call the all-in. But it's not that simple. What Matt discovered is that this great player only had to be a 53:47 favorite to make more money by calling than by folding. This is primarily because, even though the starting stack of T50,000 chips is worth $30,000 in front of this player (as compared to a value of $10,000 in front of an average player), if they call here and double their stack to T100,000, this double stack will almost double in value, and be worth almost $60,000, when wielded by this great player.

What I find most interesting about all of this, is that I've discussed this with many players who are excellent tournament pros, with years of winning results under their belts. And while they will often say that they're not going to dispute the math, they will still insist that they would not call with such a small edge, and that they are sure it is correct for them to fold. They insist that they can find a better spot in which to risk all of their chips, rather than risking them here as only a 53:47 favorite. In fact, many of them say they would fold if they were a 60:40, or even a 70:30, favorite.

I think the mistake they are making is that they are focusing too much on the downside potential, and giving themselves too much credit when they say they will find a better spot to risk it all. They often will find a better spot, but sometimes they will play smart, and yet still find they risked it all when way behind, maybe even drawing dead. Most of the time, even a great player can't avoid a cold-deck. Thus, they will usually find a better spot, but when we average those much better spots they usually find along with the sometimes worse spots they end up in, we find that their chances are probably not as good as they think. More importantly, even if they can, on average, find a much better spot to risk it all, if they take the risk now, and win, they will still be there to take advantage of these better spots that are coming along later. Thus, by risking it all now, they don't always miss out on later spots that are even better.

The math is clear, and can't be argued with unless you find that the mathematician made a mistake. So unless you find such a mistake in the math, don't even try to argue with it. But, if you wish to say that despite the math you're going to make a different decision, feel free to do so. Just make sure you understand that you're giving up EV in exchange for something else, make sure you know exactly what price you're paying, and that you are willing to pay it.

TOURNAMENT VERSUS CASH GAME STRATEGY

Here is another hypothetical I like to discuss with my students when I teach live group seminars. Imagine that the first 10 students who showed up today are going to be given a freeroll opportunity. They are going to sit at a poker table and play a tournament that is structured to last about two hours. Each will be given T1,000 chips, blinds will start at T10,T20 and increase every 15 minutes. Prizes are going to be awarded as $6,000 to first, $3,000 to second, and $1,000 to third. The first seven players eliminated will get no money at all. However, you were the first student to arrive, and will be given extra information and advice, information that only you will know. I then tell you that this isn't a tournament, but is really a cash game, and that after the end of level 2 (30 minutes), all remaining players are going to be awarded cash equal to their chip count. Thus, if you break even during that 30 minutes, you will win $1,000. If you finish with T800 chips, you win $800, T2,000 wins you $2,000, etc.

Knowing this, what should you do differently as compared to your nine opponents who don't know that this is really a cash game?

My answer? Nothing. Nothing different at all.

In a cash game, every chip is worth exactly face value. If you win a $5 chip, you win $5. If you lose it, you lose $5. This is true whether the rest of your stack consists of $10 in chips, or $10,000. In a heads-up hand, if your opponent bets all-in for $100 in chips, and there is $100 in the pot already, you should call anytime you think you will win more than 1/3 of the time. Of course, if you think you will win exactly 1/3 of the time, it doesn't matter what you do, calling and folding both have the same EV. But if you think you will win more than that, calling is worth more money than folding. One way to refer to this is that the value of each chip is linear. That is, whatever you win in chips, you win exactly that amount in money. There is never a discrepancy between these two values.

In a tournament, there is this idea that you should avoid risk and make sure you survive. In fact, years ago I used to hear players state that their strategy was to try to only play against opponents who had fewer chips than they did. Their thinking was that if they only play against people with fewer chips, they can never lose all of their chips, and therefore they'll continue to survive and eventually make money. However, our concern is not mere survival. Our concern is to maximize our EV, and win, on average, as much money (equity) as possible with every decision we make.

This strategy is partially based upon the concept that the value of chips in a tournament is not linear. And this concept is correct. However, this non-linearity in the value of tournament chips does not really come into play until very late in the tournament. It does not exist with enough effect until you are in or near the money, or until you have an exceedingly large stack. Thus, early in a tournament, you should play with the same mindset as you would in a cash game. In a cash game, you don't mind taking large risks if they are +EV, because you know you can always just buy more chips if you lose. Even though this won't always be true in a tournament, you should think of it the same way. Even though you might be eliminated from THIS exact tournament*, there is always another one coming along, and you will be able to take your money and enter the next one.

Even if this is the one and only, or the last, tournament you will ever play, playing with this cash game mindset early in the tournament is still the best

---

* If you are in a rebuy or reentry tournament, you might be permitted to pay more money and get more chips and continue to play in this tournament. See Chapter 36 for more information on these types of tournaments.

way maximize your EV. When teaching the hypothetical from chapter 1, I've often had students ask me, what if the hand in question is during the Main Event, and given their real life job, family, etc., it might be the one and only time that they get to compete in the Main Event. My answer to them is always the same. If this is the one and only time that you will get to play in the world championship, do you really want to knowingly make a decision that is less than your best? A decision that you know is incorrect? It is going to hurt me emotionally a lot less if I get eliminated in a situation where I know I made the best decision, than if I make the inferior decision now, survive this hand, but still get eliminated later. If that happens, then I'll wonder, for the rest of my life, if things might not have turned out different, and better, if I had made the decision I knew was correct in that earlier hand. What if avoiding that risky spot ended up being the difference between becoming the next World Champion, and just outlasting half the field? Unless I went on to win the whole thing, I would always wonder if that mistake made the difference.

But why is it that in a tournament, chip values are not linear? In a cash game, if you win all the chips, you win all the money. In a tournament, the winner always wins all the chips, but never wins all the money*. Thus, at some point, they must have won chips that were not worth as much as some of the chips they already had. For example, imagine an online-style sit-n-go (SNG). Ten players pay their entry fee, and the top three finishers win the prize money in a ratio of 50:30:20. If we had paid $10 each, the winners would get $50, $30, and $20. At the start of the SNG, we each had exactly T1,500, and the value of each stack was obviously $10**. But at some point, whatever the value of your stack, it cannot increase in a linear manner as you accumulate more chips. Imagine a situation where you are down to heads-up with exactly half

---

* With the obvious exception of a winner-take-all tournament, which is very rarely seen other than at some 1-table satellites. If you are in a winner-take-all tournament, you can play with the cash game mindset from beginning to end, as the chip values are always linear in such an event, just like a cash game.

** We are assuming, for discussions like this, that every player at the table is equally skilled, and has a long-term EV in the game of breaking even, ignoring the rake. Thus, since each player has the same number of chips, their chances of finishing in each spot are identical, the value of their stacks is identical, and therefore that value must be $10 each. You can do analysis wherein you take skill into account, but doing so is much more complicated and will not be done in most discussions in this book.

the chips. You are going to finish either first or second, and since you have half the chips, each position is equally likely. Thus, you will win $50 half the time, and $30 half the time, and your EV is therefore $40. However, if you win the next hand all-in, you will exactly double your chip count, but you will only increase your EV from $40 to $50.

Some people might correctly object to this analysis. They will say that the EV of your stack of one-half of the chips was not really $40. Since there were two of you remaining, you had already won $30. In effect, that $30 was already in your pocket. The EV of your stack would then be $10, or half of the difference between first and second prize money.

So, to give a more thorough example and demonstrate the non-linearity of chip values deep in a tournament, let's imagine that there are four of you remaining in the SNG, with exactly equal stacks. Since the prize pool is $100 total, and the four of you each have the same number of chips, each of you must have an EV of $25. Now imagine you double up and eliminate one of the opponents. You will have half the chips, are guaranteed a payday of at least $20, and continue playing against two opponents who each have 1/4th of the chips. What is the value of your stack now that you've doubled up? Well, whatever it is, it clearly hasn't doubled in value. It was worth $25, and the only way it can be worth $50 is if you are 100% guaranteed to win the game. And since your two opponents still have half the chips between them, it is definitely not 100% certain that you are going to win. Therefore, when you played the previous hand, you were risking your entire stack of chips worth $25 at the start of the hand, but when you doubled up you only had a stack of chips worth a lot more than $25, but a lot less than $50.

This same non-linearity exists at all stages of a tournament, but the effect is so small in the early and middle stages, when you are not yet in or near the money, that you can, as a practical matter, ignore it when making your decisions. The value of the chips in these early and middle stages is so close to linear that you can play with the same mindset and decision making processes as if you were in a cash game. In my opinion, the failure to do this is one of the biggest mistakes made by many of the best tournament pros in the world. Even though many of them will disagree with me[*], it is my opinion that despite all of

---

[*] Of course, anytime somebody who isn't clueless disagrees with you on any subject, there is always some chance that you are the one who is wrong. And the tournament pros

their skill and success, they would be even more successful if they would just overcome this issue, and be willing to take more risks early in a tournament.

Remember the hypothetical I asked my students at the start of this chapter? Now, imagine we add a twist. After providing the secret information to you, I change my mind, and tell all of them this is really a cash game. Now that everybody else knows this, what should you do differently? Theoretically, the answer is the same, and you shouldn't play any differently at all. However, in the real world, you should probably change your game quite a bit. Not because you inherently should, but because now that the other nine students know it is actually a cash game, they are probably going to play differently than when they thought it was a tournament. And since they are going to play differently, you are going to want to adjust to these differences in order to increase your EV against these players. We will explore this idea more fully in Chapter 4 about game theory.

I'm thinking of are far from clueless. Many are some of the best ever. So, of course, there must be a chance that I'm wrong about this. But until somebody can show me the math that says I'm wrong, I'm probably not going to change my mind.

ICM IS THE KEY TO TOURNAMENT POKER

When you play cash games, you use tools like pot odds, implied odds, reverse implied odds, and other math tools to calculate which decision is the best when it's your turn. When you do this math, you are working with numbers expressed in dollars. As we've said before, a $5 chip in a cash game is always worth $5, so doing the math is easy in the sense that once you determine which decision yields the highest average chip count, it is always also the decision that yields the highest EV. But as we discussed in Chapter 2, in a tournament, the value of chips is not always linear, and thus you cannot simply calculate the decision that yields the highest average chip count, but must also determine if that decision also yields the highest EV.

The key to this difference is ICM, or the Independent Chip Model. ICM is a method of determining the value of a given stack of chips at any time in a tournament. But before we dig into the details of ICM, let's start with something simpler first, something we can't forget. When you enter a tournament, you pay an entry fee (unless it's a freeroll or some such). In exchange, you are given a certain number of tournament chips. Even if there are other complicating factors, such as some players being given extra chips, dealer add-ons, etc., you can still calculate the starting value of each chip. Simply put, just take the total number of tournament chips in play, and divide by the total value of all prizes being paid. If 100 players started with T10,000 each, there are T1M chips in play. If the prize pool is a total of $10,000, then you simply do the math, and determine that T100 = $1. So, as a starting point, you might divide the number of chips in front of you by 100, and have a rough estimate of the value of your stack in dollar terms.

But clearly this rough math does not always yield the correct result. If the tournament is not yet in or near the money, and you still have T10,000, then your stack is worth something very, very close to $100. If instead you had T20,000, your stack would be worth something very, very close to $200. But if the final 10 are being paid in this event, and you are down to about 20 or fewer players, then rough estimates like these will not always get the job done. Imagine in this example with 10 players making money, you have T20,000, but you are one of the final 11 players, and two of your opponents have stacks of only T5,000 and T6,000. In this scenario, there is an excellent chance that you will be one of the 10 players who makes the money. Prizes for this event might range from $300 for 10th place, up to $3,000 for 1st. As such, your equity is probably a lot more than just the $200 we would get from doing the basic math. Now we need to use ICM to accurately determine the true value of your stack.

ICM is simply a math tool to calculate the equity of a given stack size at any point in a tournament. ICM calculates your chances of finishing in each of the remaining positions in the tournament, and multiplies those chances by the prize money that each position pays. As a simplistic example, if there are two players remaining, and you each have half the chips, your chances of finishing first are 50%, as are your chances of finishing second. You just multiply the first prize amount by 50%, the second prize amount by 50%, and add these two numbers together. This total is your current equity in the tournament, i.e., the current value of your stack. Of course, most of the times the calculations are a lot more complicated.

It is important to note that ICM is not a fixed number, either. For example, let's suppose you are in a tournament with a total of T1M chips in play, and total prize money of $1M. This does not mean that any time you have a stack of T10,000 that it is worth $10,000. Obviously, if you win the tournament, you will have T1M, but you will be paid only first prize, not the entire prize pool. Now, if you had T10,000 early in the tournament, it would be worth almost exactly $10,000. But if you make the final table with T10,000, you will win at least the 10th place prize, which is (almost certainly) more than $10,000. As an extreme example, imagine you and eight other players each had T10,000 at the final table, and the chip leader had the other T910,000. Now, while you only have a 1% chance of winning first, you have an excellent chance of finishing anywhere from 2nd-10th place, and the value of your T10,000 stack might be as high as $70,000 or more. The value of your stack depends not just upon how many chips you have, and what prizes are being paid, but also the number of opponents remaining, and the sizes of each of their respective stacks.

The basic foundation of ICM is the idea that your chances of winning the tournament are exactly equal to the percentage of all the chips that you currently possess. Although the actual value of your stack will also depend upon how the other chips are distributed, your chances of finishing exactly first are always dependent upon the percentage of the chips you possess, and nothing else*. In the hypothetical above, at the start of the tournament you had T10,000, and a 1% chance of finishing first. Even though you made the final table, since you still have only 1% of the chips, your chances of finishing first remain at only 1%.

Let's look at a more realistic scenario, and see how all of this might work. Imagine you are the chip leader of the three remaining players in a tournament. The prizes are:

1st - $1,000
2nd - $600
3rd - $300

And the chip counts are:

---

* Unless stated otherwise, we will always assume that all players are equally skilled. If you are above average in skill compared to your opponents, you will have a higher chance of winning than just your chip count alone indicates. Of course, if you are below average, your chances are also less than your chip count would indicate. Whatever your relative skill level, you can still calculate your equity using standard ICM math, and then adjust that figure up, or down, depending upon your relative skill level.

A (you, the hero) - T50,000
B - T40,000
C - T10,000

Because you have half the chips, it is easy to calculate your equity in first prize. You will win first half the time, or an average of $500 of the $1,000 in first place money. But how often will you finish 2nd or 3rd? This is a bit tougher, but ultimately some simple math will determine this with total accuracy. When you don't win, B or C will win. Overall, B will win 40% of the time, and C will win 10% of the time. Let's imagine that B wins. If that is the case, how often will you finish 2nd, and how often 3rd? If B wins, there is no reason to assume that B got those chips more so from either you or C. You have 5 times as many chips as C right now. As such, when B wins, it is 5 times more likely that you finish 2nd and C finishes 3rd, than it is that you finish 3rd and C finishes 2nd. So, when B wins, you will win the $600 2nd prize five times for each one time that you win the 3rd prize of $300.

Similarly, if we presume for a moment that C wins, you have a 5:4 chip lead over B, so it is 5:4 that you finish 2nd to C rather than 3rd. This leads to your total chances of finishing 2nd as:

5/6 x 40% + 5/9 x 10%

which is equal to 38.8%, and since 38.8% x $600 = $233, that is your equity in 2nd prize.

It is now easy to calculate your chances of finishing 3rd, and your equity in the 3rd place prize. If you are 50% to win, and 38.88% to finish second, you must be 11.12% to finish 3rd. And this equates to an equity of $33 (11.12% x $300) in the 3rd prize.

Adding these up, your equity at this moment is $500 + $233 + $33, or $766.

If we redo this analysis a little later, when C has caught up part way at the expense of B, and you have T50,000 but B and C are now tied, at T25,000, your equity or ICM value will have dropped to $750, even though you still have the same chip count. If instead B or C had eliminated the other, and you were now heads-up with half the chips, your equity would increase to $800. Again, even though you still have the same chip count, the movement of chips from one opponent to another can have a significant impact on the value of your stack. Even though your chances of finishing first will not change unless the size of your stack changes, the chances that you will finish 2nd or 3rd change as the chips move from one opponent to another.

Having gone through all of this, you may be asking yourself (and me, if I were there), what is the point of all of this? How is this going to help me play better, i.e., help me make better decisions at the table? As we discussed before, chip values in tournaments are non-linear. ICM is the perfect method for demonstrating this fact. But these changes in chip value do not have a significant impact until you are in or near the money-paying positions in a tournament. But how close to you have to be before this non-linearity should lead you to making some different decisions? And how big of an impact will all of this have anyway?

Let's look at some more examples, using the payouts above of $1,000, $600, and $300. Imagine a tournament where only these three spots are paid, but now instead of three of us left, there are 10 of us. And we all have equal stacks. One opponent moves all-in, everyone else folds to you, and you must decide whether or not to call. How often do you have to win to correctly call this shove? Obviously, with 10 of you left, all having the same chip counts, and the prizes as stated, everybody had the same equity at the start of this hand, $190 apiece. If you call and lose, you will be eliminated, and paid $0. If you call and win, you will now have twice as many chips as everybody else, and be down to nine players. If this were a cash game, the math would be easy. Call if you think you're going to win more than half the time. But this is a tournament. If you call and win, what is the equity of your new double stack? According to ICM math, my equity will not double to $380, but only increase to $353. As such, I have to win more than half the time to correctly call this shove. Specifically, I must win at least 54% of the time or calling will cost me equity. Now, this is not a huge difference, and in the real world you will never know with exactly what range of hands your opponent is shoving. As such, when you estimate their range, and estimate how often you will win if you call, there is plenty of room for error, both in your mental math, and in your estimates of their range. As such, the difference between 50% and 54% might not be that big of a deal.

But what if instead of 10-handed, we were 5-handed, everybody has equal stacks, and somebody shoves? It is folded to you, and you again must decide if you should call or fold. Before the hand started, you were one of five equal stacks, and thus had an equity of 1/5th of the $1,900 prize pool, or $380. If you call and win, ICM math shows that your stack will now have a value of $640. This is a lot less double the $380 value you had, and for this call to be correct, you now need to win at least 60% of the time. As you can see, primarily because we are so much closer to the money now, the non-linearity in chip values is becoming more and more of a concern, and having a much greater impact on your decisions.

More than anything else, this math points out two important teaching points. First, you can see the value of aggression here. If I'm the player who shoves all-in, my opponents should be more likely to fold, even in spots where they are ahead of my range. If the potential caller of this shove is holding A-Jo, for example, and puts the shover on a range of the top 20% of all starting hands, their best decision is to fold. Despite the fact that A-Jo will be the favorite against most of the hands in the top 20%, it will sometimes be in a coin-flip against an underpair (and thus a small underdog), and sometimes be in bad shape (against specifically A-K, A-Q, A-A, K-K, Q-Q, and J-J). Overall, even though A-Jo is better than most of the hands in this range, it will only win about 55% of the time. As such, you could correctly call this shove when it was 10-handed, but not when closer to the money at 5-handed. If the worst hand can make the best hand correctly fold (not just bluff, but make them correctly fold even when knowing they are a favorite, just not a large enough favorite), this shows that there is massive value in being the player who goes all-in, forcing the opponent to call or fold. It is hard to understate the value of aggression in a poker tournament.

Second, if the call is made in either of these spots, the winner does not double their equity. So where did that lost equity go? Clearly, it must now be in the pockets of the other players. In the 10-handed example, if the call is made, the winner has a stack worth $353. The other $27 in equity went to the stacks of the other eight players, who each made about $3.33. In the 5-handed example, the three players who folded each made about $40 when the other two players got their chips all-in. So while this math shows the value of aggression in poker tournaments, it also shows the value of sitting back and letting other players beat up on each other. How will we use these apparently contradictory lessons to improve our decisions? See Chapters 12, 21, and 22.

GAME THEORY AND POKER

Hopefully all the math in this book is not too concerning. Even though poker is a game of math, the math required to play the game at a high level is not really that complex. Although it is just basic arithmetic, it is pretty tough, if not impossible, to do things like ICM calculations on the fly at the table.

However, the more you do these calculations away from the table, the better you will become at closely estimating them at the table, and the better you will become at making the best decisions. And for those of you who don't believe in the math, feel free to continue. There are some great poker players whose math skills are seriously lacking, and who don't understand most of what we'll discuss about ICM, equity calculations and PokerStove (see Chapter 10), as well as this chapter on Game Theory. Most of these players are natural geniuses at some of the other key skills, such as reading tells (Chapter 29) and manipulating opponents (Chapter 31). However, if they would work on and improve their math skills, they would be even better.

Game Theory is another branch of mathematics, made most famous to the general public in the award-winning movie *A Beautiful Mind*, the partially-based-on-reality movie about John Nash, who won a Nobel Prize for his contributions to this subject. John von Neumann is generally credited with creating this branch of mathematics with the publication of his 1928 paper[*]. Game Theory has practical applications in almost all areas of business and life. What I am about to discuss is not a rigorous application of Game Theory to poker, but more of a philosophical use of its principles. But first, what is Game Theory?

Game Theory is the study of decision making in games, specifically "the study of mathematical models of conflict and cooperation between intelligent rational decision-makers."[**] But Game Theory does not only apply to actual games, such as monopoly, backgammon, poker, and the like. Game Theory is commonly used in politics, economics, military strategy, psychology, and biology, and is fully applicable to almost every subject.

Analyzing a game using Game Theory, it is potentially possible to determine what is called the Game Theory Optimal (GTO) strategy for that game. This is a strategy that if properly determined and applied, makes it impossible for any opponent to beat you in the long run. At best, your opponent can tie you, and if they play with any strategy other than GTO, they will eventually lose. In a game like chess where there is no luck factor, a proper GTO strategy can guarantee that you will win or tie every game played. In a game like poker, with its significant short-term luck factor, no strategy can guarantee that you win or tie every hand, or even win or break-even every session. But a proper GTO strategy can guarantee that no matter what strategy your opponent(s) play, your EV will be to win or break even in the long run.

There are a few important points we need to make. First and foremost, at this time, nobody has solved the game of poker so as to know the correct GTO strategy. Even the most simplistic forms of poker, if set up so as to resemble anything like what you're going to see in a real game, are too complicated for any humans or present day computers to solve. The closest we have right now are some programs that can play heads-up holdem at a level that is so close

---

* Neumann, J. v. (1928). "Zur Theorie der Gesellschaftsspiele". Mathematische Annalen 100 (1): 295–320. doi:10.1007/BF01448847. English translation: Tucker, A. W.; Luce, R. D., eds. (1959). "On the Theory of Games of Strategy". Contributions to the Theory of Games. 4. pp. 13–42.

** Roger B. Myerson (1991). *Game Theory: Analysis of Conflict*, Harvard University Press, p. 1

to GTO that very few humans can beat these programs. But to the best of my knowledge, nobody has yet to come close to a program that plays anything close to GTO for other forms of poker, and in particular for multiplayer poker games.

So, if nobody knows what correct GTO strategy for poker is, why do we need to know anything about Game Theory at all? The fact that nobody knows GTO exactly doesn't mean that it doesn't exist. Consider any mathematical proof that has ever been solved. At some point in history, we hadn't solved it yet. But that proof was still true back then, we just didn't know for sure that it was true, and at some point far enough back in time we didn't even know it might exist. Even though we don't know exact GTO poker strategy, we still should have our own basic strategy for when we play. So, even if you and I can't determine exactly the correct GTO strategy, we should still do our best to create a basic strategy that we will use, and we will stick to this strategy until we have good reason to do otherwise.

An interesting thing about GTO strategy is that it doesn't matter if your opponent knows exactly what you're doing. Even if we think of a relatively simple game, and we explain our GTO strategy to our opponent, they still can only play this same GTO strategy and tie us, or they can play with any other strategy, and lose to us. It is part of the definition of GTO that it works even when your opponent knows your strategy.

Now, this doesn't mean, in a game like poker, that your opponent is going to know your cards. Also, correct GTO strategy for poker is certainly going to include a lot of mixed plays. By that, I mean that in a given situation, the GTO strategy is probably not going to always do exactly the same thing. Instead, the GTO strategy will take one action a certain percentage of the time, and another action other times, randomly choosing between the options according to fixed percentages.

As an example, imagine you are dealt A-A preflop in a holdem cash game. Since you are holding the current nuts, the correct GTO strategy is never going to be fold. But will it call or raise? The answer is almost certainly that it will randomly pick between the two decisions, and will have a fixed percentage for each option. The GTO strategy might be something like raise 95% of the time, call 5%. In a given instance, it will randomly pick between the two, so that in the long run it is calling 5% of the time, and raising 95%. So the fact that the opponent knows the strategy does not mean the opponent knows what the GTO player is holding. When the GTO player raises, there is some chance it has A-A, some chance of K-K, and so on. So the opponent is still largely guessing as to the exact cards of the GTO player.

In the real world, none of your opponents will be playing anything like GTO strategy. They will have tendencies in their personal basic strategy that are clear errors if only they knew better. And they will sometimes provide you with tells and other sources of information that permit you to fine-tune your read on what cards they're holding. Because of all of these things, in most cases you will have a larger advantage against a player if you diverge from your basic strategy, and instead do things that you would generally consider a mistake*, but which will increase your edge against this particular opponent. In the world of Game Theory, this is called using a Game Theory Exploitative strategy, or GTE. But why should you abandon your basic strategy if you know it is a good one, and that it will guarantee you an edge in the long run? Simply put, because the edge you gain from a proper GTE strategy is so much more.

Imagine a scenario where your opponent is shoving all-in blind preflop. GTO strategy doesn't pay any attention to what your opponent(s) is doing. It just applies its fixed strategy to the situation. So, if this opponent is shoving 300 blinds, the GTO strategy is going to fold all but A-A. When the same opponent shoves the next hand, and the next, and so on, GTO does not change, and still only looks at how many blinds are being shoved, and calls only with the same tight range of top hands. But in the real world, you know that if you don't pick this guy off at some point, somebody else will, and then the opportunity will be gone. Obviously this doesn't mean you just call as soon as you are dealt a hand that is better than 50% to win against the opponent's presumably random hand. But it also means that you won't wait until you have A-A, or even K-K. Exactly where you draw the line will depend upon several factors, such as exactly how many blinds are being shoved (or how many blinds you have, if less), and how many players are yet to act behind you (and how likely are they to overcall). But certainly your EV is going to be higher if you properly adjust to this player who is shoving any two cards, and call more often than the GTO strategy of waiting for A-A. This is an example GTE strategy in action.

---

* That is, a mistake in the sense that you are no longer exactly following your GTO basic strategy.

A lot of the confusion about GTO strategy comes from the use of the word "optimal". People see that word, and they think it means that there is no better way to play. And it's true that there is no better way to play than GTO, if you completely ignore what your opponent is doing. But since the edge you can obtain is so much higher if you do pay attention to your opponent, and make appropriate adjustments, in the real world the "optimal" strategy with which to win the most money is usually nowhere near the GTO "optimal" strategy. If the other players are making lots of GTO mistakes, then a strong GTE strategy will win much more money than a perfect GTO strategy.

It is not uncommon to overhear two good poker players arguing with each other as to the correct strategy for a given hand. In many cases, they are both right, but are talking about different things. One of the players is at the level of GTO, and what would be the correct basic strategy play for a situation. The other player is at the level of GTE, and is arguing for the strategy that will be more effective against this exact opponent. If they would just realize that they are talking about different things, in many instances their argument would cease.

So I ask again, since we don't know exactly the correct GTO strategy for poker then why does Game Theory matter at all? Because it reinforces the need to develop a strong basic strategy, and to understand that you should only diverge from that basic strategy when conditions are right to use a GTE strategy. Many players focus so much of their efforts into figuring out the best way to exploit their opponents (that is, they work on their GTE strategy, though they don't think of it in those terms), that they never put any effort into figuring out a proper basic strategy. It is much easier, in the long run, to first work out a strong basic strategy, so that you can always fall back on it. And only in those situations when you are confident that it is correct to deviate from this basic strategy, do you then make use of a GTE strategy.

Let's consider a real world example. It is the river, and your opponent bets into you. You have been playing a draw, and it missed. You have a hand that beats no legitimate hands your opponent could ever be betting. Your basic strategy is going to be to fold*. However, you believe you have spotted a tell

---

* Correct GTO strategy in this situation is almost certainly going to be more complex than merely "fold". It is more likely going to be something such as fold 93%, raise 6%, and call 1% of the time.

that your opponent is weak. Should you abandon your basic strategy, and instead either call or raise here? This is a difficult decision because any tell is only partially reliable. As such it is hard to be certain when you should use such information to profitably change your strategy. If you don't fully understand your basic strategy, it is even harder to know when to correctly deviate from it. In this scenario, you must fully understand why the basic strategy of folding is correct. Without this, you will not be able to determine how reliable this tell must be before it becomes correct to use the tell to change your decision.

So, it's not that you need a deep understanding of Game Theory to be a great poker player, but you do need a deep understanding of the proper basic strategy, so you can accurately determine when the information you have gathered while playing the current game indicates that it is now the smart decision to do something else.

THE TWO HALVES OF POKER

You can neatly divide all poker decisions into two halves or portions. The first part is gathering information, and the second part is making the decision (using that information). Gathering information could also be subdivided. There is the information you can gather when you're not even playing. This significantly includes things like reading this book, talking with friends, and all of the other things you could do to better inform yourself about correct basic strategy, and about how to correctly apply GTE strategies. Then there is the information you gather when you're at the table by watching and listening to the opponents.

Gathering information at the table can be done in many different ways. At the most basic level, you should always know where you're at in the tournament, your chip count, and the chip counts of every player at your table. For every opponent you play, you should constantly be monitoring their tendencies and patterns, as well as understanding their basic playing style. By doing so you can learn some of their systematic errors, and from there best determine how to take advantage of these errors. This is one form of GTE strategy. You should also be looking for tells, especially when you have folded the current hand. By spotting these tells now, and confirming their accuracy, you will be able to make better use of these same tells later when you play against this opponent.

You should also listen to the table talk, as often opponents will simply give away their strategy, and the way they think the game should be played. Sometimes what they say is very subtle, and does not help much. But other times, what they give away can be highly valuable, and give you a significant advantage. When I have cards, I tend to sit absolutely still and say nothing. But when I'm not in a hand, I spend a lot of time chatting with others, and do so in a way that casually leads them into areas where they might give me free information.

I played the Main Event of the WSOP for the first time in 2002, the year Robert Varkonyi won. In fact, if you watch the one-hour show they produced for ESPN that year, you might spot me in the audience, and see one of my fossils on the table. My good friend Russell Rosenblum made the final table that year, finishing 6th, and had a clam fossil I gave him. I sat with his wife and other friends to cheer him on. I had gone pretty deep in that event, eventually being eliminated in about 80th place, short of the money. Near the end of day one, a player at my table told us what he was going to do. Back then, you started the tournament with T10,000, and players were a lot less aggressive than today. An average stack at the end of day 1 that year was only about T14,000, and the overall chip leader probably had something like T50-60,000. This player at my table had about T35,000, and said to the table: "I've got more chips now than I've ever had on day 1. With 30 minutes to go tonight, no way I'm going to risk taking a beat or anything. If I play a hand, I've got the nuts, so just stay out of my way. I want to sleep good tonight, so no way I'm going to risk losing a big pot now."

When he said this, I knew he wasn't kidding. While I figured he wasn't going to play only A-A, I knew his starting hand selection was going to be very tight. A few hands later, he opened for his standard raise. I knew he had a very strong hand, but also thought he would fold maybe anything but A-A to a re-raise. Sitting to his immediate left, I looked down at A-Q. Since I was holding an ace, it was that much less likely he had A-A. So I reraised. Everyone else folded, he gave me a long stare, and then called. Immediately, I knew exactly what he had, K-K. If he had held A-A, he would have reraised, probably all in. Anything less than K-K, and I'm confident he would have folded. As soon as he just called, I was pretty much 100% sure of my read. Sadly, I was behind. But fortunately, the flop came ace high. Being first to act, he checked. My initial thought was to slowplay. My second thought was don't bother, there is an ace on the board, and holding two kings he is never going to put another chip in this pot unless he catches a third king. So rather than give him a free chance to hit his 2-outer, I bet and he quickly folded, showing K-K as he did so.

The point of this story is not how great I am at reading hands. The point is if you pay attention and listen to what they're saying, sometimes they make it easy, or at least a lot easier, to read their hands.

Obviously some of the information that you gather cannot be subjected to rigorous mathematical evaluation. When they say something, or give off a physical tell, it is impossible to precisely determine the accuracy of the information. Of course, you should estimate not just what this information means, but how reliable it is. Similarly, if you are going to say something or do something in an attempt to manipulate your opponent, you can never be 100% certain it will work. While these aspects of poker are very important, they are not purely mathematical in nature, but involve psychology and intuition.

This first half of the game of poker, gathering information, involves both mathematical and non-mathematical aspects. But the second half, processing information (otherwise known as making the decision), is a purely mathematical function. It is important that you understand, even when you are applying your feel or intuition, that this is part of the gathering information step, not the processing step. You may be making a move, rather than folding, because you spotted a tell or just feel that your opponent is weak. But the proper way to use this feel or tell is to estimate its reliability and mathematically analyze that information along with everything else. You then use this extra information as part of your overall decision-making process. In some situations, no matter how reliable the non-math-based information may be, it still might not be enough to override your basic strategy. In the end, all of the information you gather, whatever it may be, can only guide your decision. The information can never make the decision.

Which brings up another of my favorite poker stories. For six years before I won the main event, I spent almost every Tuesday night at Foxwoods. This was the night of their weekly NLH tournament. It was a great event, and a significant source of my bankroll growth during those years. One night, we were down to 12 players, six of us each at two tables. I was the chip leader with about T9,000 chips[*]. The second chip leader, sitting two to my right, had about T8,000 chips. The next biggest stack was only T3,000 chips. Nine of us were going to get paid, so we were still three eliminations from the money.

With me in the big blind, it was folded to the second chip leader, who made an oversized raise to T2,000. I had a reliable tell on this guy, and knew he was weak. Moreover, given the situation, if I reraised him all-in, he would be smart to fold unless he was sure he was a big favorite. He could fold, and still be the 2nd biggest stack, but if he called and lost, he would be eliminated short of the money. The ICM math of the situation made it hugely wrong for him to call with anything less than a premium hand. I looked down at 5-5, and reraised all-in. He was looking at me, and you could just see him turning red and getting angrier and angrier. He started pointing his finger at me, and then, through clenched teeth, he spit out "I call!!" I said "Oops. I guess you must have a bigger pair than this", and tabled my 5-5. What did he show? Amazingly, he had 6-4o! At the sight of this, somebody said out loud "Why did you call?" Again, through clenched teeth and pointing a finger at me, he said "I put him on a resteal!" At which point, all four of the other players, and the dealer (but not me), said almost in unison "So what?"

Their point was, and correctly so, that even if God had come down from heaven and told him I was bluffing, he still would have been correct to fold. Thus, even with absolute certainty that his read was correct, he still should have gone with basic strategy in this spot, and just folded.

However, if instead this hand had taken place much earlier, when we were not that close to the money bubble, and he was somehow completely certain that I was bluffing, a call might have been in order. He was risking T6,000 chips to win my all-in raise of T8,000, his T2,000 that he already invested, plus the small blind and antes. He was therefore getting reasonably close to 2:1 pot odds on a call, and would have only had to win the pot about 37% of the time to break even using chip count math. And if it's still the early and middle stages of the tournament, as we've said before, the chip count (cash game) math and the ICM math are pretty much the same, as chip values are still linear at this stage. If he knew, for example, that I had a hand from the bottom half of all possible starting hands, his 6-4o will win over 42% of the chips when he calls.

---

[*] Tournaments generally started with a lot fewer chips back then, and typical structures gave you a lot less play than we are used to today.

Since he only needs about 37% to break even, it is profitable for him to make this call, even though his hand is one of the worst possible starting hands, and even though most of my bluff hands still have him beat.

But the point of this story, and of this chapter, is that no matter what information you have, in the end it is the math that reveals the correct decisions. You can gather a lot of information, including information that is completely non-mathematical in nature, but you need to do the math with all of that information, and only then reach a decision. No matter how much some of the information may push towards a specific decision, other information, and the mathematical analysis of all the information, may still mandate that another decision is the correct (highest EV) one to make.

POT ODDS

Pot odds is one of the most basic mathematical calculations you can make when playing poker. While very easy to understand, correct application of pot odds math can be difficult in practice, especially when we consider implied and reverse implied odds, which we will discuss later. For many players, one of the hardest aspects of doing pot odds math is the result of a confusion with a related concept that I call "hand odds". Let's go through these things carefully, and make sure they are as clear as possible.

Pot odds simply refers to a comparison of how much you're risking to how much you can win. More specifically, pot odds refers to how much you're risking right now compared to how much you can win right now, ignoring all future action that might occur. So, if there is $100 in the pot, and your opponent bets $100, you must risk $100 to make this call. When you do so, you can win $200 (the $100 your opponent just bet, plus the $100 that was already in the pot). It does not matter where the $100 in the pot came from. In a typical hand of poker, some of those chips out there came from you, from your antes, blinds or other bets you made earlier in this hand. But that is irrelevant when calculating your pot odds. Wherever the money came from, right now it will cost you $100 to continue, and you can win $200. Your pot odds are $200:$100, or 2:1. This means when considering only the pot odds, and nothing else, you will correctly make this call if you believe you will win more than 1/3rd (33%) of the time. If you were going to win exactly 1 time in 3, it doesn't matter what you do. One time you will win $200, and two times you will lose $100, for a net of $0. If you fold instead of call, you will also net $0 (again, for a simple pot odds analysis, we ignore the money, if any, that you already contributed to the pot).

Sometimes, my students have a hard time with this thinking. They say, but I don't break even here, I already put $50 into that pot, so if I fold I lose $50. While correct, this is irrelevant. We are talking about this moment in time right now, when you are facing the $100 bet. That $50 you put in the pot was in the past, it is already lost to the pot. Let's back up and look at the larger picture. Right now, your opponent has bet $100. There is $100 in the pot, $50 that you contributed, and $50 that the opponent contributed. You have $1,000 in chips in front of you, and you think you will win exactly 1 time in 3 if you call. Let's pretend this scenario repeats itself three times, you always call, and you win one time.

The one time you win, you will now have $1,200 in your stack. But 2 times you lose, and have only $900 in your stack. If we add these results up and divide by 3:

$1,200 + $900 + $900 = $3,000
$3,000 ÷ 3 = $1,000

So, on average, if you call, your stack will be $1,000. And if you fold, your stack will also be $1,000. This is why we say, in this spot, it doesn't matter whether you call or fold. Either way, your average result will be the same. But what if you thought you were going to win 40% (two-fifths) of the time? Now, out of every 5 times this comes up, 2 times you will win, and have $1,200. 3 times you will lose, and have $900. How does this compare?

$1,200 + $1,200 + $900 + $900 + $900 = $5,100
$5,100 ÷ 5 = $1,020

If you think you are going to win more than 1/3rd of the time, it becomes profitable to call. When you believe you have a 40% chance to win, you are making an average of $20 more by calling than by folding. What if you thought you were going to win only 25% of the time?

$1,200 + $900 + $900 + $900 = $3,900
$3,900 ÷ 4 = $975

By calling with only a 25% chance of winning, you are now costing yourself an average of $25 each time you call, because when you call, your average stack is $975, but if you fold, your stack will stay at $1,000.

In these examples, I made up numbers, saying we had a 25% or 40% chance of winning. That's all fine and good, but how, in a real hand, can we say what our chances of winning really are? Of course, unless for some strange reason we've seen our opponent's cards, we can't know exactly what our chances will be. But we can estimate those chances, and the more accurate our estimates, the more correctly we can make decisions. One complicated method for doing this involves detailed analyses of the odds of our hand beating the range of hands with which we feel our opponent is holding. For more on this, see Chapter 10. But often when we are worried about pot odds, we are in a situation where we know we are currently behind, and the question is how often will we catch up and make the winning hand? The term I use for this is "hand odds".

Hand odds is the chance that the cards we are holding will improve, and improve to the winning hand. It is the use of hand odds math that told me that I am going to win 25% of the time, or 40% of the time, or whatever it may be. As in any situation where you don't have all the information (specifically, you don't know exactly the cards your opponent is holding), you have to make some educated guesses. However, the better your education, the more accurate your guesses will be.

The first step in calculating (or estimating, same thing really) your hand odds is to count your number of outs. That is, how many cards that might yet be dealt will improve your hand to the winner? Let's start with a simple example. You are holding 6♠-5♠, and the flop is A♥-8♣-7♦. Your opponent has bet all-in, and you're deciding whether or not to call. Before we mention the pot odds, let's calculate the hand odds for your situation, that is, the chances that you will improve to the winning hand. First, we are quite confident that right now we do not have the best hand. In fact, this almost has to be true, as there are almost no hands that are not currently beating us. In this spot, even bluffing hands like Q♦-10♦, are ahead. More often than not, we expect this opponent to be even further ahead, and actually have a pair, frequently aces (e.g., they started with a hand like A♦-K♦ or A♣-J♦, and has flopped a pair). As such, we do not expect to win very often, if ever, by simply making a pair with our 5 or 6. At this moment, we expect almost all of our wins to occur when we improve to a straight by catching a 4 or 9. So, what are the hand odds for this to occur?

We have 8 outs to make a straight. There are four 4s in the deck, plus four 9s. Of course, our opponent could be holding a 9 or a 4 in their hand (A♦-4♦ or A♦-9♣, for example), and it is also possible, even likely, that one of the other players sitting at this table folded a 9 or 4, and that card we could use is now in the muck. However, at this point in time, there are 47 cards we have not seen. We know the whereabouts of the 5♠-6♠-7♦-8♣-A♥, and we can guess that our opponent will often have an Ace as one of their cards, but we only know with complete certainty the five cards we have seen. Thus, even though the dealer might be holding only 28 cards in the stub*, we cannot distinguish these 28 from the 47 total cards that we have not seen with our own eyes. It might be that the other eight opponents all folded hands that did not include any 9s or 4s, or they might have folded all of them. Since we can't know, we pretend the dealer has all 47 cards in their hand, and any one of them might be dealt on the turn or river.

We will now apply what is called the Rule of Four. Because there are two more cards to be dealt, the turn and river, we will take our number of outs and multiple by 4. Thus, 8 times 4 is 32, and we therefore have approximately a 32% chance of making our straight on either the turn or river (or both). The true answer is not going to be 32%, but something different. However, the true answer, and the approximation we get from the Rule of Four, will be reasonably close**. To convert this percentage to hands odds, we first subtract our answer

---

* The stub is the undealt cards being held by the dealer. Because they dealt 20 cards to the 10 players at the table preflop, 3 on the flop, and 1 burn card, there are only 28 cards left in the stub.

** In this case, the true answer is 31.5%.

from 100. If we have a 32% chance of making our hand, we must have a 68% chance of NOT making our hand. 68:32 reduces down to approximately 2:1. Thus, the hand odds in this scenario are about 2:1 against making the straight.

Now that we have calculated our hand odds, we can compare them to our pot odds, and make our decision. Imagine that the all-in bet was for $50, and that there was already $100 in the pot. This means our pot odds are 3:1, since we can win $150 by risking $50 more. Since the pot odds (3:1) are higher than the hand odds (2:1), we should make the call. Since 3:1 is more than 2:1, calling is profitable.

What if this all-in bet had occurred on the turn instead of the flop, and there had been only one more card to come? The analysis is very much the same, but since we only have one opportunity to catch the right card and make the winning hand, we now apply the Rule of Two, and multiple the number of outs by 2 as a means of estimating our chances of improving. We still have 6♠-5♠, but the board now reads A♥-8♣-7♦-K♠. Our opponent has gone all-in, again betting $50 into a $100 pot. What are our hand odds?

We still have 8 outs, which the Rule of Two converts to an approximately 16% chance of making the straight*. This means that there is an 84% chance we will not make our hand, and our hands odds are thus 84:16, or a little more than 5:1 against improving. Since this hand went check-check on the flop, and the opponent has bet all-in on the turn, we are again getting pot odds of 3:1. Now, with only one card to come, the pot odds are lower than the hand odds, so folding is the better decision.

As we have shown, the correct way to use pot odds is to compare them to the hand odds, and if the pot odds are higher, you should call. If the pot odds are lower than the hand odds, you should fold. But there is obviously a lot more to it than this. What if you're trying to use pot odds to make a decision

---

* If we had not used the shortcut Rule of Two, the true odds here are 8 outs from 46 cards that might be dealt on the river, which is equal to a 17.4% chance of making the straight. Although the Rules of 2 and 4 will almost never yield the exact perfect answer, what they provide is close enough. Our shortcut Rule of Two yielded hand odds of 84:16, or 5.25:1. The true answer is 17.4%, which yields hand odds of 82.6:17.4, or 4.75:1. This means that if we were getting pot odds of exactly 5:1, we would have chosen to fold using the shortcut Rule of Two, but by doing the full math we would have correctly called. However, the mistake we are making here when we fold instead of call is very small, and therefore not that important in the long run. See Chapter 33.

preflop? An opponent has bet all-in, and you have to decide whether to call or fold. Calculating your pot odds is easy, but how do you determine your hand odds? There is nothing like the Rules of Two and Four for this situation. Now, you have to determine what hands your opponent might be holding, and determine how often you will win with your hand against that range. For more on this, see Chapter 10. But once you estimate how often you will win, the rest of the math is again the same. If you're getting pot odds of 2:1 on the call, you need to win at least 33.3% of the time to correctly call (because in this spot, you would lose about 66.6% of the time, and 66.6:33.3 is 2:1). It is still simply a question of whether or not the pot odds are higher or lower than the hand odds.

But the real complicating factor is most of the times the bet is not all-in, and there remain more chips that might be bet on later rounds. Now, how do we use pot odds, hand odds, and the like to help in making the best decision? We have to introduce two new concepts, implied odds and reverse implied odds.

Implied odds are the chips that you can win on future betting rounds. As we learned above, if you have an open-ended straight draw, 8 outs, and are only considering the one next card to be dealt, your hand odds are about 5:1 against. Let's imagine that there is $100 in the pot, and your opponent has bet $50, as they did above. This yields pot odds of 3:1, which is a lot less than the 5:1 hand odds of improving on the next card. If this bet were all-in with one card to come, it would be clearly correct to fold. But here, we are looking at the single next card on the turn, and we are assuming that both you and your opponent have a lot of chips left after this $50 bet. Specifically, let's assume that if you call here, the effective stack* remaining will be $1,000. This means that if you call this $50 bet, you can win $150 that is in the pot now, plus potentially up to $1,000 more that might be bet and won by you AFTER you make your straight. This means that your total implied odds are $50 to win $1,000 + $150, or $1,150:$50, or 23:1! This is a lot higher than the 5:1 hand odds,

---

* The effective stack is the smaller stack between you and your opponent. If you start a hand with 100 chips, and your opponent has 200, the effective stack is 100, as that is the most either of you can win or lose. If the opponent instead had 50 chips, the effective stack would be 50, even though you have more. Again, 50 is now the most you can win or lose in this hand.

so it would seem that calling now becomes an easy decision.

But there is another factor to take into account. Reverse implied odds. These are the chips that you can lose on future betting rounds. Some of the time you will make your straight on the next card, but that same card might also give your opponent a flush. And even if the turn card that makes your straight doesn't also give your opponent a better hand, the river card might give your opponent a flush or a full house, and you will lose. Thus, it is seldom 100% certain that you will win every time you improve by catching one of your outs. And the concept of reverse implied odds is one way to take this into account.

Going back to our example, your pot odds were 3:1, your hand odds were 5:1, and your implied odds were 23:1. How do we use this information correctly to make our decision? Well, if we're in the same spot as discussed earlier, we are holding 6♠-5♠ on a flop of A♥-8♣-7♦. Any 9 or 4 that is dealt on the turn cannot also make a flush or better for our opponent. If the turn is a 4, we will have the nuts, and can only lose if the river card improves our opponent's hand to something even better. If a 9 is dealt, it is possible we didn't improve to the best hand, as our opponent could possibly hold 10-6 or J-10, and just made a higher straight. However, the chances of this being the case are very low, and most of time we can ignore this possibility. So this means we are assuming that every time we catch a 9 or 4 on the turn, we will have the best hand at that moment. So unless our opponent also makes a flush draw with the same 9 or 4, and then catches another card of that suit on the river, or if our opponent has two pair or trips on the turn, and makes a full house on the river, we will win. Again, these are both very unlikely scenarios, and we can mostly ignore them.

So, should we call? We still need to do a little more analysis. Our hand odds are 5:1 against, and our pot odds if we make the $50 call are 3:1. This means we need to make up this difference with the implied odds for the call to be correct. That is, since our hand odds are about 5:1 against, and our opponent has bet $50, we need to feel certain that we will win, on average, at least $250 total when we make the call, AND a 9 or 4 is dealt on the turn. That means, in addition to the $150 already out there, we need to feel certain that we will get at least another $100 out of our opponent, on average, every time we call and then make our hand. But, since there were some reverse implied odds considerations, we should bump this number up a little. Instead of expecting an average of at least $100 more when we call and make our hand, we should probably believe that we will average somewhat more than that before we elect to call. How much more? That is hard to say exactly. But since in this scenario the chances that we make a straight and then lose is fairly remote, I would say that we only need to increase the number a little bit, to maybe something like $125 more.

If the board had been a lot scarier for a straight draw, we would bump this number up more, maybe even a lot more. For example, instead of holding 6♠-5♠ on a flop of A♥-8♣-7♦, what if the flop were A♥-8♦-7♦? Now, our opponent could have hands like A♦-K♦, where whenever we make a straight with the 9♦ or 4♦, we don't improve to the winning hand, but instead improve to a very strong losing hand. And even if we catch one of the non-diamond 9s or 4s, the opponent will still catch a diamond on the river about 20% of the time, and beat us out of what is likely to be a lot of chips, maybe even all of our chips. If our opponent has a set on the flop, even if we make the straight on the turn, the board will pair to give them a winning full house (or quads) about 23% of the time, again costing us a lot of chips.

The more coordinated the board, the more likely it is that we will lose, even if we improve our hand. Also, even if we don't lose, the more coordinated the board, the more it might look scary to our opponent, and therefore they might fold rather than pay us off after we make our hand, thus eliminating the implied odds we were counting on when we made the call.

How can we deal with the issue of calculating our hand odds when the board is coordinated, or we are otherwise not certain of all of our outs? Again, in this example of 6♠-5♠ on a flop of A♥-8♦-7♦, we have 8 outs to a straight, but two of those outs also put a potential flush on the board. We don't know if we actually have 8 outs to a winning straight, or only 6 outs if the 9♦ and 4♦ beat us rather than make us the winner. Of course, what if the opponent were actually bluffing when they bet this flop? Maybe they have something like K♥-Q♥. If that is the case, we don't have just 8 outs, we have 14 (four 9s, four 4s, three 5s, and three 6s). Instead of hand odds of about 5:1, we might have hand odds of 7:1 (for 6 outs) or 2.5:1 (for 14 outs).

The best way to deal with this is to estimate the number of outs we think we have on average, and proceed from there. Most of the time, catching a pair on the turn when a 5 or 6 hits the board will not win us the hand. Even if our opponent has K-Q, if they continue to bluff, it will frequently work, and we will fold if we don't make better than one small pair. So we can probably ignore those outs for the most part. And when we make the straight, even if it is a diamond, it will usually win us the pot. We might want to think of this situation as if we had 7 outs instead of 8. Although we expect to win more than half of the time when the 9♦ or 4♦ is dealt, we also expect that the opponent will be that much less likely to pay us off, possibly folding even a strong hand, since both the straight draw and the flush draw got there.

So, assuming 7 outs, we convert this to hand odds using the Rule of Two, or 14%. 86:14 is about 6:1, and the immediate pot odds are 3:1 as we are facing that $50 bet. We need to make up another $150 with implied odds to correctly call here. Plus, since we might make the straight and still lose, we will bump this up to $200. Therefore, we should only call for $50 if we believe that we will, on average, get at least $200 more from this opponent after we make our straight on the turn.

I teach a lot of live poker seminars every year. In addition to lecturing, I spend a lot of time doing what I call live hand exercises. In these, I am the dealer, and the students at my table have play chips and we play hands of NLH as if it were a real game. The students are told to play their very best, and make the same decisions they would make if this were a real big buy-in event, and at the end of the hand I critique their decisions.

One of my most common comments when evaluating a student's preflop decision to play a hand is for me to tell them they chose to play a reverse implied odds hand. For example, let's say we're simulating the very beginning of a tournament, and the average stack is 100 or more big blinds. One student raises to 2.5xBB, and another calls. Just considering what we've discussed above, part of their mistake might lie in the fact that they are getting immediate pot odds of 2:1, 3:1, or even more (especially if other players have already called the raise). Moreover, they are getting huge implied odds, maybe 50:1 or more. So they call the raise with a hand like K-9o, and think "Hey, I'm getting 3:1 right now to call that T250 raise, plus I could win as much as T20,000 more if I hit the right flop."

But they are forgetting to take into account the reverse implied odds of the situation. While it is true that they could win another T20,000, it is equally true that they could lose another T20,000. And K-9o is the kind of hand that, in my experience, tends to lose more chips than it wins in postflop betting. When you do hit the flop, most often it is one pair. And this just isn't the hand that often wins a big pot with one pair. If you do have the best hand, you usually won't get a lot of action, and will only win a small pot. If you don't have the best hand, it is still top pair, which means you can't just check-and-fold, and instead will tend to lose somewhere from a medium to a very large pot in the process. Even though you can't do detailed pot odds math with any accuracy for these preflop situations, you should keep in mind the question, if I play this hand, is it the kind of hand that will tend to win or lose chips, on average, in future rounds of betting?

Early in a tournament, when all or most players have deep stacks, it is often going to be more correct to play small connected and/or suited cards (e.g., 7♠-5♠, 9♣-8♦, even 4♥-3♥) than it is to play two unsuited high cards (e.g., K♦-10♠, A♣-9♦). Most of the time, your cards will miss the flop completely. And most of the time you do hit the flop, you only make one pair. Lots of (weak) players will always play hands like K-10 and A-9 if there are not multiple raises preflop, and they will often lose a lot of chips when these hands flop one pair. But how often do you put a lot of chips in the pot after flopping one pair with cards like 7-5s? With these hands, you are looking to hit big draws, a pair plus a draw combo , or better. Otherwise, you know to proceed with caution.

Late in the tournament, when stacks become shallow, then the small connected and/or suited cards lose most of their value, while high card hands go up in value. Now much more of your equity results from getting chips in preflop while ahead, as there are fewer chips left to win or lose in postflop betting. Early in the tournament, the importance of implied odds and reverse implied odds is huge, whereas late in the tournament the importance of implied odds and reverse implied odds has gone down dramatically.

PREFLOP BET-SIZING

While it is a very complicated question to determine whether or not you should bet or raise, HOW MUCH you should bet or raise is typically a much simpler decision. At least at the Game Theory Optimal level, that is. At the Game Theory Exploitative level, it is as complicated as anything that involves reading players and taking maximum advantage of their weaknesses.

The overriding consideration with bet-sizing, both preflop and at any point during the hand, is consistency. If you bet or raise different amounts, you could be giving away the strength of your hand, and making it easy for your opponent to better decide how to respond. It was not uncommon in the past to see players who made larger bets/raises with their strong hands (presumably because they felt more confident they would win, and therefore wanted to build a bigger pot), and smaller bets/raises with their weaker hands. It quickly became easy to fold when they bet or raised a large amount*, and either call (or reraise) when they bet or raised a smaller amount.

If you are currently betting different amounts at different times, you

---

* Unless you had a very strong hand, or the stacks were deep and you were going to consider implied odds, try to draw out on them, and then win a really big pot.

may think that you are mixing it up and do not have a pattern. You are probably wrong. Humans are horrible at being random, yet very good at spotting patterns. That is one reason you see so much faulty thinking at a casino. We evolved the ability to spot patterns, and tend to believe what we see. It was very useful to notice that the flood waters tended to return a few days after a certain migratory bird showed up, and we would learn to use that information to our advantage. But, when there has been a 6 on the flop for 8 out of the last 10 hands, that doesn't mean 6s are hot, and we should play any hand with a 6 in it. In fact, the knowledge of what cards hit prior flops is so irrelevant to reality, that it is surprising we even notice such a thing. But we evolved the skill to spot any pattern, even those we're not actively seeking. So if there is any pattern to your bet sizes, it will be noticed.

So, now that you are going to be consistent in your bet-sizing, how much should you raise preflop? In the old days, well before the poker boom, preflop raises of 4xBB to 10xBB were common. The prevailing attitude was you should raise big to protect your hand (unspoken rule, you only raised with the stronger starting hands), and make sure that you either take down the pot immediately, or at least make sure you got as few callers as possible. The problem with this strategy was that you were risking too much compared to what you could win. Preflop, if nobody else has opened the pot, there is only 1.5xBB in the pot, or 2xBB to 3xBB if antes are in play. If you raise to 5xBB, you are risking 5xBB to win 1.5-3xBB, and this means that you must be successful a significant majority of the time to come out ahead.

Just before the poker boom, the standard preflop raise amongst better players had come down to 3xBB, but it turns out that was still more than necessary. As the poker boom progressed, the better players started trying smaller and smaller preflop raise amounts. If you were raising 3xBB as your standard, you were going to get everybody to fold some portion of the time. Let's pretend that for a period of time in a specific game, you were getting them all to fold about half the time, 50%. But, in trying smaller amounts, we learned that if you instead made your preflop raise 2.7xBB, they would still all fold almost as often, maybe 47% of the time instead of 50%. And if you tried 2.5xBB, they all folded 45% of the time. And if you raised just barely more than 2xBB, it would still get them all to fold more than 40% of the time.

With this new method, you were raising something like 2.1xBB instead of

3xBB, and therefore risking about 30% fewer chips. And you were stealing the blinds more than 40% of the time, instead of about 50% of the time, a decrease of only about 15-20%. Thus, raising preflop to steal the blinds was much more profitable. So, not only did this mean you were making more profit from pre-flop raises, but it was now correct to raise more often, since it wasn't as risky to do so. Then, since you were raising more often, your range of hands was a lot wider, meaning it was that much harder for an opponent to read your hand, which leads to you being tougher to play against postflop, and increasing the likelihood that your opponents make mistakes in their postflop decisions. As such, this reduction in the average size of preflop raises has been a large part of the reason that poker games are much tougher now than they were before the poker boom, and why the games are also so much more aggressive than before.

In today's poker world, a lot of players are min-raising, literally putting in the minimum amount for a legal raise. Thus, if blinds are T500,T1,000, they raise to T2,000. In theory, this is correct, and should be slightly more prof-itably than raising slightly more. However, in practice, for reasons of ego or otherwise, I find that if you min-raise to T2,000, the player in the big blind just feels they cannot fold. But, for some reason that really makes no sense, if you raise to T2,100, they feel they can fold their worst hands. For this reason, I prefer what I call the mini-raise (T2,100 in this example), rather than the min-raise (T2,000). In this one spot, I feel that the extra chip does make a noticeable difference in getting people to fold, especially the player in the big blind. Therefore, when you are opening the pot preflop, and choose to raise, I recommend the mini-raise to just over 2xBB.

But what if you're not opening the pot? What if other players have limped in before it's your turn? In this case, you should raise more. One simple method is to just add in the amount of extra chips. That is, if you would have opened for 2.1xBB if you were the first player to enter the pot, but somebody has called, now raise to 3.1xBB instead. If two players have limped in, make it 4.1xBB, etc. I tend to do this, but add a little less than one full big blind to the amount. So, for zero limpers, I tend to raise 2.1xBB, for one limper, 3xBB, for two limpers, 3.9xBB, and so on.

Let me reinforce the main lesson of this chapter, it is more important that you are consistent with what you do, than it is whether you prefer bet sizes that are higher or lower than what I use. In other words, in the future, somebody might do some detailed analysis, and come up with convincing evidence that I should use amounts that are higher or lower than what I've been using, and this won't surprise me very much unless they are recommending amounts that are significantly more or less. But if somebody comes along and says that my use of consistent amounts is a mistake, I will be very surprised, and probably require exceptional proof before changing my mind.

How about the situation where you are not opening the pot, and somebody else has not just limped in, but has raised before you? I still believe very much in being consistent here, but the standard rules are a little more complicated. At the most basic level, I like to reraise about 3x the amount of their raise. Any smaller than that, and there is very little chance they will ever fold preflop. Of course, sometimes you have a hand that is happy to get action, and sometimes you have a hand where you want everybody to fold. But since we are going to be consistent, we can't raise less with stronger hands that don't mind action, and more with weaker hands that want everybody to fold. This is too transparent, and easy to take advantage of. So we raise or reraise a consistent amount, and since we sometimes want them to fold, we must pick an amount that is large enough to make this reasonably possible. And 3x their raise is the smallest amount, in my experience, that can motivate them to fold some of the time.

So why haven't I told you to just always make it 3x the previous raise? Mostly because in many cases the raise you are facing is either too big or too small, and as such you should adjust. It is not uncommon to see a situation where several people limp in, and then somebody min-raises. Maybe they play too much limit holdem, maybe they live-misclicked*, who knows. But if you reraise to 3x their amount, it will only be for 6xBB. There is already about 7-9xBB in the pot, so if you raise to a total of 6xBB, you will be offering pot odds of about 3:1 for the players who have already limped, and almost 4:1 for the raiser. They have already indicated that they have "playable" hands, so it is very unlikely they will fold in this spot to your 6xBB reraise. As such, you will almost certainly want to raise more.

---

* Misclick refers to a common online poker mistake, where a player intends to click one button, perhaps to fold, but instead clicks the wrong button, and unintentionally calls or raises instead. When a player makes a silly mistake playing live poker, it is now often referred to as a live-misclick. An example would be mentally intending to bet T2,100, but instead of grabbing 2-T1,000 chips and 1-T100 chip, the player grabs 1-T1,000 chip and 2-T100 chips, and makes it T1,200 by accident.

In this situation, the original raiser would have been better off raising to about 4-5xBB, in which case you would have reraised to about 12-15xBB. But they didn't. However, instead of tripling their bet to 6xBB, or making it the 12-15xBB as you would have chosen had their raise been bigger, pick a bet size in-between these two amounts, something like 8-10xBB. This is enough that the limpers might all fold, and the raiser might fold as well. And if they don't all fold, that's fine. You shouldn't be choosing to reraise in this spot with a junk hand (stuff like Q-5, 10-4, 7-2, and the like), as doing so would often leave you in a situation where you would have to make tough decisions post-flop. And if you ever do reraise in a spot like this with a junk hand, there should be really strong evidence supporting this GTE play.

You should also consider adjusting the size of your raise based upon your position relative to the other players. If you are in position compared to all of the other players who have voluntarily entered this pot so far, your standard amount can be smaller, as it will be easier to motivate them to fold. Everything else being the same, a good player is less likely to continue when out of position, and more likely to continue when in position. As such, you can raise less when you have position, and contrarily raise more when you are out of position. In the paragraph above, where I suggest 8-10xBB, you would raise 10xBB when out of position (usually when you are one of the blinds), 8xBB when on the button, and 9xBB when in late position but not on the button. The point here is to still use consistent bet sizing (the variation is based upon these other factors of position and the bet size you are facing, not upon your cards) so as to not provide information about the strength of your hand, and to select the smallest bet size that creates a reasonable chance that all the players might fold.

All of the discussion up to this point has assumed that your stack size, and that of all or at least most of your opponents, is not too small. If you find yourself in a situation where your standard consistent bet or raise amount is about 1/3rd or more of the effective stack, your GTO strategy should be to bet or raise all-in instead. For example, if three players limp in and the next player raises to 5xBB, your normal reraise would be to about 15xBB. But if you have only about 45xBB or less in your stack, then you should probably raise all-in instead. Any time you put about 1/3rd or more of your stack in the pot pre-flop, you are virtually never going to fold if somebody else reraises. So why let them make the all-in move? If you shove, they might fold, and you win what's out there now. And if they call, you win when you have the best hand at show-down. But if you raise less than all-in, and then call for the rest of your chips, you can only win when you finish with the best hand at showdown.

Of course, if you have A-A or the like, you will probably want them to get all-in with you, rather than getting them to fold. But, if you raise to 15xBB when you really want action, and shove for 30-45xBB when you want them to fold, they might catch on to this pattern, and be able to make better decisions.

Plus, there are many times when even if you are quite likely to have the best hand, you would still prefer them to fold. In this same scenario, three players limp in, the next player raises to 5xBB, and you have 40xBB and are holding J-J. You are very likely to have the best hand right now, but what would be better for you, to reraise your normal amount (or even a bit less), and hope the original raiser shoves (so you can call and be the favorite to win a big pot), or shove all-in and get everybody to fold? Obviously the answer depends upon exactly what cards the original raiser is holding.

But imagine they have K-Q, a perfectly legitimate hand for this raise. If you reraise to 15xBB or less, they may feel that there is enough chance you will fold that they choose to 4-bet all-in. And if you don't fold, they know they will be behind, but usually have between 30-45% equity in the pot. If you get all-in with them preflop, there will be about 85xBB in the pot, and you will win almost 56% of the chips, on average. Thus, while you will end up with either 85xBB or nothing, you will have, on average, a stack of 48xBB if all the chips go in. But what if you shove instead, and they fold preflop? Now you will still have the 40xBB you started with, plus you will win their raise of 5xBB, the 3xBB in limps, and the 2xBB or so in blinds and antes, for a total stack of 50xBB. Thus, when they fold, you end up with more chips, on average, AND there was no risk of being eliminated. Win-win.

Even when we look at the entire range of hands for them, if they're going to have something within the top 10-20% of all starting hands to make this raise, your edge with J-J is only going to be about 60:40. At that point, your equity is pretty close to the same whether they fold or go all-in with you. So, if it's about the same, the play that involves no risk of going broke must be better, even early in the tournament before ICM affects the math.

Everything up to now in this chapter has been about GTO strategy for preflop bet-sizing. And unless you have a very good reason to do otherwise, you should stick to your GTO strategy. But sometimes the evidence is there, the information has been provided to you, whether it is a pattern, a live tell, or something else, and you should do something other than your GTO bet-sizing, because you firmly believe that some other amount will give you an even greater edge. What are some of those things?

One of the main reasons to bet more is when you have an opponent who is calling larger raises just as often as smaller ones, and you have a hand where you want to get more chips into the pot now. You see this a lot in cash games. Players tend to have much deeper stacks, in terms of number of blinds, in a typical cash game as compared to a typical tournament hand. With such deep stacks, a lot of players like to regularly make opening raises of 3xBB or more. In many cases they are wrong to do this, but the right time to do it is when you have a very strong starting hand, and would like to build a bigger pot as soon as possible. If you know the player(s) behind you are just as likely to call (or fold) for a raise of 4xBB as they are for a raise of 2.1xBB, then it makes sense to raise 4xBB with hands that want action, and 2.1xBB when you're stealing. Obviously, this flies in the face of most of the advice in this chapter, which is to use consistent bet-sizing so as to not give away the strength of your hand.

However, there will be times when giving away information is not a concern. Maybe since you've been moved to the table, you've observed this tendency of certain players to be insensitive to the size of raises, but you have not yet been the preflop raiser yourself. As such, if you open for 4xBB now for the first time, there is no pattern, as one incidence of anything cannot create a pattern. If, however, you have already made your standard raise of 2.1xBB several times, it will likely arouse suspicion if you raise more this time, and should probably not be done.

One of the best times to adjust your preflop bet-sizing is when you are doing so for the purpose of making it more likely that you are the player who can make the all-in raise, if it comes to that, rather than the player facing the shove by another.

For example, a player limps, and you know they like to limp-reraise fairly often (meaning, they don't always have a super-premium hand when doing so). Also, when this player reraises somebody preflop, they consistently triple the bet. Between you and them, the effective stack size is 25xBB. This means that if you make your normal raise of about 3.1xBB in this spot, their normal reraise will be about 9xBB. But since 9xBB is more than 1/3rd of the effective stack, they will likely just shove in instead. Therefore, it might be better for you to raise to a total of 2.5xBB this time. Facing this raise, they will likely reraise to about 7.5xBB (rather than shoving), and you can then you can be the player who moves all-in for 25xBB. Now, because you have reduced your normal raise amount, you have manipulated the situation such that you can force them to call your shove (or fold to it), rather than you having to make that difficult and critical decision.

Of course, there are millions of potential tells, patterns, and situations where you might prefer to alter your bet-sizing. However, I would resist these temptations until you are extremely confident that you have properly analyzed all of the information, and you are certain that a different amount is preferable. The more you diverge from your standard bet sizing, the more likely it is that you are creating a pattern. Your smarter opponents will figure out the pattern, and thus do a much better job of reading your hands. If I can accurately deduce your cards much of the time, you really have very little chance of beating me. Likewise, if I give away such information to you, I will be the one who can only win by getting lucky. Our goal is to be the player who always wins when they run good, and usually wins when their luck is average, not the player who wins only when they get lucky.

POSTFLOP BET-SIZING

You should consider numerous factors when determining whether to bet or raise postflop (i.e., on the flop, turn, or river). At a minimum, you need to consider your hand, the range of hands you believe your opponent(s) to be holding, how they are likely to play those hands (both in immediate reaction to this bet/raise/check, and on future streets), the value of giving or taking a free card, the benefits and detriments of making the pot larger now, and many other things. But once you do the difficult analysis and determine whether to bet or raise, how much is usually an easy decision.

Just like we discussed for preflop bet-sizing, the key to good postflop bet-sizing is consistency. Again, you want to make sure that you are not betting more or less based upon the strength of your hand, or how much you desire the opponent(s) to fold. If you do, your tougher opponents will pick up on this fairly quickly, and seriously outplay you with this knowledge.

Before we discuss how much you should consistently bet, let's first discuss what exactly it means to make a pot-sized bet or raise. If you are making a pot-sized bet, the math is easy. How much is already out there in the pot? If three of you each put T500 in preflop, there is T1,500 out there now, and a full pot-sized bet is exactly T1,500. If you bet T1,000, you're betting 2/3rd of the pot. T750 is half the pot, and so on. What if there is T1,500 out there, and somebody else bets first? Now how much is a pot-sized raise? For some reason, this calculation causes tremendous confusion for some players. But it's actually not that hard. If you are facing a bet, and want to make a pot-sized raise, the first thing to do is imagine you have called the bet. Then, add up how much is out there in total, and raise that much more.

For example, T1,500 is in the pot, and somebody bets T500. It's your turn, and you want to raise the pot. How much do you make it? Imagine you had called the T500; how much would be out there? There would be T1,500 (the pot) + T500 (the bet) + T500 (your call), for a total of T2,500. Thus, for you to make a pot-sized raise, you would put out T500 + T2,500, or a total of T3,000. For some reason, a lot of players tend to forget about the bet and the call, and think that a pot-sized raise would be a raise of T1,500 on top of the T500 bet. But even though the dealer hasn't scooped those chips into the middle, as soon as they are bet, those chips are in the pot. What if another player had called the original bet of T500 before it was your turn? Now, it's all the same, but the pot is T500 larger when it comes to you, so your new total to make a pot-sized raise is T3,500.

What if you didn't want to make a full pot-sized raise, but instead wanted to raise half the pot? The math is similar. T1,500 in the pot, the opponent bet T500, and you imagine you called the T500, making a pot of T2,500. Half of T2,500 is T1,250, so a half-pot raise would be T500 + T1,250, and you would raise to a total of T1,750. As you can see, the player who thinks a pot-sized raise is T500 + T1,500 (the amount in front of the dealer only), is actually making a raise that is closer to a half-pot raise, not a full-pot raise, in this instance.

So now that we know how much a pot-sized raise is, how much should you raise? There is a lot of latitude here, but again, be consistent. I advise that you bet/raise the same percentage of the pot every time, and that you pick a number between 50-100% of the pot for that amount. I will admit, 50-100% is a very wide range, so you would think that some part of this range would be a lot better than other parts. The answer is yes and no. Some players prefer to play bigger pots, and make bigger bets. They are more comfortable with this. Other players prefer smaller bets. So you should feel free to find out what size works better for you. But once you pick your size, say for example 70%, then all of your bets and raises should be 70% of the pot. Besides just fitting the size to your natural style, what else might guide your selection between larger and smaller standard bet sizes?

One of the most important factors is how you rate your skill level as compared to the other players at your table right now. If you think you are the best or nearly the best at your table, you would usually prefer to pick a standard bet-size that is on the smaller side, i.e., 50-70% of the pot, for your bets and raises. This is the heart of the "small-ball" style of poker. The idea is that if your bets and raises are smaller, it takes more of them to reach that point in a hand where somebody is all-in. That is, instead of needing there to be four bets and/ or raises before somebody is all-in, it will require five bets and/or raises to reach that point. This means one more decision must be made before reaching the final all-in decision. And if you're the better player, it is because you make better decisions. If you make better decisions, you want each hand to require more decisions be made.

Obviously, the opposite is also true. If you know that you're outmatched by the players at your table, you should choose to make larger bets and raises (in the range of 80-100% of the pot). This will result in fewer decisions, and give them less of an edge against you.

Taking this concept to the extreme leads to the strategy I had my Mom use in our team tournament. Essentially, depending upon how many big blinds are in the stack of the player, they either shove or fold preflop, and never do anything else. Although this method will not make the person a long-term winning (+EV) player, it minimizes the edge that the better players have against such a total novice. If you follow this strategy, even if you tell your opponents exactly what you're doing, there is not much they can do about it. They can either be dealt a strong enough hand to call against your (quite strong) range when you shove, or correctly fold. That's it, there is no better strategy for them to use.

The other significant factor in choosing how much to make your standard bet is how much does it take to get the job done? Whenever you bet or raise, most of the time, you prefer that everybody folds. And I don't say this because you are trying to avoid risk, and want to just take down the pot now. If you're bluffing or semi-bluffing, you obviously desire everybody to just fold. But even when you are betting what you know is probably the best hand, usually you would prefer that they all just fold.

For example, you raise preflop with A♠-K♠, and get two callers. They both check to you on a flop of A♥-Q♦-9♥, and you bet your standard amount given the size of the pot. Are you going to be glad if one or both of them call? If you get a caller(s), you might be beat already, as they could be slow-playing two pair or trips. Even if you have the best hand, no matter what card hits the turn, it could beat you. Any heart could make a flush, any king, jack, ten, or eight could make a straight. And any of these cards, plus all of the deuces through sevens could make somebody two-pair or a set (even though the non-heart deuces through sevens are rather unlikely to beat you, it is possible). This means that if you get called, no matter what card is dealt as the turn, you are in a position where it is very hard to be certain you have the best hand. As such, should you bet the turn and not give a free card to somebody who is still drawing to beat you, or should you take a free card because you're the one who is currently behind?

The point of all this is simply that even in situations where you bet, knowing you are very likely to have the best hand right now, often it is better for you if everyone folds. Because as soon as they don't fold, the odds of you being behind go way up, as do the odds that they have a strong chance to catch up. Therefore, since most of your bets and raises prefer that everybody folds, and since you want to always bet the same amount compared to the size of the pot so as to not reveal the strength or weakness of your hand, the best thing is to find a standard bet size that is as small as possible, so as to risk the least, while still being large enough that it will get the job done and get the opponents to fold.

If you bet too small, they will hardly ever fold. If the bet is small, they can't intelligently fold unless they are quite certain they are behind, and also quite certain that they have little chance of catching up with the next card. Also, many players see a small bet, and it will make them think you are weak and uncertain, thus inducing them to try a bluff. If you bet too large, you will do a great job of getting them to fold whenever they have the worst hand, but you will be losing too much all of those times they have the stronger hand and don't fold. For example, if you choose to make your standard bet three times the size of the pot, it has to succeed three times for every one time it fails for you to just break even, and this is asking too much.

Most of the time, I pick a range of 50-70% of the pot for the size of my bets and raises. And my starting point is usually about 50%. If this amount is not getting players to fold very often, then I increase it. If it is working well, I lower the amount and see if it continues working. If it stops working, I move back up to a percentage that was working.

You also need to consider how the bet size compares to stack sizes. If you are early in the tournament, starting stacks are T30,000, and blinds only T50,T100, your postflop bet of 80% of the pot will probably have about the same success rate if the pot size is T600 or T3,000. However, if you are now in a very large pot for this early stage, and somehow five of you have put in T2,000 each preflop to build a pot of T10,000, your bet of 80% of the pot is likely unnecessary, and betting 50% of the pot will work just as often. This is simply because either bet size represents such a huge portion of each player's stack, that anybody who might call the 50% bet of T5,000 is probably not going to fold just because you made it T8,000 instead. Both amounts represent so much of their stack that they are going to think of it as being for essentially their whole stack, and they will either fold, or be willing to play for all their chips.

You should also be aware of pressure point considerations for certain players. It might be quite common early in a tournament to find some weak and/or inexperienced players at your table who are typical calling stations. And when everybody has 10-30,000 in tournament chips, they are happy to almost always call bets for a few hundred chips. But once you move into the range of betting thousands, they become uncomfortable calling so much, and scared of being eliminated.

Thus, you might find that a player will call successive bets of T400, T800, and T1,200 on each street, but if instead you had bet T400, T800, and then T2,000 or more on the river, they will fold unless their hand is very strong. For that many chips, even though the bet size is quite reasonable when compared to the size of the pot, they get scared and fold. So you will want to learn this about these players, discover (mostly by observing them in pots where you have already folded) their pressure point numbers, and make sure you tend to bet less than their pressure point when you want a call, and more than their pressure point when you prefer a fold. This can be very hard to do, as these numbers are not written in stone, and will change as the blinds and antes increase, and as their stack size fluctuates. But this is a common mistake you can exploit with proper GTE strategy modification.

It can also be a good idea to vary the size of your bets based upon the texture of the board*, but you must be careful that you're not subconsciously varying your bet size based upon your hand. What do I mean by this? Some boards are clearly expected to favor one player over another, or at least they are expected to be very unlikely to have hit multiple players. On a board like this, the most likely situation, if we could see the cards, is that one player is far more likely than their opponents to have hit the board, and to have the best hand, with the others having little chance of catching up and beating them.

As a clear example, imagine a flop of A♥-A♠-6♦. This board offers no straight draws, no flush draws, and is unlikely to have improved anybody's hand unless they are holding an ace. If you make a bet on this board, a bet of any size, your opponent is limited to very few possibilities. If they call, they either have an ace, have something less that they believe is the best hand, or they are floating** you and plan to bluff on a later street. But very few people are going to float here, and even if they call with a 6, a pocket pair, or even just K-high or Q-high, they will more often fold those hands now, and frequently fold them later if you bet again. If they raise, they either have an ace, or they are bluffing. But again, this is a tough board to attempt a bluff, as they know you are much more likely to have an ace than any other specific card, simply because you chose to not fold preflop.

The most important point here, is that if they are going to fold when you bet this flop, they are probably just as likely to fold for a bet of 50% of the pot as they are for a 100% pot-sized bet. In fact, they will often fold for even quite a bit less than 50% of the pot. Who wants to call now, for let's say 30% of the pot, knowing that if they decide to call you down, your flop bet of 30% will often double on the turn, and double again on the river? At that rate, they would be calling, in total, 210% of the current pot. That means they are calling 210 units to win 310 units, and must believe they are going to win over 40%

---

* See Chapter 9 for more on board texture.

** Floating is calling a bet on one street with a hand that is unlikely to be ahead, and which has very little chance of becoming the best hand, with the intention of bluffing on a later street. Essentially, by just calling now, it appears you must have some sort of reasonable made hand or a good draw, and this can make your later bluff look stronger.

of the time to just break even. If they have a marginal hand for this flop (and any hand without an ace is marginal here), they will often choose to just fold now and minimize their losses.

Now if we change the board a bit, and make it A♥-10♦-8♦, you will often want to make larger bets rather than smaller bets. Even if you have the current nuts on this flop, a set of aces, there are a lot of dangerous cards for your hand. If any diamond, king, queen, jack, 9, 7, or 6 is dealt on the turn, it could give your opponent a flush or straight. That doesn't leave many safe cards. Therefore, how much you bet can have a large impact on whether or not your opponent will call. Depending upon how deep the stacks are and other considerations (tells, tendencies, position, etc.), they might be much more likely to call a 50% pot-sized bet than they would be to call a 100% pot-sized bet. Players with only gutshot straight draws and weaker straight draws will be much more likely to fold for the larger bet sizes. Even flush draws might fold due to the larger bet, combined with concern that you might have a higher flush draw (especially if they think you could have the ace-high flush draw, which is also top pair).

However, the key here again, if you choose to vary your bet sizes for this reason, is to make sure you are consistent. Issues like whether you actually hit this flop or are bluffing have a lot to do with the decision of whether or not you will bet or raise. But once you determine that you should bet or raise, the amount should be consistent. Either it is always the same for the given pot size, or it varies for reasons that have NOTHING to do with your hand. It is fine to bet or raise smaller on a flop like K♥-K♦-7♣ that is unlikely to have hit anybody, and to bet or raise larger on a flop like K♥-10♥-7♣ that is more likely to have connected with your opponent's hand. Just make sure you don't bet bigger on a flop like K♥-10♥-7♣ only when you miss it, or bet smaller on a flop like K♥-K♦-7♣ only when you hit it. If you're going to vary your bet-sizing based upon board texture, you need to vary it every time, and only vary it based on the board, not because of how well this board hit your hand this time.

BOARD TEXTURE

One of the most important factors to take into account when making your decision whether to check, bet, raise, or fold, as well as how much, is the texture of the board. When we refer to the texture of the board, we are only talking about the cards on the board, and not the cards you are holding. Board texture is often referred to as coordinated or uncoordinated (the terms wet and dry are also often used). A coordinated (wet) board is one that has more than average potential for straights, flushes, and draws to the same. An uncoordinated (dry) board has below average potential for straights, flushes, and draws.

Sometimes the rank of the cards is also taken into account, as a board that has mostly higher ranking cards is more likely to have hit a typical starting hand than a board that has mostly lower ranking cards. For example, if the players were holding random cards, then a flop of J♠-10♠-9♦ and a flop of 6♣-5♣-4♥ should both be equally likely to have connected with their cards. But in the real world, people are more likely to play starting hands that connect with the J♠-10♠-9♦ flop, and are more likely to fold starting hands that connect with the 6♣-5♣-4♥ flop.

By considering board texture, you can do a much better job of determining if you should check, bet, call, or raise. The more coordinated the board, the more dangerous it might be to give the opponent a free card. And if you're thinking of slow-playing, board texture is one of the most important factors to consider (see Chapter 16).

Overall, the most important thing about board texture, is that the more coordinated the board, the more likely it is to have connected strongly with the opponent's starting hand. The ultimate wet board would be a flop like J♥-10♥-9♥. On this flop, anybody with two hearts already has a flush, and anybody with one heart has a flush draw. There are already three starting hands that have made a straight (K-Q, Q-8, and 8-7), and every hand that includes a king, queen, 8 or 7 has a straight draw. Additionally, since players are more likely to play coordinated starting hands (hands where the two cards are the same suit and/or close to each other in rank), a player is more likely to have flopped two-pair on a coordinated flop than a dry flop. Compare this flop of J♥-10♥-9♥ to a completely dry flop like K♦-8♥-4♣; most players are much more likely to play J-10, J-9, or 10-9 as compared to K-8, K-4, or 8-4.

Therefore, whether you are playing a pot that is already heads-up, or still multiway, the more coordinated the board, the more likely it is that one or more of you have connected with the flop. And of course we're not just talking about the flop either. You will want to pay attention to how coordinated the board is on the flop, turn, and river. Even a very dry flop like Q♠-8♥-5♦ can quickly become rather wet when the 9♠ is dealt on the turn. All of a sudden two different made straights are possible, a flush draw has just materialized, and numerous straight draws are now possible as well.

In addition to considering board texture, you should also consider how likely it is that this board has connected with your opponent's range of hands. If your opponent was the last aggressor, they are probably more likely to have higher cards, so the higher the cards on the board, the more likely this board has connected with their hand. It will of course be obvious to you whether or not your hand has connected with the board, but you also need to keep in mind the concept of whether or not the board is likely to appear to your opponents to be a board that has connected with your hand. If they are likely to perceive the board as one that hit you, you probably have more room to bluff, but less room to extract value (when it actually has hit you). No matter which person you are at the moment, some boards look like they are more likely to have connected with the aggressor, and some boards look better for the caller(s).

And as we will discuss in a lot more detail in Chapter 19, when the turn and/or river cards are dealt, you should be considering whether those are cards that appear to be good bluffing cards, for you and for your opponent(s). If one player has been calling on a wet board, and the next card might have completed their flush and/or straight draw, any good player will realize that the caller might now easily have the best hand. As such, you should expect that player's perception of the relative strength of their hand to change significantly.

Just remember to always be aware of the board texture, as in many cases it will be more important than even the two cards you are holding in determining your best decision.

POKERSTOVE AND MORE ICM

In Chapter 3 we discussed ICM, or Independent Chip Model, a method for determining the value of your stack at any point in a tournament. To review a few things, ICM is unnecessary during all but the later stages of a tournament, as the chip values will be linear until you are in or very close to the money. In a typical tournament that pays about 10% of the field, ICM will have little effect until you are down to at least about 20% of the field. But once you are down to these later stages, when you are actually playing tournament poker, you need to keep in mind that the chips you win when you win a pot are not worth as much, per chip, as the chips you lose when you lose the pot.

Let's look at a basic example. You are well into the money-paying positions, and at the final table. You start a hand with T100,000 chips, and we could use ICM to calculate the value of that stack, given the current stack sizes of all remaining opponents and the payouts for each position. If you were to play and win the next hand, and now have a total of T120,000 chips, clearly the value of your stack will increase. However, the amount of that increase, whatever it is, will be a smaller number than the value you would lose if instead you play the next hand and end up with T80,000 chips. That is, if it turned out to be worth $100 to increase your stack from T100,000 to T120,000, it would cost you more than $100 if you instead lost and were down to T80,000. The T20,000 chips you win are not worth as much as the T20,000 chips you lose. This is why it can be prudent to avoid risk deep in a tournament.

Of course, there is typically dead money in a pot, which you cannot forget to factor in. If you put T20,000 chips into the pot, you will almost always win more than T20,000, due to antes, blinds and bets from players who folded. And this does help somewhat with the ICM issue and non-linear chip values.

The simplest scenarios for applying ICM to help in making a decision is when an opponent has moved all-in (or bet enough to put you all-in), and you are the only player left in the hand. If you fold, you know exactly how many chips you will have. If you call, win or lose, you also know what your new chip count will be. And you will also know everybody else's chip counts. Since we are so deep in the event, the prizes are certainly published by now, so you have all of the information you need to use ICM to calculate dollar values of each potential outcome. Let's look at a representative example of how to do this.

You are 5-handed at the final table, with payouts of:

1st - $10,000
2nd - $6,000
3rd - $4,000
4th - $3,200
5th - $2,800.

The blinds are T100K,T200K with a T25K ante. You have open-raised from the cutoff to T425K, and the button has shoved all-in for T2M (you started the hand with T3M), and the other players have all folded (and will finish this hand with chip counts of T2M, T3M, and T4M no matter what you do). How often do you need to win to correctly call? If we were doing a cash game analysis, the math would be relatively simple. They have raised T1.575M more, and there is T2.850M in the pot. To break even here you need to win more than 1.575 ÷ (2.850 + 1.575), or more than about 36% of the time. Most of your hands are going to have more than 36% equity unless the button's range is extremely strong, meaning you are correct to call. However, this is cash game analysis, and ignores the ICM considerations.

Without going into all the details of the analysis, we can calculate the value of your stack for all three possibilities. First, you fold, leaving yourself with T2.6M, and an equity in the remaining prizes of about $5,000. If you call and lose, you will only have T1M, and an equity of about $3,800. If you call and win, you will have about T5.4M, and an equity of about $6,800. Knowing this more accurate information, how often do you need to win in order to correctly call? If you fold, you have a stack worth $5,000, so you can't correctly call unless the average value when you call is more than $5,000. For the average of $6,800 and $3,800 to exceed $5,000, you need to win over 47% of the time! 47% equity is a lot higher than 36% equity[*], and now you will often want to fold, even some fairly strong hands. More importantly, as you can see with this example, which is a very realistic scenario at this stage of the tournament, there is a huge difference between the chip count (cash game) math answer, and the real money (ICM) math answer.

Although you will not be able to do such detailed analysis as this at the table, you can do it away from the table, and you should. You should imagine scenarios that seem reasonably possible to you, and go through this analysis to see how much of a difference there is between the cash game math and the ICM math when this deep in a tournament. And try the same scenario when you are quite a bit further away from the first place finish as well, and compare. When you run into these scenarios in the real game, write down some notes when the hand is over, so you can do the detailed analysis later. Eventually, you will find that you can provide yourself with a reasonable estimate, in real time, as to how much of an adjustment you should make in the chip count math due to ICM considerations.

Now that you know for this scenario that you need 47% equity to correctly call (rather than just 36% equity), how do you figure out or estimate whether or not you have that much equity? Of course, until you call and see the opponent's cards, you'll never know exactly where you stand, but you can usually come up with some kind of range of hands that you think your opponent is likely to be holding. In this example, everybody is relatively short-stacked, only having from 10-20xBB to start the hand. As we will discuss later

---

* Duh!

in Chapter 12, this means that when the opponent shoves, they are doing so either because they think they have the best hand, because they think you will fold often enough, or some combination of both factors. Depending upon their image, the image you think they have of you, live tells, past tendencies, and numerous other factors, you need to make an estimate of how strong of a hand they would require before making this shove, and how often, if ever, they would do this with a weak hand. You then compare this estimated range of hands to your two cards, and again estimate how often you will win, lose, or draw, and thus your total equity in the pot if you choose to call.

But how do you do this last step? Fortunately there is a great and free tool out there for you to use to do the work for you. It is called PokerStove*, and it calculates the equity of one hand against another, one hand against a range of hands, or even one range of hands against another range. In this case, let's say you are holding AsTc, and you believe that your opponent would make this shove with any hand that is in the top 20% of all starting hands. This range would include all pairs 6-6 and above, A-4s and above, A-9o and above, any two Broadway cards, and a few combinations of other high and middle cards that are suited. As such, even though many of these hands are ahead of A-10o preflop, against some of these hands your A-10o is the favorite. Running this matchup on PokerStove, it turns out that your A-10o is actually the overall favorite, winning more than 51% of the time, and you therefore will realize more EV by calling than by folding.

But what if your opponent was only raising with the top 10% of all starting hands? Almost every hand in this range has you beat now, and you will only win about 38% of the time. This makes it an easy fold for this stage of the tournament. But, if we were still early in the tournament, where the chip count math and ICM math are going to produce almost exactly the same answer, then it would be slightly correct for you to call. What if the opponent was only going to raise with hands that had you beat (pairs and better aces), but would

---

* PokerStove was written originally by my friend Andrew Prock, who also was the biggest investor in my bankroll, aside from myself, when I won the Main Event. He turned his $5,000 investment into about $360,000. However, PokerStove has not been updated for quite a while. You can still find it as a free download by searching its name in your browser. But there are more up-to-date software programs that also perform the same functions, and more. The publishers of this book recommend Equilab, which you can also find as a free download by searching its name in your browser.

also throw in quite a few "bluff" hands, like small suited connectors? If they are bluffing with these weaker hands often enough, your equity will rise to the point where it again becomes correct to call.

As you can imagine, we can do this kind of estimating and running the analysis over and over, each time trying different ranges of hands that you think the opponent might be holding. If you do these analyses often enough, you will eventually find that even in the heat of the moment at the table, you can quickly estimate where you stand with fairly high accuracy. That is, for example, if you are facing a shove holding a hand like K-10s and think your opponent has a top 30% hand, you will be able to think back to all of the times you have run PokerStove in the past, and be able to make a good estimate of the correct answer. While your estimate might not be the actual answer of 45%, if you've done this enough, your estimate will be reasonably close to this number.

I promise you, the more you use this software, the more your game will improve. Just take notes whenever you are at the table facing these sorts of decisions. Then later, when you have time, run the situation on PokerStove, and see how much equity you would have had against the range of hands you thought your opponent was holding. In combination with the ICM analyses you also do, you will learn to integrate this analysis into your everyday game.

MORE MATH – THE UNEXPLOITABLE SHOVE

The Unexploitable Shove is a beautiful example of math in action at the poker table. The concept applies in situations where if you were to shove preflop, you could show your cards to the opponent(s), and yet still be in a +EV situation. Obviously, you will be better off if you don't show your cards, but the point here is even with full information available to them, all your opponent can do is call if they have a better hand, or fold if they don't. And whenever your hand is strong enough (and it doesn't have to be as strong as you might think), you will be in a profitable situation.

If your hand is the best, A-A, then clearly your opponent would never call (unless you were shoving for so little that they were getting the right pot odds to call against anything) and you would always win the blinds and antes. And if you showed 2-3o, they would always call, and they would always be the favorite. But what about everything in-between? Let's say you have something quite good, like A-Jo. With this hand, your opponent will only be ahead about 9.5% of the time. But, if your stack is too small, the opponent might have pot odds to call even when behind. If your stack is too big, they will only call the 9.5% of the time they are ahead, but you will lose so much when called that it will exceed the profit you make the 90.5% of the time they folded. The key isn't just which cards you are holding, or your stack size, but the combination of both.

Let's look at a specific example. If you were holding Q-10s, and were going to do this play, how many blinds would be too many? If your opponent gets to see your Q-10s, they will correctly call whenever they have you beat or tied. So if you shove 10xBB, is that too many? 15xBB? When I first learned this concept of the unexploitable shove, I was amazed at just how deep you could be and still turn a profit with this play. Let's figure out the answer together here.

When you shove all-in with Q-10s, and show it to a single opponent, they will know that they are correct to call with any pair, as well as any hand that is A-high or K-high, plus Q-J and Q-10. If they are holding any other starting hand, they will know they are behind, and will correctly fold (again, unless your all-in is for such a small amount that they are getting the correct pot odds to call even when behind). Overall, this adds up to them calling about 35% of the time, and therefore folding 65% of the time. When they fold, you immediately win about 2.5xBB, as you are winning their big blind, your small blind (it was already in the pot before you acted, so it was no longer yours), plus the antes. While the size of the antes varies from level to level and tournament to tournament, we will assume that the total of the antes is equal to 1 big blind, as that is a typical amount.

But what about the 35% of the time they call? In every one of those cases, you are behind (except when they also have Q-10 and you are tied), but that doesn't mean you will lose every showdown. Using PokerStove, it turns out that your average equity will be about 43% of the pot when they call. When I first learned this stuff, I was surprised this number was so high. This is a situation where the Q-10s is called only when it is behind, yet it is still winning a rather large percentage of the time. But the thing is, many of the hands with which you are being called consist of one higher and one lower card, such as K-5 and A-7. And even though in each of these match-ups you are the underdog, it is not by much.

To determine the maximum stack size with which you can shove, we will first determine at what loss (when called) you would break even given that you are winning 2.5xBB when they fold. Since they call 35% of the time, and fold

65% of the time, with "A" representing the amount you can lose, we can say:

2.5xBB x 65% = A x 35%
Solving for A, we get A = 4.64xBB

When you are called, the pot size will be 2n +1, where n is the number of big blinds that were in your stack. It will be this size because the pot will consist of n big blinds from you, the same amount from the opponent, plus 1 big blind from the antes. As we just calculated above, you can profitably make this shove (while showing your cards) whenever your average loss, when called, is 4.64xBB or less. When you are called, your loss will be n (your stack before being called) minus 43% of 2n+1 (your average stack after being called).

n - (0.43)(2n +1) = 4.64
Solving for n, we get n = 36

This means that even if we have as many as 36xBB in our stack, if we shove a hand as moderate in strength as Q-10s, it is still strong enough that we can break even when we show our cards to the opponent, and let them make a perfect calling decision. And for any number below 36xBB, we are making a profit with this play.

Now none of this should be interpreted as advice that this is the best way to play your hand. First, if you don't show your cards, then your opponent might not call with the correct range of hands. In this example, if instead of calling with the 35% of their hands that are beating Q-10s, they only call with the top 20% of hands, you will win even more on average. While your average equity when called will decline from about 43% to about 41%, you will now win the blinds and antes uncontested 80% of the time instead of only 65% of the time. Instead of breaking even when shoving with 36xBB, you will now be making an average profit of almost 1xBB. Similarly, if your opponent is calling with more hands, you will steal the blinds and antes less often, but you will now have the best starting hand some of the time when called. So if the opponent still calls with the hands that beat or tie Q-10s, but also adds in a few more worse hands, now calling you 42%

of the time, your equity when called will increase to about 46%. This means you will lose about 2.5xBB when called, but still win 2.5xBB when they fold, and since they are folding 58% of the time, again you are turning a profit when shoving 36xBB.

Of course, it is pretty obvious that you shouldn't show your cards to your opponent while they are still making their decision. But even beyond this blatantly obvious point, I'm not saying if the table has folded to you in the small blind, you have 20xBB and are holding Q-10s, that going all-in is the best choice. It is quite likely that some other strategy would be even more profitable. Depending upon the opponent, it might be much more profitable, on average, to just make your standard raise right now, and then see what they do. If they fold, fine, take the blinds and antes. If they call, continue with your normal postflop strategy. If they reraise, make a decision, possibly a difficult decision, as to how to best proceed.

What I am saying is that folding as your first decision would NEVER be correct. Maybe your normal strategy with this hand and this stack size is to open-raise your standard amount, for example, 2.2xBB. However, if the player in the big blind is a very tough and tricky player, you might be in a situation where they are going to outplay you often enough that you will tend to lose money, on average, in playing your normal strategy against them. If that were the case, then you might be inclined to fold. However, given this hand and your stack size, clearly an unexploitable shove is better than folding. Again, don't shove and then show, but shove and know that no matter where they draw the line between calling and folding, your decision to shove will be profitable.

Let me say again, I am NOT saying you should open-shove when it folds to your small blind and you have 25xBB or less. If you have about 10xBB or less, then you should probably always shove. But when you have more than about 10xBB, but less than about 25xBB, then open-folding is unlikely to be the best choice. And if it is the best choice, it would have to be for GTE reasons, or ICM reasons, and should not be your basic strategy in such a spot. Most of the time, with 10-25xBB here, you are going to be open-raising a standard amount, or open-calling, not folding.

Included herein is a list showing, for a selection of starting hands, the maximum number of big blinds up to which you can execute an unexploitable shove. As we determined above, the number for Q-10s is 36xBB. If your stack size is more than that number, you cannot profitably make an unexploitable shove, whereas if your stack size is 35xBB or below, you will be in a +EV spot if you shove, no matter where your opponent decides to draw the line between calling and folding.

However, you are almost never correct to open-shove if your stack is more than 25xBB. As discussed above, with that deep of a stack, doing something else (folding, calling, or raising a more typical amount) is almost always going to be a better choice. And with 10xBB or less, you are always shoving (with possible exceptions for ICM reasons). As such, the list only includes those hands having an unexploitable shove number above 10xBB and below 25xBB. Starting hands that are stronger than those shown in the list have numbers above 25xBB, and weaker hands than shown have numbers below 10xBB. It is interesting to note that there are no pairs in the list, as all of them have numbers well above 25xBB.

It is also important to note that there is a big difference when antes are present, as that makes it much more correct to shove for a given stack size. That is, the unexploitable shove cutoff number goes up significantly with the added dead money of antes in the pot. For example, you can profitably execute an unexploitable shove with K-5s with a stack size of up to 15xBB if there are no antes in the pot, but that number increases to about 24xBB if there are antes present.

With antes in the pot, the maximum stack size for this play is:
24xBB for K-5s down to 20xBB for K-2s
25xBB for Q-9s down to 12xBB for Q-2s
20xBB for J-9s down to 11xBB for J-5s
17xBB for 10-9s down to 11xBB for 10-7s/9-8s
24xBB for K-8o down to 15xBB for K-2o
24xBB for Q-10o down to 10xBB for Q-2o
18xBB for J-10o down to 11xBB for J-7o/10-9o

With no antes, the maximum stack size for this play is:
24xBB for A-2s
23xBB for K-9s down to 12xBB for K-2s
25xBB for Q-Js down to 10xBB for Q-5s
18xBB for J-10s down to 10xBB for J-8s
12xBB for 10-9s
24xBB for A-6o down to 19xBB for A-2o
25xBB for K-Jo down to 10xBB for K-2o
17xBB for Q-Jo down to 10xBB for Q-8o
12xBB for J-10o

As mentioned many times, you are never going to actually show your cards before the opponent acts. As such, they will almost never draw the line perfectly, and will call with or fold some hands mistakenly, at least in the sense that they would have made the other choice if they had seen your cards. What if you think the opponent is so tight that they will only call with the top 10% of all starting hands? In that case, you can profitably open-shove anytime you have 25xBB or less, as the opponent is folding so often, that it is fine that you are way behind when called. Even if the opponent is calling with up to any top 20% hand, shoving with 25xBB or less is always profitable.

STACK SIZE STRATEGY

One of the greatest improvements in NLH tournament strategy, developed primarily since the poker boom, and driven mostly by online poker pros, are the ideas behind stack size strategy. Simplistically, the main concept behind stack size strategy is that you should be the player who goes all-in, rather than the player calling all-in. Also, when you do move all-in, it should be for enough chips that your opponent(s) might fold, but it shouldn't be for so many chips (compared to what's already in the pot) that your risk/reward ratio is too high.

As we've discussed, the advantage of being the first player to move all-in is that you will win whenever everyone else folds, and when called you can still win by having the best hand at showdown. In contrast, if you are the caller, victory only occurs when you finish with the best hand. Therefore, even if the call is correct, victory is never certain, and the risk of being eliminated increases. However, even though you want to be the player who moves in, doing so if the size of the all-in is too much compared to the size of the current pot doesn't make sense, as in that case too many chips are being risked compared to the amount of chips won when everyone folds. Therefore, the key is to time the sequence and/or sizes of your bets and raises such that you will be the player going all-in, and doing so for enough chips that you have a reasonable chance of getting all opponents to fold, but not for so much that you are risking too much compared to how much you can win.

In determining the size of your stack, we compare it to the current blinds. Thus, having T100,000 sounds like a lot, and it is if the blinds are T400,T800. But if the blinds are T4K,T8K, then you don't have all that much. In the former case, you have 125xBB, but in the latter, only 12xBB. What hands you should play and how you should play them will vary dramatically between these two situations. We will discuss four different stack sizes in this chapter, the very short stack of 10xBB or less, the short stack of about 10-20xBB, the medium stack of about 20-35xBB, and the large stack that is more than 35xBB.

If your stack is very short, approximately 10xBB or less, there really aren't many reasonable options. In fact, with very few exceptions, there are only two. Either go all-in preflop, or fold. There is some disagreement amongst the top players as to where to draw this line. Some advocate that the line isn't until you are down to 8xBB, others say it starts at 15xBB. In reality it is not a completely rigid line that is always the same. It does depend somewhat upon the size of the average stack, as well as who exactly is at your table, and how tight or loose they play preflop. More specifically, how tight or loose will they play when comparing how they respond to a shove from a very short stack, versus how they respond when that same very short stack raises a standard amount. If they are rather likely to call either bet preflop, but will tend to check-and-fold if they miss the flop, then you should not start shoving all-in until your stack is getting closer to 8xBB. If the opponents you're facing will be much more inclined to fold to a shove, but much more likely to call if you make a standard raise, then you should first start shoving when you still have about 12-15xBB.

When else might you choose to do something other than shove or fold when you have a very short stack? First, let's make it clear that if you only fold or shove when you get down to having a very short stack, you will almost never be wrong. It may be that there were times when you shoved and should have folded, or when you folded but should have shoved, but the times when you should have selected a third option will be extremely rare. One exception might be if several players have limped into the pot, and it's your turn to act in the small blind. In this situation, there will be hands with which you are better off calling and seeing a cheap flop, as opposed to folding or shoving. Similarly, if several players limp to you on the button, even for the cost of one blind, you might be correct to also just call preflop, and see what comes. But in both cases, do NOT do this with hands that will require great judgment as to when to correctly continue after the flop. In either case, what would you do post-flop with A-rag on an A-high flop? You will have the best hand right now too often to just check-and-fold, but you will be beat very often whenever the opponent is willing to put more chips into the pot. To correctly call preflop, you should have a hand that defines itself very well on the flop, like suited connectors or small pairs, or a hand that is two high cards but was not so strong that you thought it correct to shove preflop (e.g., A-10, K-J).

Why is it so correct to only fold or shove with this stack size? Consider the math. First, let's put you nearer the top of this range, with 10xBB. If you shove preflop, anybody thinking of calling is risking 10xBB to win your 10xBB plus the blinds (and antes, if any). They are getting pot odds of about 6:5, and this means they can't correctly call unless they think they are going to win over 45% of the time. Plus, they often have to worry about players behind them who are yet to act. And this means they have to be even more certain that they will win often enough against you. And in the real world, many players won't call when they think it is correct, but just barely so, to make the call. Many players want a large edge before taking any risk. The only player who doesn't have to worry about a third person coming in is the big blind, who is also getting a better price on the call, about 4:3. This means they still need to think they will win over 40% of the time to correctly call.

In my experience, you will successfully win preflop with these shoves about 50-80% of the time, depending upon just how big your stack is, and how tight the table is playing. When you get called, you are often behind, but will still usually have 30-50% equity in the pot. Therefore, over half the time you will win the 1.5-2.5xBB that are in the pot preflop, and the rest of the time you will either go broke or double up. When you do get called, the pot will be about 21xBB, and since you started with 10xBB in this hypothetical, and will have about 40% equity in the pot, you will win back just over 8xBB on average. Thus, you lose about 2xBB when you get called, win about 2xBB when you don't, yet you will be getting called significantly less than half the time. Thus, if your timing and hand selection is good, you will find these shoves to be very profitable.

But remember, the most important lesson, if you only ever shove or fold preflop when you have a very short stack, you will seldom be picking from the wrong choices. Even a full-time tournament pro, out there playing 100+ events per year, will find a situation only a couple of times per year where a third option was the better choice.

What if your stack is too big to only shove or fold preflop, yet is still a short stack? When you have about 10-20xBB, this is called a 3-betting stack, and you are primarily looking for a good situation to reraise all-in. By this I mean when someone makes an opening raise of 2-3xBB, you are now holding the perfect size stack with which to shove all-in, and force them to make a tough decision. The best situation for this move is when the opening raise has been made by a player who is very loose and aggressive preflop, but who is not so silly or ego-driven that they will call your shove even with their weaker hands.

It is quite common amongst the best players to play a lot of hands when they have a chip lead, or when the table is passive. As such, they are opening the pot for a raise with not just premium hands, but also small pairs, suited connectors, and other hands that I like to call "playable junk". If this opponent makes their opening raise, is doing so 40% of the time they are in that position, and you then shove all-in for 10-20xBB, they will usually be smart to fold. Of these 40% of hands with which they are raising, they will probably only call with those in the top 10-20%, and thus they are folding between 50% and 75% of the time when you shove. When they fold, you win the blinds, antes, plus their bet, or about 4-5xBB. When they call, you are usually going to be behind, but again not that far behind, and will probably have about 40% equity on average. Presume you do this with a stack of 20xBB. When they call, the pot will be about 42xBB, and you will win about 40% of this, for a return of about 17xBB, or a net loss of 3xBB on average. This means that even if they are calling your shove half the time, you will win about 4-5xBB when they fold, and lose about 3xBB when they call. Again, a very profitable situation for you to make this shove.

The key to doing this correctly is to pick a spot where either you happen to have a very strong hand, so that even if they call you will probably be ahead, or where there is a very good chance they will fold. If the player making the first raise is very tight, and only opens with premium hands, then they are probably calling your shove with almost all of them. This means you have very little

FOSSILMAN'S WINNING TOURNAMENT STRATEGIES

fold equity, and will typically be behind when they call. It's OK to usually be behind when they call, but only if there was also a very good chance that they wouldn't call. If the chance that they will fold is high enough, you can shove with this stack size holding any two cards, even if there are still several players behind you yet to act.

What if your stack is bigger yet, a medium stack of 20-35xBB? This is called a 4-betting stack, because you are looking for a good spot to 4-bet shove all-in. In a typical game today, the first raise (2-bet) will be to 2-3xBB, and the typical 3-bet will be to a total of about 5-9xBB. Thus, when you shove all-in for 20-35xBB, it will be a large enough raise that there is a significant chance everyone will fold. The math here is similar to what we did for the shorter stack sizes. Because your raise all-in is big enough, you are probably getting everybody to fold much of the time, and when they do, you are picking up about 10-14xBB. When you get called, you are often further behind, and you are risking a lot more chips, so you tend to lose more than in the previous examples. Still, you will find that you will win preflop half the time or more, and the 10-14xBB that you win preflop is about the same, or more, than the number of blinds you lose on average when called.

The most common situation for this 4-bet shove is when you make the first raise, get 3-bet, and then shove all-in. It is much less common that you will find a correct situation to 4-bet shove as your first decision. Most of the situations where it is correct to 4-bet shove occur when you are in late position or you are the small blind. When it folds to you in late position, or the small blind, you are a lot more likely to raise than when it folds to you in early position, and your opponents know that. Therefore, when you open-raise from the small blind or late position, it is more likely that you will get reraised (3-bet) than if you had open-raised from early position. Since they are 3-betting more often, they must be doing it with weaker hands, on average. As such, when you 4-bet all-in, they will be correct to fold those weaker hands.

The best situation for this play is when there is somebody behind you who is very loose and aggressive, and will frequently 3-bet you light*. If they are this loose and aggressive, their range of hands will include many weaker hold-

---

* "Light" here means not heavy, or not strong. Players often refer to a bet or raise as light when it is not a hand that is generally considered strong enough to justify the bet or raise. If somebody raises, and you reraise with a weaker hand, you are "3-betting light".

ings, and it will be a mistake for them to call your shove with such hands. So as long as they are not ignorant of this fact, or so ego-driven that they call even when they know they are behind, they are the perfect target for this play. If instead the players behind you are going to usually just call your first raise with their marginal hands and playable junk, and only reraise when they have a very strong starting hand, they are the wrong targets for the 4-bet shove.

Finally, what do you do if you have more than about 35xBB? Now, you just play poker. This stack is large enough that getting it all-in preflop is not something you expect to happen very often. Here, you play your normal game, adjusting to the situation, and everything else we discuss in this book, to pick the best play.

BANKROLL CONSIDERATIONS

A lot of players try to make it as poker pros, but most fail. In many cases, they overrate their skill level, and aren't actually good enough to be long term winners, or at least cannot win at a high enough rate to pay their bills while maintaining their bankroll. Even more common is the player who is capable of playing well enough to make a living, but fails to do so, or loses their poker profits on "leaks", such as sports-betting, playing in the pit, overspending on luxuries, or drinking and drugging it away. If you're not a full-time pro, you don't necessarily need to concern yourself with bankroll management. Since you are paying your bills and taking care of yourself (and your family) with the money you earn from your regular job, the only problem if you lose your bankroll is that you have to stop playing. But if you are a full-time pro, earning your living on the felt, then you must abide by proper bankroll management rules, or you will eventually go broke, no matter how skillfully you play.

The most common bankroll guideline you will hear is the 100 buyin rule. If you play by this rule, then you will only play in games where your bankroll totals at least 100 buyins for the game. For example, do you have enough bankroll to afford to play in the 5,10 blind NLH game, where one buy-in is $1,000? The answer would be yes only if your bankroll were at least $100,000. You may not believe me, but it is not that hard for even the best players to experience a bad run where they will lose 100 or more buyins. Therefore, if you continue to play in games where you don't have at least 100 buyins, eventually you will hit that truly bad run, and you will go broke. To make it even more real, the 100 buyin rule is not even that conservative. If you want to be truly cautious, and make sure you never go broke at the table, you should have 200 buyins, or more.

What about tournaments? Same rule. If the tournament buyin is $1,000, your bankroll should be at least $100,000, or you shouldn't enter. However, the 100 buyin rule is even less conservative for tournament pros, and if they wish to be truly safe, they should actually have at least 200 buyins, and probably quite a bit more. Because so few tournament pros have bankrolls this large, there is a lot of trading pieces, staking, and borrowing in this segment of the poker world.

How does all of this work in practice? Let's say that the games typically available in your local poker room are 1,2, 2,5, and 5,10 NLH, and each game has a buyin cap of 100xBB, or $200, $500, and $1,000 respectively. If your bankroll is $100,000 or more, you can play in the 5,10 game. But if your bankroll drops below $100,000, then you need to step down to the 2,5 game until you rebuild your bankroll to at least $100,000. If your bankroll drops below $50,000, then you no longer have 100 buyins for that game, and need to move down to the 1,2 game. Unfortunately, very few poker pros stick to bankroll guidelines like this, which is why so many of them are broke so often.

As mentioned above, because so many pros do not live by these bankroll rules, and because so many of them go broke or at least run low on money, you do see a lot of borrowing and lending, as well as staking, in the poker room. My rule with respect to this? Don't borrow or lend, ever. I have never leant money to somebody who is broke, and presumably I never will. If they're such a good friend that I would even consider it, then I believe that I'm better off just giving them money, and not considering it a loan. If they later get financially healthy, and give it back, great. If not, it was a gift, and I'm not upset that they did not repay it.

When I have lent money, it has been in situations where I fully believe the player has the money, just not on him at the moment. In one example, I was playing a 400-800 mix game at the Bellagio, and a friend lost all of his chips.

He had four more hands until it was his big blind, and asked to borrow some money so he could play those free hands*, at which point, win or lose, he would take a break, go to his safe deposit box, and get out more money. I believed him, and lent him $5,000. If I hadn't, he would have had to take a break immediately, and miss out on four hands that were worth about $200 in equity. Within 15 minutes he paid me back. In other examples, I wasn't expecting to get paid back within minutes like that, but I was fully confident the player had the money and would pay me back very soon.

If we are going to do a fully mathematical job of determining the necessary bankroll for a game, we actually need to go much deeper than just counting the number of buyins available. For a truly accurate job, we need to know, or at least estimate, how much you will win per hour in the game, and how much variance will be associated with that win. Essentially, the higher your win rate as compared to the size of your typical swings, the smaller bankroll you need. Contrarily, the larger your swings as compared to the size of your win rate, the more bankroll you require. As you would imagine, if you and I are both playing in the same 10,20 blind NLH game, and you average a profit of $50/hour, and I average $25/hour, I will probably need a much larger bankroll than you to ensure I don't go broke. However, if you play so much more loosely and aggressively than me that your $50/hour win rate is accompanied by typical swings of +/- $1,000/hour, while my $25/hour win rate has swings of +/-250, then you would actually be the player who needs a larger bankroll.

Even though this is not strictly the right place to discuss it, I also would like to talk about game selection. The better and more disciplined you are in game selection, the smaller a bankroll you will require. Another big reason that so many pros go broke too often is because they fail to quit bad games, and fail to select the best game available in which to play. Frequently, you will see a pro who has the bankroll for the 5,10 NLH game, the biggest game in the room, and so whenever they show up to play that is the game they choose. However, on some nights, that game will be tough, and their edge will be small. On such a night, they should either move to another table and play a smaller game, or just not play at all.

However, in most cases, their ego will stop them from doing this. In their

---

* Free hands in the sense that he had already paid his blinds for that orbit, and could be dealt into those four hands without having to involuntarily put in money.

mind, they are now one of the big guns in this room, and therefore feel they should only play in the big game. But if the lineup is so tough tonight that instead of their usual win rate of $50/hour (+/- $500), they are going to more realistically only win $10/hour (+/- $1,000), they might be inadequately bankrolled for the game. Moreover, in many cases, they could just quit the 5,10 NLH game and instead sit in the 2,5 NLH game, where the lineup is still so soft they can average $30/hour (+/- $200). Thus, not only do they have a sufficient bankroll for the smaller game, they will actually average a higher return, given tonight's cast of players in each game. They are hurting themselves (and more importantly, their bankroll) a lot if ego prevents them from seeing, and acting on, the correct game selection for this situation.

In tournament poker, you can't pick the table you're at, as it is randomly assigned. But you can still practice game selection in terms of deciding which tournaments to enter. When it comes to picking which tournament to play, I often see two huge mistakes. In the first case, I see many pros make their decision based upon the expected first prize of each tournament. Whichever event they think can potentially make them the most money is the one they prefer to play. However, it's much more important to estimate how much you expect to win in each event, on average, than how much you will win when you finish first. Even in a small field it's hard to win the tournament, and therefore rather unlikely. But I can estimate how well I will do on average, and use that information to compare events. So, should I pick the smaller tournament where my average result will be a $2,000 profit with a first prize of about $100,000, or should I enter the bigger tournament where my average result will be a $1,500 profit with a first prize of about $500,000? Unless there is other information to consider, the answer to me is obviously the smaller tournament. Yet many pros will pick the larger one because the $500,000 first prize is so enticing.

Another big mistake I see is the manner in which some pros put so much of their attention into the structure of the tournament. Of course, it is true that the slower the structure, the more it will tend to favor the skillful player. And since we're talking about full-time pros, by definition they are more skillful than average. Thus, if everything else is the same, a pro will average a better result if the structure is slower, and thus make a higher average profit in that event. However, I believe that the average skill level of the field is much more important than structure when it comes to quantifying my edge. I would prefer to play a tournament with a faster structure, but weaker opponents, as compared to a tournament with a slower structure, but tougher opponents. The structure does matter, and it should be considered in deciding where to play, but I think more about the expected skill level of the field at each event, and give that factor much more weight in my decision.

13

TOURNAMENT EQUITY AND GOALS

As we discussed in Chapter 2, when it is early in the tournament, you are really just playing a cash game. The only reason that you shouldn't play exactly the same way you do in your regular cash game is that your typical tournament opponent is playing differently than your typical cash game opponent. As such, the Game Theory Exploitative strategies you select will be different, because the tournament player is making different mistakes than the cash game player. It is not until the late stages of a tournament, when you are in the money or at least getting very close to it, that you really start to play tournament poker.

Why is this? Again, we look back to chapter 2, and the discussion of how early in a tournament, chip values are linear*, whereas now that we are deep in the tournament, in or near the money, chip values are now noticeably non-linear. Since the chip values are non-linear deep in the tournament, the ICM considerations we discussed in chapter 3 come into play, and we are now truly playing tournament poker.

If you have much experience in playing both cash games and tournaments,

---

* Or so close to linear, that we can ignore the minor amount of non-linearity that does exist.

you know all of this, even if you don't realize it. When you are near the bubble of a tournament, how often have you seen a player with the largest stack at the table (or at least one of the largest) simply run over the table? Everybody else at the table knows that this player is raising not just with premium hands, but also with a lot of very weak ones. Yet they continue to fold to this aggression. Why? Why is this so common that we've all seen it (and even done it ourselves)? It is because all of us at that table are playing tournament poker. There is so much value in surviving the bubble that many players will not take the chance of get- ting involved in a pot against the aggressor unless they have a truly premium hand. And since the aggressor knows this, they are raising, and will continue to raise all, or at least many of the hands, as long as this condition lasts.

The shorter stacks are playing extremely tight, because the ICM value of the chips they could lose right now, on the bubble, is so much higher than the value of the chips they could win. Thus, those blinds and antes are ripe for the picking by the chip leader. In the real world, many players are even more risk averse than they should be on the bubble, making this extra loose-aggressive play even more enticing to the chip leader. However, even if everybody at the table is a world-class player, and is making all the smartest decisions, it is cor- rect for the chip leader to be more aggressive, and for the other players to be more risk averse, than in most other situations.

Let's look at a SNG example showing just how large this ICM (non-linear chip value) discrepancy can be. Imagine an online SNG where we each paid $10 to enter, and the final three will be paid $50, $30, and $20. Starting with T1,500 each, we are now 4-handed, with you and I starting the hand with T4,500, and our two opponents holding T3,000 each. You and I each get T1,500 into the pot. That makes a pot of T3,000, and each of us has T3,000 remaining in their stack. You move all-in. What is the math guiding my deci- sion?

If this were a cash game (or early in the tournament), the math would be easy. There is T6,000 in the pot (counting your bet), and it will cost me T3,000 to call. I am getting pot odds of 2:1, and should call if I believe I will win more than 1/3rd of the time. Please notice that I have not mentioned whether all of this is preflop, or on any other street. Even on the river, the math is the same. The question is simply do I believe I will win more or less than 1/3rd of the time?

But this isn't a cash game, or early in a tournament, so the math is quite a bit more complicated. Let's start by looking at each alternative. What if I fold? In that case, I will have T3,000 chips and be facing opponents holding stacks of T3,000, T3,000, and you with T6,000. Using an ICM calculator, my stack has a value of $22, meaning the two opponents who also have T3,000 stacks also have $22 each in equity, leaving an equity of $34 for you. If I call, then what? If I lose, my stack is worth $0 as I'm eliminated in 4th place. You will have T9,000 vs. two stacks of T3,000, which will give you an equity of $41 and each of them $29.50. If I call and win, then your stack is worth $0, and I'll have the $41 stack.

Notice something important here. If I call your shove, then win or lose you and I will have stacks worth $0 and $41, giving our two opponents a combined value of $59. But when I folded, the combined value of their stacks was $44. You and I clashing on the bubble of this SNG gave $15 of equity to our opponents. Each of them went from $22 to $29.50, an increase in value of more than 34%! This is why it can be valuable to just sit back and let your opponents butt heads late in a tournament. If everybody else is playing very loose and aggressive, you can make a lot of money by just sitting back, waiting for premium hands, and watching the carnage.

Back to your shove. If I fold, my stack is worth $22; and if I call, my stack is going to be worth either $0 or $41. At what point is the average of 0 and 41 more than 22? It turns out that for me to correctly call your shove, I have to win at least 54% of the time. This is a huge difference from the cash game math. Instead of needing to win at least 33.3%, I now need to win at least 54% of the time, or I should fold. And this difference exists because the value of the chips that I can win is much lower than the value of the chips I can lose, on a chip-by-chip basis. If I call and lose, I lose T3,000 chips that would have been worth $22. That is equal to $0.0073 per chip. If I call and win, I win T6,000 chips that increase the value of my stack by $19 (to a total of $41). Those chips, when added to my stack, are worth only $0.0032 per chip. In this scenario, if I call your shove, each chip I lose is worth more than double the value of each chip I win.

One table SNGs that pay multiple winners will have some of the most extreme examples you can find with regard to non-linear chip values. About the only other situation you will find that has such extremes will be in super-satellites and survivor tournaments that pay multiple identical prizes (see chapter 35). In a typical tournament that pays multiple winners with more money to first and lower amounts to other winners, you will not find such a large discrepancy between the value per chip of chips lost vs. chips won.

But this discrepancy does exist, and it makes it even more important in a tournament that if somebody is going to shove all-in, that you be that player, thus forcing your opponent to fold, or make what could often be a mistaken call. Looking back at our SNG example just above, what if you shoved knowing that each of us was exactly 50% likely to win? You have now forced me to fold, or to make a call that is a mistake. If instead I had been the one to move all-in, I would be putting you in this horrible spot, where you must fold (while getting 2:1 pot odds on a coin flip) or make a bad call. In that situation, it is the player who moves all-in first who wins, so to speak.

Now that we've seen how much the tournament math can change your decision, as compared to the cash game math, what should you do to help yourself make the best tournament decisions? Interestingly enough, the first thing you should do as you're facing the decision in a tournament, is to do the cash game (chip count) analysis. If you are still early enough in the tournament, you can just make the best decision based upon this cash game math. If you are extremely deep in the tournament, in the money or close to it, then we need to look a little closer. If the cash game math shows one decision is significantly better than the other(s), it is very likely still the best decision even in a tournament situation. But if the cash game math shows that two decisions are reasonably close in value, then it is probably more profitable to select the low risk choice (that is, the choice that carries the least risk of losing all or most of your chips).

What about the idea, which you will hear often from tournament players, of passing up on a given spot that is profitable, because you believe that an even better spot will present itself later? Early in a tournament this is just silly. Let's presume that you are a great player, with a significant edge on the field. You know from the history of tournaments you have played, that you will double your stack in a tournament before you go broke about 80% of the time. Notice we're not talking about making the money, or winning, just the concept that if the tournament started with T20,000, that you will, with about 80% certainty, reach T40,000 or more at some point before you are eliminated.

Now, you are faced with an all-in situation, where you believe you are 70% likely to win. If you call, you will double up when you win, and be eliminated when you lose. But if you fold, you know that by continuing with your normal game you will double up at some point with about 80% certainty. Does this mean you should fold this hand where you're a 70:30 favorite?

Sorry, but if you said yes, you need to think about it some more. The real question isn't which decision gives you the greatest chance of doubling up. If this were a $100 buyin tournament, and you had made a bet with a friend for $10,000 that you would double up at some point in this event, then yes, you should probably fold in this spot. But ignoring such silliness, the real question isn't which decision is most likely to double you up, but which decision, on average, makes you the most money. If you call now and lose, it is true, you will miss out on those future opportunities in this tournament where you would have gotten your chips in good, and frequently (80% of the time) doubled up to T40,000. But when you call now and win, you will have doubled up right now, AND you will still be there (70% of the time) to enjoy all of those future opportunities. You might say that if you call now and win, you have become something like an 80% favorite to triple up at some point in this tournament, because those opportunities wherein you would have won those other chips will still be there for you.

Only at very end, when you are down to the last few players, should you consider passing on a profitable but risky spot, in order to wait for a better spot that you are confident is going to come along. Here is a common example. You are down to three players in the tournament, and your two opponents are both very passive and relatively tight players. It is obvious they are not used to playing short-handed, and do not understand that they need to play a wider range of starting hands than when the table was full. As a result, you have been able to raise preflop, and steal the blinds and antes frequently, and you believe that you will be able to continue doing so, even when it gets down to heads-up play. Now, you raise again, and one of the opponents moves all-in. You actually have a very strong hand this time, and even when carefully doing the ICM/tournament math, you know it is profitable to call. But should you? Maybe not. If these opponents are going to let you slowly grind them down, one blind at a time, with a very high certainty, then why play a huge pot, even when you are a significant favorite to win? This is a time where you can go beyond the math, and realize that the more profitable play might be to fold. In essence, what you are doing here is giving up on a call that is clearly correct as a Game Theory Optimal play, and pursuing your Game Theory Exploitative strategy of grinding the players down instead.

However, when it is still early in the tournament, it simply won't be more profitable to pass on risky hands where you have the advantage. With so many players still left in the field, you can't know that you will be able to win using conservative strategies. Even if the opponents you're facing now would permit this as a reasonable possibility, you will be facing many other opponents as you proceed in the tournament, and it is highly unlikely they are all going to let you grind them down slowly and surely. Early in an event there is so far to go, and so many chips yet to be won, that there is always a lot of risk awaiting you. As such, it simply won't be profitable to avoid risk early simply for the sake of avoiding risk. If the situation you find yourself in involves a lot of risk, but also gives you a significant edge, then it is a risk you should take if you want to maximize your long-term profits.

Something else I want to discuss in this chapter, because I really only see this in tournaments, by tournament players, is the setting of goals. My only goal, in a cash game or tournament, is to do my best to make the most profitable decision every time it is my turn. I see a lot of players who set more specific goals. In most aspects of life, it is better to have specific goals rather than general goals. A goal that is too general, like I'm going to write this book by the end of the year, isn't all that helpful, as such a goal might not motivate me when it's February. But if my goal is more specific, such as I'm going to spend at least one hour a day writing, it will be more helpful to achieving the ultimate goal of getting the book done by the end of the year. But in poker, I find that specific goals are actually counter-productive, and will probably hinder, rather than help you, achieve your ultimate goals.

When I play in the WSOP Main Event, everybody knows that it is a long, hard road to the final table and the bracelet. The starting field in recent years has averaged over 6,000 players, spread out over three starting days. Typically less than half of this number will be eliminated by the end of the first day. Many players set a goal to double their stack by the end of the day, so that they will be above average for day 2. However, this goal is silly, and more likely to lead to mistakes than if you just play your best game.

Imagine you set the goal of doubling your stack to at least T100,000 by the end of the day. With 30 minutes left to go, you've done quite well, and have a stack of T90,000. With so little time remaining, there is a good chance that your normal game will yield a result of little to no change in your stack size. And this means you will not reach your goal of T100,000. Therefore, when somebody opens for a raise in early position, maybe you decide to play a hand you would normally fold. But if your normal strategy is correct, then you are folding this hand because that is the most profitable decision. But that normal strategy, while correct, does not in this case give you the best chance of achieving your short term goal. And thus you might play a hand you normally wouldn't. If it works out, great, you will reach or at least come closer to your short term goal. But you might instead find yourself being eliminated, or losing a lot of chips you never should've lost, because of this self-destructive goal. Does it really matter in the end whether you get to T100,000 today, rather than some other time later in the tournament?

Other longer term goals, like deciding you will win a bracelet this year, or get your first 5-figure (or 6-figure) score, or anything like that, are equally harmful. There is too much variance in poker for such goals to be achievable just because you stick to them. It would be like me setting a goal of not just writing a book, but winning the Pulitzer-prize. Even if I write the greatest book of which I am capable, and most of the critics felt it was the best book, there is still a huge chance it won't win the Pulitzer. But I can set a goal of getting the job done, and doing my best possible work. And even if that doesn't get me the Pulitzer, if I have enough talent and work hard enough, I will be able to make a living as a writer. Similarly, if you make sure you work hard on improving your game, and always play the best you can, you will be a winning player. But don't set results-based goals in poker, as these will actually reduce your chances of meeting the more important goals that should be your true focus.

TIGHT IS RIGHT

I've been playing poker seriously for over 20 years, and not once have I ever seen somebody who is too tight to be a winning player. I have seen very tight players, and I have seen lots of players who are consistently too tight in certain situations. But I have never seen anybody who was so tight with starting hand selection that I thought "They are just too tight to ever be a winner." The funny thing is, when I talk to students at my seminars, many of them tell me that they think they are too tight, and they need to learn how to "open up their game" in order to become a better player. Again, it may be that these players are too tight in some situations, but it never turns out, when I watch them play, that they are just too tight overall.

My point is, if you think you're too tight, you're wrong. You may need to loosen up in some spots, but I can promise that overall you're looser than you should be, and it's likely you will fix more leaks by tightening up, rather than loosening, your overall game.

Let's talk about some of the ways that some players are too tight in certain situations. Many players take an overly simplistic approach to poker in general. And some of these players are aware enough to realize that you can't play lots of hands and expect to be a winner. So they learn to fold many hands. But because their approach is too simplistic, too one-dimensional, some of them fall into the trap of simply categorizing hands into two groups, playable and unplayable. What happens is they are playing too many hands in early position, because they are entering the pot with any and all of their "playable" hands, but then they are too tight in late position, because they are still folding all of their "unplayable" hands. Because position is so important, especially in big bet games like NLH, it is essential that you play many fewer hands out of position, and many more hands in position.

It is easy to imagine two players who each average a VPIP* of about 20% at a full table, wherein one of the players is a world-class highly profitable player, and the other a huge loser. The world class player might have a VPIP of only about 5% when UTG**, but a VPIP of 40% or higher on the button. If the other player is too simplistic, they might be playing fairly close to 20% VPIP in all positions.

It is also important to play a lot tighter, or looser, depending upon what has been done by the players acting before you in the hand. Your VPIP should be a lot higher (that is, you should play more hands) if the action folds to you, than if there has already been a raise.

Another common example of being too tight in some situations is the player who doesn't loosen up enough when the game becomes short-handed. Again, looking at VPIP, a good player's stats might be 15-20% at a full table, but more like 25-35% at a 6-handed table, and at 80-95% when heads-up. It is not uncommon to find very experienced tournament players who just don't have enough experience and knowledge about short-handed and heads-up

---

* VPIP = voluntarily put into pot, a statistical indication of how tight/loose you are playing preflop. If you voluntarily put any chips into the pot preflop, whether by raising or calling, even if you later fold preflop when somebody else raises or reraises, your VPIP for that hand is 100%. If you fold preflop, your VPIP for that hand is 0%. If you check your option in the big blind, then that hand doesn't count either way for purposes of this statistic. Thus, if you were dealt 100 starting hands, and put chips into 30 of those pots (beyond just the blinds and/or antes you were required to post), then your VPIP for those 100 hands would be 30%.

** UTG stands for under the gun, a phrase referring to the first player to make a decision on the first round of betting in a hand of poker. In a game with blinds, UTG is the player to the immediate left of the big blind. In a game like stud, UTG is the player to the immediate left of the bring-in.

play, and who therefore fail to loosen up enough in these situations. They may be way too loose at a full table, with a VPIP of 25-35%, but then too tight when heads-up, with a VPIP of only 50-60%. Thus, while this player is much too loose at a full table, they are now much too tight for heads-up play.

You will also sometimes see the player who is not too tight, nor really too loose, in a typical situation, but who is way too tight when it comes to pulling the trigger in special situations. For example, there are many players who are generally pretty solid, but who fail to take advantage of special situations. They might not loosen up enough and steal all the pots they could when they are the chip leader on the bubble. They might not reraise (unless they happen to be dealt a very strong hand) when a great squeeze play opportunity presents itself. In general, this category of player, one who fails to loosen up at the times they should, is not simply a player who is too tight. They are actually a player who was learned an overall tight style (which is a good thing), but lacks the ability to correctly loosen up when the situation is right.

Related to this issue of tight vs. loose, is that of passive vs. aggressive. A worse mistake than playing too loosely is playing too passively. The ultimate bad player is the calling station, the person who just calls almost all the time. They don't fold anywhere near often enough, but they also don't raise enough either, doing so only when they have a truly strong hand. Why are there so many calling stations? I believe the answer is fear. This player is afraid they might fold the winning hand, so they never fold if they think they have any chance. Similarly, they don't want to risk more money by raising, because they are afraid they might lose. Thus, unless they are certain their hand is no good (and has no chance of catching up), or certain their hand is going to win, they just call. In their mind, they are following a sensible, cautious, middle-of-the-road approach. They are not nits who fold, and they are not maniacs who raise all the time. However, in poker, this middle-of-the-road approach is worse than either extreme. Nobody is a more consistent loser than the calling station.

How do you overcome this fear? I'm not a therapist, so if that is what you need, I can't be of any help. Having said that, I believe the answer is fairly simple. What is there to be afraid of? We are playing a game. Presumably, we are playing with money we can afford to lose*. Do you get afraid when you play

---

* If you're playing with money you can't afford to lose, please seek professional help. Seriously.

Monopoly? Scrabble? In any game, you have to make decisions. If you're playing to win, you will make the best decision you can. But win or lose, all you can do is make that decision, and live with the results. Poker is the same. Simply make the best decision you can, and live with the result.

After the game, of course, it is a good thing to review your decisions, and work on improving your game, so you will make better decisions next time. Presumably, that's part of why you bought this book. But in the moment, what is there to be afraid of? Sure, you might get bluffed. Of course, you might pay off the better hand. But that's just part of the game. When you make a wrong decision, take some notes, and review and reconsider the hand later. If you still believe you made the best possible decision at the time, given the information available to you, then it was just bad luck that you lost. But if you determine that you didn't make the best decision at the time, that's good news, because now you've learned something, and will play even better in the future.

But fear just isn't part of the equation. We are all going to make wrong decisions, even the greatest of players; and even the worst players will sometimes make the right decision. All you can do is focus on making the smartest possible decision in the moment. Fear is for the other guy.

SLOW-PLAYING

This chapter is NOT about playing slow, that is, taking a long time to make your decisions. This chapter is about slow-playing, or just checking and calling (rather than betting and raising) with a hand that is highly likely to be the best. But first let's talk a little about the other thing, playing slowly. Don't do it.

There are going to be times where you just don't know what decision to make, where all choices seem utterly wrong, and you spend extra time thinking. First, if the choice is really that close, then in the long run it doesn't matter. Somebody raises you all-in, and you feel that your equity when folding is just about equal to your equity when calling, whichever decision you make, it will average out the same in the long run. And if the equities are not close, then what are you waiting for? Make the decision you think has the higher equity, and live with the result, good or bad*. Second, regularly taking too much

---

* There are many times when a player is facing a bet for all or most of their chips, and they take a long time before calling. Then, when I see their cards, I know the delay was silly, as they were never going to fold. It just took them a long time to call because they were afraid they might lose. As discussed in Chapter 15, such fear is only going to hurt your chances, and is something you want to move past. Fear is for the other guy.

time on decisions will hurt the game. Other players might realize they're not thinking enough, and start playing better. If your game had been moving along quickly, with people having fun and gambling, slowing it down might change that mood, making the game less profitable. It's fine to never snap out a decision, but taking 3-5 extra seconds is not at all too much, and usually enough to avoid a truly silly mistake. Any more than that, other than in rare spots you didn't see coming, and you're hurting yourself more than helping.

Now, on to slow-playing. Let's start by saying, don't ever slow-play unless you have very specific reasons to do so. Most players slow-play way too often. In fact, I'm sure you have all seen the players who will almost always slow-play whenever they have a very strong hand. They are so worried you will fold and not pay them off, that they regularly slow-play their strongest hands after the flop. But think about this, if I always slow-play my strongest hands, then every time I bet or raise, you know I have a medium-strength hand at best. Even if I seldom bluff, and you know I have at least a decent hand, you also know I don't have an extremely strong hand. If I bet into you when a possible straight flops, you know I don't have it, and your set or two-pair is almost certainly the best hand. Whether we're considering the issue of slow-playing, or any other poker situation, you shouldn't always do the same thing, or you will become too easy to predict, and will be dead meat to be eaten by your skilled opponents.

When players consider reasons to not slow-play, the first concern is the risk of giving the opponent(s) a free card, and how often this free card might give them the better hand. When this disaster happens, you will lose a big pot instead of winning a small one. Given this, should you rarely slow-play hands that are vulnerable (e.g., 10♠-10♦ on a J♦-10♥-4♠ flop, or A♠-J♠ on a K♦-Q♦-10♥ flop), but always slow-play hands that are practically unbeatable (e.g., 10♠-10♦ on a 10♥-5♣-5♠ flop, or Q♥-J♥ on a 10♥-9♥-8♠ flop)? The answer is still no, you should rarely slow-play. It is not just the concern that the next card could beat you, but the chance that the next card might be more likely to kill your action rather than create more of it. Let's look more closely at some examples.

Consider again the situation where you are holding 10♠-10♦ on a 10♥-5♣-5♠ flop. Any opponent can have at most one or two outs to beat you[*]. Somebody holding A-A, K-K, Q-Q, or J-J has two outs, and somebody

---

[*] We are ignoring the very unlikely situation where the opponent has 5♦-5♥ for quads. If that happens, you just say "FML" as you lose a huge pot.

FOSSILMAN'S WINNING TOURNAMENT STRATEGIES

with a 5 has one out. And not only can your opponents either be drawing dead or at least very slim, it is highly unlikely that anybody else has hit this flop. For them to have improved with this flop, they must be holding the last 10, or one of two 5s, which is very unlikely. So this seems like a perfect situation to slow-play. And if you are ever going to slow-play (and obviously you should at least some of the time), this is a very good time to do so. But against what hands might you get action now (when you don't slow-play), and against what hands might you get action later but not now (when you do slow-play)?

If your opponent has any pocket pair, then this looks like a good flop for them, especially if they are holding an overpair (A-A, K-K, Q-Q, or J-J). But even with a smaller pair, 9-9 and below, this looks like a good flop. It would seem unlikely you have a 5 in your hand, as that is not a common card to play. And while you might have a 10, that is the only overcard to their pair on the board, and they know you aren't that likely to have a 10. Therefore, if you bet after they check this flop, there is a reasonable chance you will get called (or check-raised) by these hands. What if they don't hold a pair, but instead just two high cards, such as A-J or K-Q? Again, this is the driest of flops, and is un-likely to have hit you. If they believed they had the best hand preflop, they will probably believe that they still have the best hand now. As such, it is unlikely they will just check-and-fold, and will at least call your bet.

What if they have an even worse hand? If they called your raise preflop, they might be holding a hand that is now fairly hopeless, such as suited con-nectors (e.g., Q♠-9♠ or 7♦-6♦). With these hands they can only bluff or fold, and if you bet the flop, they might choose to check-raise bluff, or call (float) now, and then bluff later. The main advantage of slow-playing this flop, is that when you check behind, they might be inspired to bluff the turn or river, whereas if you bet the flop, they might just fold.

One of the best reasons to slow-play the flop is that the opponent might make a pair or a draw on the turn, and then pay you off (or be inspired to bluff, as we discussed above). But if they have nothing on the flop, then they have at most six outs on the turn to make a pair. Depending upon their exact hand, there might be many cards in the deck that are higher than both of their cards that could hit the turn instead. In most cases, there are going to be a lot more cards in the deck that scare the opponent, as compared to cards that improve their hand.

Consider the same hand, where we have flopped a full house, 10s full of 5s, and let's consider an opponent holding 9-9. The pair of 5s on the board will scare them a little, and the 10 a bit more, but they know that if their pair was ahead preflop, it is probably still ahead now. But if you slow-play, how are they going to react when an A, K, Q, or J is dealt on the turn? They are now going to be that much more concerned that they don't have the best hand. Of course, when instead the turn card is anything 8 or below, their confidence level will go up, but they are still unlikely to put a lot of chips into the pot, on this board, unless they catch one of the two 9s in the deck. Your slow-play might gain you a few extra chips some of the time, but most of the time it will cost you chips instead.

Many of those who slow-play all the time reinforce their mistake by assuming, when they do get a call on the turn or river, that if they hadn't slow-played they would not have won those chips. But much of the time, they could have gotten the same call on the flop, and possibly even more chips on the turn or river. And frequently, you just won't get any more chips out of the opponent no matter what you do.

More than any other street, slow-playing happens on the flop. As we'll discuss in the next chapter, if you were the preflop raiser, you are going to often be betting the flop, hit or miss. In this case, it is even more of a problem if you slow-play too often, as it will become even more apparent, and rapidly so, that a bet from you means a weak to semi-strong hand, and a check means you've hit the flop big time.

The best time to slow-play is not when you have the strongest hand, or when you are in the least danger of being outdrawn, or when the board is the very dry. The best time to slow-play is when you are against an opponent who will potentially go overboard in trying to steal the pot whenever they (think they) smell weakness. If you raised preflop, got called, and then bet again when checked to, this opponent may feel that bluffing is a mistake, because there is no reason to think you aren't strong. But if you check the flop, instead of sensing a trap, they might be inclined to believe this signals weakness, and attempt to steal the pot. If you're facing this type of situationally aggressive opponent, slow-playing becomes much more likely to be the best play. Contrarily, if the opponent is unimaginative, will never start betting or raising without a good hand, and won't even call unless holding a fairly good hand, don't bother slow-playing unless your hand is unbeatable. All you're doing against this type is giving them a free card if they do happen to have any outs.

CONTINUATION BETTING

Continuation betting, commonly referred to as "C-betting" simply means to bet when you were the last aggressor on the previous round of betting. Most often, this refers to making a bet on the flop when you put in the last raise pre-flop. When you make the last aggressive action on a round, you are saying you have the best hand. Even if you're bluffing when you do it, you are still telling the story that you have the best hand. Therefore, if you had the best hand, you will probably still have the best hand after the next card is dealt, and therefore it is expected you will continue your aggression, and bet.

More important than whether or not you actually have the best hand, is the fact that your opponent only called your raise. Therefore, they either believe your story (though not enough to fold), they are trapping with a strong hand, or they are exercising pot control and intend to call you down but don't want to grow the pot too big by raising. Of course, preflop, they often believe you have the current best hand, but they have a hand where they wish to try to outflop you. For example, if you raise in early position, and I am in middle position with a small pair or suited connectors, depending upon a variety of other factors, I would often tend to just call your raise and see the flop. But if the flop does not improve my hand, I will often fold to your C-bet. This is true of most opponents, so it is important that you C-bet much of the time you are the preflop aggressor.

As is so often the case, one of the most important factors when making a decision is to not fall into a pattern that gives away the strength of your hand. If you C-bet only when the flop is favorable to your actual hand, it will become easy to know when you are weak (and bluffable) and when you are strong (and shouldn't be paid off). If you do the opposite, then we'll learn to gladly take the free card when you check, and steal the pot with a raise when you bet. Of course, you can try to randomize your decisions, but humans are horrible at faking randomness, as we all tend to fall into patterns. Instead, I use the following guidelines, which tend to obscure my hand as well as achieve my goals.

If I have a single opponent, I always C-bet. Whether the flop hit me or not, whether the flop looks like it would be favorable to me (the raiser) or my opponent (the caller), no matter what the stack sizes, I always C-bet into one opponent. The only exceptions to this rule are based on GTE considerations. Thus, if I believe that the theoretically suboptimal play of checking instead of C-betting will produce a superior result against this opponent at this time, I will check. But this deviation is rare. Seldom will you want to check rather than C-bet.

No matter what the flop, there is a very good chance that it missed your opponent. Although some hands can hit more flops than others, overall you will hit the flop only about 1 time in 3. This means that if you missed the flop, there is still a good chance that your opponent also missed, and that they will fold if you bet. But if you check instead, they might become motivated to bluff. And if you really did miss, there must be a decent chance this bluff will work. Therefore, it is important that you bet every time you miss, so that you can take advantage of the fact that your opponent probably also missed, and get them to fold.

But if you always bet when you miss, you must also always bet when you hit, or the strength of your hand will become obvious. As said before, the only reason to check is if you are certain you are going to get raised and will have to fold, or if you are choosing to look weak to trap the opponent. But both of these are GTE plays, and are technically incorrect from a GTO viewpoint. You should only check against one opponent when you are certain, for reasons of

17

live tells and such, that doing so is superior to C-betting on this occasion.

Against three or more opponents, I never C-bet. And if you are playing against somebody else who is a competent player, you should expect them to also take this line. While some players will C-bet 100% of the time, against any number of opponents, a good player knows that against three or more callers there is just too great a chance that at least one of them hit the flop. This means that you really don't want to bet unless you have also hit the flop, and hit it well enough that it is correct to bet.

So, when I say I never C-bet against three or more opponents, I don't mean to say I never bet. I just don't consider it a C-bet. Just as you don't expect another competent player to automatically C-bet when against three or more opponents, you won't either. This means that if I call a raise preflop, as do two or more others, I don't expect the raiser to always C-bet. And since I don't expect them to automatically bet, I will sometimes choose to bet myself. I might bet because I hit the flop, I have what figures to be the best hand, and I don't want to risk giving a free card. Or, I believe I have the best hand, and I believe that somebody else will raise me, and that I can get a lot of chips into the pot now; whereas if I check, I might give a free card, and I might miss a chance to build a big pot with the best hand. In other words, when there is a raise and three or more callers, I am pretty much just as likely to bet whether I am the preflop aggressor, or one of the callers. Being the last aggressor doesn't have much impact on the decision.

The trickiest situation is when you get exactly two callers. It is fairly close to 50:50 whether or not one of them hit the flop. Thus, when you missed the flop, you hate to check, because about half of the time they will both have missed as well, and a C-bet might have won the pot now. But if you C-bet all of the time, you will be betting into the superior hand too often. So we want to balance our action here, and not go with one absolute (always C-betting) or the other (never C-betting). You could try to randomize your actions, but as I said before, humans are very bad at this, and you will probably fall into a pattern. Instead, we're going to use the flop to randomize the decision for us, in a sense.

Imagine you are watching a game from the rail, somebody raises preflop, gets two callers, and the dealer puts out a flop. When you see that flop, you probably think the flop is either one that is good for the raiser, or one that is good for the callers. For example, almost any flop with an Ace in it probably looks better for the raiser than for the callers. Contrarily, a flop of all middle cards looks more likely to be beneficial to the callers. My guideline is to C-bet every time the flop looks good for the raiser, and to never C-bet when the flop looks good for the callers.

It is important to note that I am not talking about whether or not the flop actually hit my hand. If I raised with 5-5, and the flop is 9-5-4, I'm going to check. This flop is all middle cards, and it looks more likely to have helped my opponents (the callers) than to have helped me, even though it is actually one of the best flops I could hope for. Similarly, I'm going to bet the flop of A-J-9 with my pocket fives, even though this is a horrible flop for my hand. The A-J-9 flop looks like one my opponents expect to have hit me. Therefore, they are unlikely to continue in the hand unless this flop connects well with their hand. And even if they hit this flop, unless they have an Ace or better, there is still a good chance they will fold. For example, if you called a preflop raise holding 9-8s, would you want to call a C-bet on this A-J-9 flop?

Let's examine more closely some examples of this concept. Imagine a flop of 10♥-9♠-7♠. Since players often raise with big cards, and are more likely to call with hands like suited connectors and small pairs, this looks like a flop that is much more likely to have hit the calling hands. If this flop missed me, it really missed me. Unless I have an overpair, or two big spades (such as A♠-J♠ or K♠-Q♠) and flopped a flush draw, this is almost always a bad flop for me. Or, I might have hit this flop, with hands like 7♥-7♦ or J♣-10♣, in which case I have two pair, trips, or a pair plus a draw.

Notice that in almost all cases, it is not really a bad thing if I give (or take) a free card. I either have a hand that figures to be a solid favorite, or a hand that might be the best and has outs to improve if it isn't. Only if I completely missed the flop with a hand like two overcards and no draw (e.g., A♥-Q♦), or a small pair or suited connectors that didn't hit (such as 3♦-3♣ or 5♠-4♠), am I missing out on a chance to steal with the worst hand. By always checking these sorts of flops against exactly two callers, I am balancing my range. I will sometimes be checking the (likely) worst hand, and probably giving up on the pot. But I will also sometimes be checking the best hand, and am either going to call or raise if one of my opponents bets. Most importantly, because I am always checking such flops in this situation, my opponents cannot know, just because I checked, whether I missed or hit the flop. The fact that I'm checking has no correlation to the actual strength of my hand, but only to the perceived strength of my range on this flop.

Another factor you might consider taking into account, when deciding whether or not to C-bet into exactly two callers, is position. Some flops obviously fit the standard of looking good for the raiser, and others obviously look favorable to the callers, but many are somewhere in the middle. Where you draw the line to separate the two can be moved depending upon position. If you are first to act, be more inclined to check. That is, draw the line so you are C-betting only flops that clearly look favorable to the raiser, but checking flops that look good for the callers, or are somewhat in-between. Contrarily, if you're in position, and both players check to you, be more inclined to C-bet. Draw the line where you're only checking flops that clearly look very favorable for the callers, and C-betting all that are clearly favorable to the raiser, or in-between. Because both players have checked to you, that is extra evidence (though nowhere near conclusive) that they missed this flop, and are therefore more likely to fold to your C-bet. In any situation, if the evidence suggests they are more likely to fold, your standard play should be weighted more towards betting, whether you think you have the best hand or not.

The size of all of your C-bets should be a consistent amount, and never based upon the strength of your hand, as we discussed in Chapter 8. If you are going to vary the size of your bets, it should be for reasons related to stack size more than anything else, and possibly based upon the texture of the board. For example, a common play is to C-bet smaller when the flop looks obviously favorable to the raiser, and especially so if it's the kind of flop that is very unlikely to have hit more than one person.

Consider a flop like A♥-A♦-6♠. It is clearly possible that two players could be holding an Ace. But this is unlikely. If the preflop raiser C-bets this flop, with what hands can the caller ever continue? Unless the caller is going to float or otherwise make a play at stealing this pot without a hand, there are really only two possibilities. The caller can have an Ace, in which case they almost always have the best hand and are a huge favorite to win the pot. Or, the caller can have a 6, or a pocket pair, and believe there's a decent chance they have the best hand. In that case, the caller is probably going to either call down the pre-flop raiser, or maybe call now, and reevaluate later (that is, either continue to call, or change their mind and fold). This means that if the preflop aggressor C-bets into this pot, the size of their bet can be very small. The caller who has nothing is going to fold most of the time for any size bet, and the caller with an Ace is never going to fold. Only the caller who is in-between, with a 6 or a pocket pair, might be influenced by the size of the bet, and this opponent is going to be very cautious on this flop regardless of your bet size.

The main point is that if you C-bet this flop, and you have trip Aces or better, you're unlikely to get action, and you don't mind if you do, so betting small is fine. And if you don't have such a hand, you can probably bluff just as successfully with a small bet, so why risk more than needed?

While this idea would be much less applicable on a flop like A♥-K♠-9♦, it is still true that most of the time, if your opponent doesn't hold an Ace, or better, they are not going to like this flop. As such, you can bet smaller than you typically would, because the smaller bet is almost as likely to get them to fold. Just be sure that when you vary your bet size, it is based only on board texture, position, or other such factors, and not upon the actual strength of your hand. Only at the GTE level should you ever let the actual strength of your hand affect your bet size.

17

THE VALUE OF SURVIVAL

I've never been a big fan of analogies and truisms, in all facets of life, but especially in poker. I use them at times to convince people of a point I'm trying to make, but in reality they are frequently useless, and often misleading[*]. Poker is full of these common wisdoms that seem valuable in educating a poker player, but will more likely lead the student down the wrong path, or at least slow down their progress.

Here's a saying you hear often at the beginning of a tournament that will last many days, "You can't win this today, but you sure can lose it." This truism is indisputable, yet totally useless. You usually hear it spoken to a player who is taking a lot of risks, or maybe playing too many pots. The purpose of the statement is to make the point that they shouldn't be trying to win every chip, because no matter what, they aren't going to win this tournament today. The best they can hope for is to make it back to play tomorrow.

But if the aggressive player is making the decisions with the highest EV,

---

[*] A bird in the hand may be worth two in the bush, but if you're trying to feed your family, you should probably drop the hummingbird in your hand and go after the two turkeys in the bush.

maybe because their opponents are letting themselves be bullied, then why should they slow down? If their decisions are -EV, as they are being too loose and aggressive, then they should slow down, not because they can't win the tournament today, but because they could be making better, more profitable, decisions. In reality it doesn't matter whether this tournament is going to be done six hours from now, or six days from now, you want to be making the decisions with the highest EV. Sometimes loose and aggressive play is correct, sometimes not. But the amount of time left in the tournament is not a significant factor when playing each individual hand.

I mention all of this because it relates to another common mistake made by tournament players, including some of the best pros in the world. They place too much emphasis on survival. You often hear statements about "somebody risking their tournament life", and that "you can't win it if you're not in it". Obviously you can't win a tournament once you've been eliminated, but again, does that really matter? When we do our analysis of pot odds, implied odds, ICM adjustments, and the like, we are determining which of the decisions available to us has the highest EV. If one of the decision paths we're considering involves the risk of losing all of our chips, then we are already taking survival into account when we determine the value of that path. There is no need to then add extra value to other paths, just because they don't carry the risk of elimination. In other words, forget completely about survival! Focus instead on EV, and which decision will lead to the highest EV, whether or not survival is at stake. If it is, then you will have taken survival into account already, as long as you did your analysis properly.

Let's consider some simple situations. The flop is 10♦-7♥-3♥, and you have A♥-K♥. The pot is heads-up and your opponent has moved all-in. You feel their most likely hand is one pair, in which case you have as many as 15 outs twice to make the better hand. Of course, they could also have a stronger hand, in which case you have less chance of winning; but they might also be semi-bluffing a hand like a straight draw or an inferior flush draw, in which case you are an even greater favorite. Combining these possibilities, your chances of winning this pot are probably close to 50%. If this is early in the tournament, we don't even care how much your opponent bet and how much is in the pot. Even if the all-in bet is T20,000 and the pot size only T2,000, you are 50% to win and are getting pot odds of 22:20, so a call is +EV. Half the time you will win a pot of T42,000, and half the time you will lose T20,000, for an average profit of +T1,000. Let's look at three scenarios within this fact pattern.

First, you have a huge stack, T100,000, so even if you call for T20,000 and lose, you will still have a large stack. Most pros would make this call every time, because they know it's profitable, and even if they lose, they still have a big stack, so they don't mind taking the risk. In a second scenario, you only have an average stack at the moment, about T40,000, meaning that if you make this call and lose you will become a short stack. This is a spot where many players, including a significant fraction of tournament pros, will elect to fold. But they will be making a mistake when they do so. Calling here is still profitable to the tune of +T1,000, so they are giving up that profit when they pass. How often can you pass up on profitable situations and still be a winning player? If you try too hard to avoid risk, you will also end up avoiding too many profitable situations, and become a losing player instead of a winner.

Finally, what if T20,000 is your entire stack? In this case almost all players choose to fold. But again, this is part of the reason why most players are long-term losing players. They have been fooled by the truisms and sayings about the value of survival into thinking that even if this play is profitable in terms of chip count, it is somehow a money-losing play because it risks elimination. But as we discussed in more detail in Chapters 2 and 3, early in a tournament the chip count math and the money math are identical. This means if it is a profitable play in terms of chip count, it is a profitable tournament play as well. If we were instead very close to the bubble, or past the bubble and in the money, ICM considerations would affect the math, and it might be that this edge is too small. That is, winning a T42,000 pot half the time might be worth less than the T20,000 we will have every time if we fold.

Remember, when you do your analysis correctly, taking into account pot odds and ICM and every other factor that you can use (e.g., live tells), then your analysis already takes into account the disaster of being eliminated. Don't make the mistake of adding extra value to mere survival. It is not just a question of whether or not you survive, but on what terms.

BLUFFING

Bluffing is a big part of the game of poker, but it is often a bigger part of the game than it should be. Most players bluff too often. Reflecting on the theme from Chapter 18, you often see a player attempt a pretty obvious river bluff after they miss a draw, and after getting called, they say "Well, it was the only way I could win." And when you hear them say this, they are almost always correct. But does that mean they were correct to attempt the bluff? Of course not. Just because it's the only way you can win doesn't mean you should try to bluff. But anytime a player feels they don't have the best hand, they are going to be tempted to bluff. None of us like to lose, not even one pot. So it is always tempting to try to bluff whenever you feel you will otherwise lose.

But the point is, you should never bluff, unless bluffing is more profitable than the alternatives. Just like every decision in poker, you need to determine what options are available to you, and estimate the value of each option. If one of the options is bluffing, you assess its value just like any other decision. If bluffing is the decision you estimate as having the highest EV, then you should bluff. If another decision has a higher EV, then obviously you should go with that decision instead.

But the most important factor in determining the value of a bluff attempt (and more specifically, estimating its chances of successfully getting the opponent(s) to fold), is answered by asking yourself a question, and answering it honestly. If I attempt this bluff, am I telling a believable story? When you hear the losing player say it was the only way they could win, it is often a situation where this player was calling bets on previous streets, with a board showing one or more obvious draws to be possible. Then, the river card was a blank, not completing any draw, and suddenly this player who had been checking and calling comes out with a bet. What story does this tell?

Let's assume the flop was A♥-9♥-8♣. This player called a raise from the big blind preflop, and has now called another bet on the flop. The turn is the K♠, and this player checks and calls again. Now the river card is the 4♦, and this player suddenly bets out. What hands would they logically play in this manner? The possibilities are few. Maybe they had A-4, have just rivered aces up, believe it to be the best hand, and also believe that the opponent will often check behind on the river. In that case, a bet makes sense, as they are trying to extract value from the hand. Nothing else really comes to mind.

Now consider what other hands might be played in this fashion? Maybe they flopped a big hand, two pair or better, but wanted to wait and see a safe runout* before betting, for fear that their opponent would make a straight or flush. If this is the case, they let the opponent pay the minimum to try to make the draw, and now they're betting into a hand (a busted draw) that can never call. Better to check again in this case, and try to induce one more bluff from the opponent who has been semi-bluffing all along.

Fairly obviously, the most likely hand for this player to be holding is a busted draw. They were calling, hoping to hit, and now they missed. Bluffing is their only chance to win what has become a sizable pot. So they make the attempt. Usually, it is a futile attempt, because everything about this bet says "I'm bluffing". The opponent is unlikely to fold here unless they also have a busted draw. And even if the opponent also has a busted draw (or other weak hand), if they are any good at all they will raise rather than fold, because the nature of this

---

* Runout means the turn and river in a flop game like holdem. It is used to distinguish these last cards from all the prior ones that were dealt. An example of the term in use might be "After I flopped top set, the runout prevented me from betting any further, as all the draws hit."

bluff is so obvious. Although bluffing truly was the only way to win the pot, it was also the only way to lose even more chips.

So how do you decide when it's a good time to bluff? Simply put, when it is likely enough the opponent will believe the story you're telling, and fold. The stronger the hand your opponent is holding, the better your story has to be. When we discussed C-betting in Chapter 17, if you raised preflop and only got one caller, you should C-bet all flops, even those that missed you. And clearly when you bet after missing the flop, you are bluffing. But this is a believable story, even though you C-bet every time in this situation. You were the last aggressor preflop, and your story preflop was "I have the best hand now". Since your opponent just called, they are saying they believe this story so far (or they have a premium hand and are trapping you). Therefore, when you C-bet, all you are doing is continuing to tell the same story you told preflop. In fact, you're not even saying that you hit the flop. You're saying whether I hit the flop or not, I still believe I have the best hand. And this is a believable story, or at least, it is believable enough that your opponent will often fold all their weaker hands.

More generically, when you are considering a bluff, you have to do some math, based upon some estimations. You have to consider how much you will win when it works, and how much you are risking to attempt the bluff. You then estimate how often the bluff will work, and compare these numbers. Thus, if you are considering a river bluff, there is T5,000 in the pot, and your normal bet size here is T3,000, then you need this bluff to work at least 3 times out of 8 (37.5%) in order for it to be profitable*. If you estimate the opponent will fold more often than this, you should attempt the bluff. If you think they will not fold this often, don't bluff.

The more complicated scenarios occur when the bluff is going to take place over multiple streets, and involve cards yet to be dealt, as part of the equation. Consider this hypothetical. You call from the big blind with 10♠-9♠ in a heads-up pot. The flop is 5♦-4♦-2♥, you check, and the preflop raiser C-bets. If they are a decent or aggressive player, they are C-betting here every time, so you

---

* Why 3 times out of 8? You are risking T3,000 to win T5,000. If you succeed 3 out of 8 times, then 3 times you win T5,000 (T15,000 total), and 5 times you lose T3,000 (T15,000 total), for a net result of breaking even. So this bluff must work 37.5% of the time, or more, to be better than just giving up on this pot.

know there is no specific reason to think this is a good flop for them. And given the nature of this flop, it is unlikely to have improved their hand. Their range includes lots of hands that consist of two high unpaired cards, such as A-K, A-9, K-J, J-10, and the like. But all of those hands still have you beat. Your choices here are to fold, or attempt a bluff. In order to make the best decision, let's estimate the value of each play.

First, you can just fold. This play leaves you with exactly the number of chips still in your stack. The chips you already put into this pot preflop are gone, so you can't count them. The EV of folding is 0.

If you bluff, there are several lines you might take. The most basic would be to check-raise the flop, and hope that your opponent folds now. The math here is basically the same as our river bluff scenario above, that is, how many chips would you bet as a check-raise, how many chips will you win if they fold, and how often do you estimate they will fold? If the pot was T2,000, the opponent bet T1,000, and your check-raise amount would be T3,000, then you are risking T3,000 to win T3,000. This would be a profitable bluff attempt if you estimate the opponent will fold over half the time.

What if you check-raise the flop to T3,000 and the opponent calls? Should you try to bluff again on the turn? There is now going to be T8,000 in the pot, if your normal bet would be T5,000, then trying again would be correct if you honestly estimate the opponent will fold more often than 5 times in 13 (about 40%). But clearly the turn card will have a big impact on how likely it is that they will fold to this second barrel bluff. If they have an A-X hand, then if the turn is an Ace they just made top pair, and if the turn is a 3 they made a wheel, and you wouldn't expect them to fold. Similarly, any K, Q, or J might give them top pair. In each case, you can't know. But clearly you should be more inclined to attempt another bluff bet on the turn if it is not a high card or a 3, and more inclined to give up if it is one of those cards. You should be a lot more inclined to bluff again if the turn is a 6, as that could sell the very believable story that you flopped a pair plus a straight draw (with a hand like 4-3), and have now made the straight. Other good cards for you are 8, 7, 5, 4, and 2, as these are unlikely to improve the opponent's hand, but could look like they helped you. If you turn a 10 or 9, and make top pair, you are no longer bluffing if you bet, as you would believe you probably made the best hand, though you will now face the equally tough decision of whether or not you should value bet.

What if the turn is a good bluffing card for you, but the opponent calls again? The math for the river is similar, though the thought process to estimate their likelihood of folding is getting harder. What if they are holding a medium or large pair, and have been planning on calling you down? Or even calling you down with Ace high? If you bet again on the river, it becomes harder for them to imagine you're bluffing, as that would mean that you have bluffed all three streets, something not too many players will do. So it has, in some ways, become easier for them to believe your story.

But on the other hand, people hate to admit they're wrong. If they fold now, they have to admit, at least in their mind, that they were wrong to have called your flop and turn bets. Many players have too much of their ego involved to do this. They would almost rather call you down, lose, and fold their hand unseen. They can then claim to have held the best possible hand that still lost. This means that against some opponents, the third barrel bluff is hopeless, while against others it is almost mandatory. Accurately determining into which category this opponent falls is not easy to do. And many opponents will be in one camp, and then switch to the other, as their fortunes at the table change.

Another way to bluff at this flop is to float. "Float" is a relatively modern term, one I don't recall hearing until well after the poker boom started, at least a couple of years after I won the Main Event in 2004. Although the term is new, the concept existed well before then, though I don't think there were very many of us doing it yet. Floating means to call a bet with a hand that is unlikely to be the best hand now, and has no real drawing potential either. In our example, we are holding 10♠-9♠ on a flop of 5♦-4♦-2♥. While it is true we have overcards and could make top pair, this is not what you would normally refer to as a drawing hand, and calling here only to try to catch a 10 or 9 on the turn would be a truly weak play (that is what calling stations do).

We should only be calling in this situation if we are floating. We call because that sets up the story that we have hit this flop. We then prepare to bluff on the turn or river, depending upon what card is dealt and what our opponent does. For example, if a blank hits the turn, and we check, it will not be that surprising if the opponent checks behind. There is a reasonable chance they have two overcards, and no pair. Thus, if the river is now not an Ace or a 3 (and to a lesser extent, not a K, Q, or J), then we make a bluff bet on the river. The combination of this board of low cards, plus our opponent checking the turn, let's us tell the story that we have at least a medium pair. Thus, this bluff will often work if our opponent does only have A- or K-high.

If instead they bet the turn, we can either give up on the float attempt and fold, or we can check-raise bluff the turn. Again, the check-raise on the turn tells a very believable story, as we could easily have flopped two pair, trips, or even a straight, and we were trapping with our previous checks. This play is extremely likely to succeed if the opponent has no better than A-high, and is reasonably likely to get them to fold most one-pair hands. Even if the opponent has A-A, they know they are only going to beat us when we're bluffing, because if we're not bluffing, we almost always have better than one pair to play our hand this way. Although this bluff attempt can be costly, it also has a high chance of success. As always, the hard part is estimating the likelihood of getting the opponent to fold.

One of the most important concepts to keep in mind when considering a bluff, is don't turn a good hand into a bluff. You see this mistake reasonably often, especially in preflop raising wars. Somebody makes a raise or reraise with a fairly-strong to strong starting hand, then folds to the next raise. While this can be the correct way to play the hand, it is often a mistake. In most of these cases, unless you are very certain that the opponent can only raise you back with a better hand, and could rarely be bluffing, this raise just turned what might have been the best hand into a bluff.

Let's examine such a preflop scenario. You are the short stack in this situation, and are open-raising on the button with A♠-Q♣. You start the hand with T15,000, blinds are at T100,T200, and your open-raise is your standard amount of T450. Now the big blind reraises to T1,100. Even in the face of this 3-bet, you still believe you are highly likely to have the best hand right now. That would seem to be a compelling reason to 4-bet, and it is.

But what might happen here? If you 4-bet to T2,700, your opponent might 5-bet and put you all-in. Would you still believe that A♠-Q♣ is the best hand, or would you now reconsider that opinion, and fold? You need to decide this before you make your 4-bet, because that 5-bet is coming often enough to be a concern. If you know this opponent quite well, and they would never 5-bet without holding an extremely strong hand (specifically, A-K, A-A, K-K, Q-Q, and almost never anything else), then 4-betting and folding when reraised is a good option. But would they ever 5-bet bluff? Would they 5-bet with smaller pairs? How small? What about hands you're currently beating, like A-J, K-Q, etc.? If there is enough chance their 5-bet is a worse hand, then you can't fold. But if you fold anyway, then you just turned A-Q into a bluff.

Given all of this, if the opponent is a loose and aggressive player, maybe you're better off just calling their 3-bet to T1,100, and playing the flop. If you hit big, you will now be a favorite to win a nice pot. If you miss, you will be in a tough spot, because they might have also missed, and now their C-bet might get you to fold. But, for probably the same price as your 4-bet preflop, you can call their flop bet. That is, instead of investing T1,600 more in your preflop 4-bet, this opponent will probably bet T1,600 or less on the flop, and you can call that bet, even if you miss. Now, with position, you can evaluate again on the turn. You might decide you're beat by a small-to-medium pocket pair, but maybe feel confident you can bluff this opponent because of the overcards to their pair that are on the board. Or, you might get lucky and hit the turn. Or, you miss the turn, they bet again, and now you can feel more confident that if you fold, you are folding a hand that is beat. Playing this way can lead to both higher rewards, and lower risks, on average.

Similarly, let's look at a flop situation. There are plenty of chips still in play, so all-in anytime soon is not a concern. Your opponent raised in early position, and you called from late position with 10-10. The flop is J-7-2 rainbow, and your opponent makes a standard C-bet. You believe there is an excellent chance you have the best hand. Should you raise? A major part of that decision will be determined by first asking this question. If I raise here, and they 3-bet, will I fold? And if they do 3-bet, will that mean they almost certainly have a better hand than 10-10 right now? If you can be certain of this, then raise and fold to the 3-bet, knowing that while losing is unfortunate, you played the hand well.

But if there is going to be a lot of uncertainty, then it is probably better to just call the C-bet. The only downside to just calling is that you will, in effect, be giving a free card to this player. It may be that you are ahead now, but they will catch a card on the turn to take the lead. However, you must balance this risk against the risk of raising now, getting reraised, and being bluffed off of the best hand. An important point to make again is that if you just call the flop bet, you can call the turn bet (that is presumably coming) for about the same number of chips as it would cost to raise now.

Because of this desire to not turn the best hand into a bluff, you will sometimes lose a pot that you would have won, because you just call and your opponent, who would have folded to your raise, instead is still in and catches a card to beat you. There are also times when you catch a card that improves your hand, and you decide that it is now strong enough that bluffing is no longer the best decision, and you lose to a slightly stronger but still weak hand that would have folded to your bluff.

There have been numerous times where my opponent has been the aggressor, but because of live tells or otherwise, I believe there is a good chance that I can bluff them. For example, on a board of medium cards, I have A-5s. My opponent C-bets into me, I sense weakness, and raise as a bluff. But they call. However, their call took some time to make, and I am confident they have a very small pair or a no-pair hand like A-K or A-Q. Because of this read, I have decided to bluff the river. The river is dealt, and it's a 5. They check, and now I don't choose to follow through with my bluff, because I just took the lead against much of the range that I thought would fold to my bluff. I just beat all of their A-K and other high card hands, as well as their smallest pairs (22-44). Before I hit the 5 on the river, my bluff was going to be profitable, if my estimate of how often they would fold was correct. But now, many of the hands I would be causing to fold will lose anyway when I check. And that means that the ratio has gone down when comparing the hands I can bluff to the hands I can't bluff. Let's look into this more closely.

It might have been that about half of their hands were hands that were beating A-5, but which they would fold if I bet again on the river. The other half were hands that were beating A-5, but were not going to fold. This means that if the pot were 5 units, and I was going to bet 3 units as a bluff, half the time I would lose 3 units, and half the time I would win 5 units, making this a profitable bluff attempt. In two such attempts, I would win 5 and lose 3, for a profit of 2 units, or 1 unit per attempt.

But now, after I paired my 5, the situation might be more like half of the time they will not fold and I will lose my 3 unit bluff bet, one-fourth of the time they will fold a hand that still has me beat (such as a middle pair), and one-fourth of the time they will fold a hand that loses anyway to my pair of 5s. This means that if I bluff, I still make the one unit of profit per attempt. But if I don't bluff, I will lose this 5-unit pot 3 out of 4 times, and win it once. This is an average profit of 1.25 units, which is higher than the average of 1 unit of profit when bluffing. So, I will choose to check rather than bluff. But it sure does suck when you check, get shown 6-6, and know that if you had not improved on the river, you would have bluffed and successfully stolen this pot.

Bluff equity (or fold equity) is merely a term that refers to the fact that even when you know you have the worst hand, if there is any chance you can successfully bluff, then you still have some equity in the pot. If bluffing did not exist as an option, it may be that you face a situation where your opponent has bet into you, and although there is some chance you currently have the best hand, and/or some chance you could draw out and make the best hand, these factors do not give you enough equity to correctly call. But, if we can now add in the chance that instead of having or making the best hand, you might also be able to successfully bluff, this might add enough value (enough bluff equity) to make it correct to not fold. Just don't put too much value into this concept, as it seems to become harder and harder to win by bluffing as the game and our knowledge of it progresses.

19

POT CONTROL

Pot control refers to the concept of playing in a manner that avoids creating larger pots, and thus avoids large risks to your stack. More specifically, players exercising pot control will pass up on opportunities where they feel they are a small favorite if they bet or raise, and instead choose to check or call, because doing so will ensure that they do not lose all (or a large portion) of their chips.

As I've discussed, you should be making the decision that is the most profitable (i.e., the highest EV), regardless of the amount of risk that comes with the play. And, I've described how if it is early enough in a tournament, where you are not yet in or almost in the money, the EV of each choice when analyzed by chip count is essentially identical to the EV of each choice when analyzed by money value (using ICM considerations). There are many times a player will believe they are exercising pot control when they are actually using ICM. That is, in their situation, betting or raising would maximize value in terms of chip count, but to maximize money value (because of ICM considerations), the player should just check or call instead.

Distilling this down, the entire concept of pot control is either a mistake, or a misdescription of what is really happening. If it is early in the tournament, you shouldn't be worried about minimizing risk, but only with maximizing value, so there is no good reason to exercise pot control. If it is late enough in the tournament that there are now discrepancies between maximizing chip count value, and maximizing money value, you should try to make the decision that best maximizes money value. The fact that such a decision might also avoid risk, whether for reasons related to pot control or otherwise, is irrelevant. Therefore, in the strictest sense, you should entirely ignore the concept of pot control.

Having said that, there are many situations where players will describe a decision as being driven by pot control, even early in a tournament, and be both right and wrong. They are wrong in the belief that the decision is correct because of the idea of pot control, yet the decision itself is still correct. But it is correct for some other reason. One of the most common of these "other reasons" is the concept of "way ahead or way behind". There will be many situations where there is a significant chance that you have the best hand on the flop or turn. And if you do have the best hand, you will be a large favorite for that hand to hold up and still be the best hand at the river. But if you are wrong, and do not have the best hand, then it is instead your opponent who is a large favorite now, and a large favorite to still have the best hand at the river.

Here is a very straightforward example. You are holding K♠-Q♦ and the flop is A♦-K♣-7♥. If you have the best hand right now, then your opponent is way behind. In fact, any hand they are holding that is currently behind has at most five outs to become the best hand on the next card. This means that you are at least a 4:1 favorite to still have the best hand at the river. However, if you do not currently have the best hand, then it is you who has at most five outs, and is at best a 4:1 underdog.

If you are in position this hand, and your opponent checks to you, should you bet? The answer to that is very complicated, but you will often hear a player who checks in this spot say they did so for reasons of pot control. But even if their check was correct, pot control was not the correct reason. A better reason would be the idea of way ahead or way behind (and there are many other good reasons as well). If you bet here with the best hand, and the opponent folds, you have gained very little. They were drawing thin, so you were not saving yourself from being outdrawn very often.

But if you bet here when behind, unless your opponent makes an unexpected fold, you are putting more chips into a pot you are very unlikely to win. Therefore, it might be a more profitable play to check here, as the risk of giving a free card is minimal, but the risk of losing chips might be quite high. Also, by checking behind, you might convince the opponent that their inferior hand is actually the best, and convince them to mistakenly invest more chips in this pot on future betting rounds. You also might motivate them to bluff with a hand that they know is not the best, since you "showed weakness" when you checked. Therefore, because you are either way ahead or way behind, you chose to not play aggressively on this round of betting, and by doing so you will, on average, lose a smaller pot when you lose, yet maybe win a larger pot when you win.

What about if you were holding A♠-2♠ on a flop of A♦-10♥-8♦? Would this be a good hand to check behind? It might be correct to check behind, but not because of the way ahead/way behind concept. On this flop, even if you are currently ahead, your opponent might be holding a hand that is drawing to a lot of outs, maybe as many as 15. In fact, your opponent could have so many outs that they are actually the favorite to win, even though they are currently behind. Thus, if you check behind here, you would have to do so understanding that you could easily be giving your opponent a free draw at numerous outs. The concept of way ahead/way behind would simply not apply in this situation.

There are two major drawbacks to checking when you are either way ahead or way behind. The first is simply that you might have lost value by doing so. Maybe this opponent would have called you down if you bet the flop, turn, and river. By checking the flop, you only got in two streets of value, and missed the third (and most valuable, as it would have been the largest bet). Also, you might have gotten called if you had bet the flop, but the next card further convinces your opponent they are beaten, and they choose to check-and-fold rather than pay you off.

The second drawback is that by taking the "weak" line of checking behind on the flop, you are somewhat forced to call down your opponent if they bet on future rounds. As we discussed, one advantage of checking the flop was it might induce your opponent to bluff, or mistakenly value-bet, on the next round. Well, if part of the reason you checked was to induce these bluffs, it would be pretty silly to fold when your opponent makes them. But sometimes this will cost you chips, as it turns out you were way behind, and if you had bet the flop, you might have folded sooner and lost fewer chips. But now you pay off two bets instead of folding after making just one bet yourself.

Remember, the real lesson here is to ignore the concept of pot control, and instead focus on the concept of maximizing value, i.e., money value, at all stages of the game.

20

PLAYING THE SHORT STACK

21

Before I discuss anything further about playing with a short stack, I must make sure I refer you back to Chapter 12, where I discussed stack size strategy. In that chapter, I didn't compare your stack to the field, as that wasn't the concern. If you have 10 or fewer blinds, even if that is an above average stack, you should be following the advice in that chapter of either folding or shoving all-in preflop. Overall, the advice in Chapter 12 is going to dominate the advice in this chapter. Keeping that in mind, this chapter will discuss what to do when you have a short stack as compared to the other stacks at your table, regardless of how many big blinds that may be.

In theory, how your stack compares to your opponents as a group isn't that important when determining the correct strategy. What really matters is the size of the effective stack, i.e., the size of the shorter stack between you and your opponent(s) in the current hand. If you have 100x big blinds, and your opponent 50x, you should theoretically play the same as if you were the player with 50x, and your opponent had 100x. But in practice, it doesn't work this way, and a majority of players place an oversized emphasis on whether it is them, or the opponent, who has more chips.

Again, referring to Chapter 18, The Value of Survival, most players place excessive emphasis on survival. As such, they believe that it is much more correct to play against an opponent whom they have covered, as compared to playing against an opponent who has them covered. In the past, I used to literally hear players say that their strategy was focused on only playing against opponents with fewer chips, as that way they could never go broke. And it's true, if you never played a hand against anybody with more chips than you, you couldn't be eliminated. Yet despite its veracity, this statement leads to a strategy that is completely useless.

What does matter is the perception of your opponents. If you notice a player is very concerned with whether or not they have an opponent covered, you should be much more inclined to steal/bluff against this opponent when you have them covered, and much less inclined to do so when they have the larger stack. Of course, since they will be folding less often when they have you covered, you can also make more thin value bets against this opponent.

On the flip side, you should expect this opponent to be playing more aggressively, and bluffing more often, when they have you covered, as they probably expect you to be more likely to fold. Thus, it is going to be more correct to trap and slow-play this opponent when you are the shorter stack, and much less correct to do so when you are the larger stack. While an opponent with this mindset is going to be much more likely to try to bully you when they have more chips, they are also going to be much less likely to bully you when they do not. So when putting them on a range of hands, take into account your relative stack sizes, and weight their range accordingly.

This mindset, which is moderately commonplace, of putting so much emphasis on relative stack sizes, is a significant mistake. But when you take this mindset into account, you are not making the same mistake. You are merely using your opponent's thoughts to correctly put them on a narrower range of hands, and to predict their likely future decisions with the hands within that range. Just make sure when you are doing this that you don't go too far with it, and start playing with this mindset yourself.

One of the best things about having a short stack is that it is relatively easy to make the optimal playing decisions. While it is not always obvious where exactly to draw the line between which hands to fold and which hands to shove, it is usually not that hard to draw the line reasonably well. This means that you will either always be making the right decision, or at least your mistakes will be minor ones. Of course, you might not feel this way emotionally, as every time you play a hand you will probably be risking all or at least a significant portion of your chips. And when it goes wrong, you will probably tend to second-guess your decision, especially if it resulted in your elimination. However, you need to remind yourself when this happens that poker is a game of decisions, not a game of results. And if you continue to make the best decisions, you will eventually achieve the results your decisions deserve.

The toughest thing about having a short stack is the negative mindset it creates in many players. Often, the reason you have a short stack is from recently losing several pots, or losing one big pot. But it does not matter what is causing the negative mood. What is important is the impact that a negative mood can have on your ability to make quality decisions. One of my favorite tricks, whenever I have a short stack, and especially if I have just lost a big pot, is to count my stack, and imagine how I would feel if I had just doubled up to this number.

For example, let's say I am doing well in a tournament with T70,000, almost double the average stack of T40,000, then I lose a big pot and only have T20,000. Whether I took a bad beat, got caught by a cold-deck, or made a mistake doesn't really matter that much. Any time you lose a large pot there is a good chance you will find yourself in a bad mood. Instead of letting that bad mood linger, count again your stack of T20,000. Now pretend you had T10,000 at the start of the last hand, and doubled up. How would you feel then? What would your mood be? Although it is very understandable that you are unhappy after losing a big pot, there is no rational basis to feel any different about your T20,000 stack, no matter how you got there.

If you're a kid and find yourself in Disney World, do you really care how you got there? It might have been a lot less boring to fly to Orlando rather than take a 2-day car ride with your parents, but either way, now that you're there, you will probably feel just as good. And even though having half the average stack is not a good thing, it is a lot better than being eliminated. So focus on the positive, and renew your commitment to making good decisions going forward. That is the most you can do to maximize your chances of obtaining a good result in this tournament.

PLAYING THE BIG STACK

You are probably going to have a lot more fun when you have the big stack. Most of the time, you are going to have a lot more options, and it is likely going to be correct to play more hands than when you have a short stack. Yet while there can be a lot more fun and excitement, this also means that you are going to be making a lot more decisions, and will be putting yourself in position to make a lot more mistakes.

Many of your decisions as a short stack involve folding or shoving all-in preflop, which means that you only have to get one decision right per hand to maximize your EV. By comparison, when you're playing a big stack correctly, you are going to make a lot of decisions that do not involve just folding or shoving, which means a lot of room to get it right and dramatically increase your chances of winning, or to get it wrong and lose your status as the big stack.

When most people think about how to play a big stack, they think about playing very loose and aggressive. That is, they are thinking about running over the table, forcing opponents to fold, and taking down one pot after another. While it's true that you are more able to run over a table when you have the big stack, this is the correct way to play only if your opponents are going to let you do it. By far the biggest mistake made by inexperienced players with a big stack is to try to win every pot they enter. As we discussed, it is often the case that other players will be more likely to back down in the face of your aggression, simply because you have more chips. And this does mean that everything else being the same, you will be correct to play both more loosely, and more aggressively, when you are the chip leader. But this is not the case for every opponent in every hand, and it is never the case for some opponents.

Before the poker boom, some of the most successful tournament players were simply unrelentingly aggressive. If it worked out early, they built a big stack. And once they had a big stack, they continued their aggressive play. And it often worked, as many players were timid about getting involved against the bigger stack. In the modern poker world, players are much less concerned about survival just for the sake of survival, and more focused on maximizing their chances to win (or at least place very high in) the tournament. This means that these players will not back down to your loose, aggressive play just because you have them outchipped. They will pick intelligent times to play back at you, and they will trap you with their good hands, whenever it is profitable to do so. And this is the correct way for them to play.

Therefore, once you have the big stack, it is not your job to attack the shorter stacks all of the time. It is not your job to pummel them all into submission. Your job is exactly the same as it was when you were a short stack, or when you were an average stack; it is to make the most profitable decision available to you every time it is your turn. If the other players are folding too much, then yes, you should play loose and aggressive, and take advantage of this mistake. But if they are not backing down, and are willing to risk all of their chips even in spots where they probably should fold, then you should be the one backing down, unless your hand is strong enough to merit the action.

Also, another common mistake made by chip leaders is a fixation on eliminating players. While it is always a good thing to take out an opponent, unless you are in or near the money, the only benefit to eliminating somebody is that you are winning chips in the process. And even if you are extremely deep in the tournament, your job is always maximizing your EV, not knocking people out. Knocking players out is merely a side effect.

Essentially, what this all comes down to is the fact that poker is always a reactive game, not a proactive one. In most human activities, it is a good thing to be proactive, to go out and make things happen, rather than wait for them to happen to you. However, in poker, you simply cannot make things happen. You can bet and raise and do everything to win a pot, but if the opponent is simply not going to fold this time, then you had better have the best hand at showdown.

Even when you are betting and raising and it works, you should not pat yourself on the back for "making it happen". If you played the hand right, then you can give yourself credit for recognizing a good opportunity to bluff and steal a pot, but you didn't make it happen. Instead, you recognized the opportunity, and didn't let it pass by.

That is the essence of good poker, knowledge and attention, so you see the opportunities that exist, and take full advantage of them for maximum profitability. But sometimes, all you can do is minimize your losses. When it's one of those times, don't fall into the trap of thinking you should make something happen. Instead, stay alert so that when it is time to start winning again, you take full advantage of the opportunity.

22

PLAYING AGAINST AN ALL-IN

Given the nature of tournament poker, you are going to see a lot of all-ins, many more than in a typical cash game. Once an opponent is all-in, if the pot is not heads-up, correct strategy changes significantly. Since this is a common situation, you must learn to make the proper adjustments when an opponent goes all-in.

If a player has already gone all-in, and it is your turn to act, of course the first decision is whether or not you should fold. If it is correct to fold, you should do so, regardless of the fact that your presence in the pot might increase the chances of the all-in player being eliminated. If it is otherwise not +EV for YOU to continue, it does not usually become so just because you can eliminate an opponent. However, there are some circumstances where it will become correct to continue in a hand while holding cards you would normally fold.

For example, imagine a short-stack player raises all-in for just double the big blind, and one or more players call. It is now your turn to act in the big blind, and you have a horrible hand that you would normally fold, despite being offered these very high pot odds to call. Even if you are getting pot odds of 8:1 preflop, you should usually fold a hand like J-5o, simply because it is such a horrible "reverse implied odds" hand. That is, even though your hand is not an 8:1 underdog against the field, folding is still correct because this is the type of hand that tends to lose a lot more chips than it wins, on average, in later betting rounds. Given this, even if you are getting pot odds of 8:1, and you might only be a 6:1 underdog against the multiple opponents if there was no more betting possible, you will fold in this spot because you will be so likely to lose more chips postflop, rather than win or break-even in the postflop betting.

But here, where the first raise was all-in, you should probably call. With a player all-in, a large majority of players will only bet or raise postflop if they have a very strong hand. Some players go so far as to only bet or raise in this spot with the absolute nuts. They believe it is so important to "gang up" on the all-in player, to maximize the chances of their elimination, they will always check postflop unless they make a hand so strong that it is virtually guaranteed to beat the all-in player.

Because there are so many people who play this way, you will now frequently have the opportunity to see more cards (i.e., the turn and river) for free than in a typical pot where nobody is all-in. Because of the all-in player, you are not as worried about your hand's reverse implied odds postflop, because it is likely that your opponent will not bet into your J-5o when the flop comes Q-8-5, whether or not they hit the flop. And if they do bet, it is that much less likely that they are doing so with hands that cannot currently beat your bottom pair. As such, it is much easier to correctly fold on these flops when somebody bets, and free to stick around when they don't bet, giving you a chance to either reach showdown with the best hand, or improve to the best hand if your little piece of the flop isn't enough already.

But what about you? How differently should you play in order to maximize the opportunity to eliminate the all-in player? Should you check (or just call) with hands that would normally merit a bet (or raise)? Is it correct to keep the other players in, so if you don't beat the all-in player, they are still around to maybe eliminate them? As always, the correct answer lies in EV. It is irrelevant whether or not the all-in player is eliminated. All that matters is that you make the decision which, on average, will yield the highest EV for YOU. If it is not late in the tournament (that is, not in or almost in the money), then there is almost zero value in eliminating an opponent.

Again, at this stage, you should think like a cash game player. In a cash game, would you care that a player got felted, if the pot is going to somebody else? Of course not. All you care about in a cash game is winning the most chips while losing the least. When somebody else wins a pot, it doesn't make any money for you. Likewise, unless you are very deep in the tournament, if somebody is eliminated by another player, this does not do you any good. Your goal at this stage is accumulating chips, not knocking out opponents[*]. Therefore, if you think it improves your personal equity, you should bet and/or raise postflop, in order to either bet the other players out of the pot, or to try to get them to put more chips into the side pot for you to win. Of course, the fact that one opponent is all-in, and that you have zero bluff equity in the main pot, does factor heavily into your decisions.

What about preflop; should you isolate? That is, if the short stack has already raised all-in, and you decide that folding is not the best play, should you reraise in order to get others to fold, or should you just call to make it more attractive for other players to stay in? Again, the simplistic answer is you pick the option that you believe will provide the highest EV for you. If it is the bubble or very close to the bubble, this would often lead you to play in a way so as to invite others into the pot, as this would increase the odds of eliminating the all-in player right now. But I must reiterate, if it is not late in the tournament, you never care about anybody being eliminated, as this does not, in and of itself, make you any money. And even if it is late, if you invite others into the pot, not only do they reduce the chance of the all-in player winning the pot, they also reduce YOUR chance of winning the pot. So factor this into your decision.

Any time you reraise after a short stack has gone all-in, the other players know that you are isolating the all-in player so as to beat them heads-up. This will often lead them to adjust their opinion with regard to your range of hands. That is, they might decide that your range does not include some of the very strongest starting hands. They know that you don't have a weak starting hand, because if you did, you would just fold as you are unlikely to be ahead of the all-in player. However, since you reraised, they may tend to believe that your hand is not extremely strong, as you would not mind if other players also joined the pot.

A typical example might be where action folds to the button preflop, who moves in for 8xBB. The player in the small blind now reraises to 16xBB, where

---

[*] Unless you're playing a bounty tournament. See Chapter 37.

the effective stack between themselves and the player in the big blind is significantly larger, like 50xBB or more. In this scenario, many observers will assume that the small blind has a decent hand, something that is at least tied with the range held by the button, but cannot be holding a hand like A-A or K-K, as they believe the small blind would just call with such a strong hand, so as to entice participation from the player in the big blind.

Of course, it is true that if you hold something like K-Q in the small blind, you don't want to fold, as you are ahead of the button's likely range, but you also don't want to invite the big blind into the pot as well, as their presence will reduce your equity in this pot. However, if you were to only reraise with decent hands that don't also want action from the big blind, you are being too predictable. You should at least sometimes reraise even when holding very strong hands like A-A, so as merge your ranges and make it impossible for the opponent in the big blind to accurately (and narrowly) predict your hand range. Once you decide that folding is not an option, think further about how you expect the big blind to react if you just call, as compared to when you reraise, and weigh the value of each choice, taking into account potential postflop action.

Up to now, we've examined scenarios where the all-in player is the one who bet all-in. Obviously, sometimes a third player has made a bet or raise that is larger than the all-in player's stack, and the all-in player called. In these scenarios, there is often immediately a side pot that can be won by you and the other players, but not by the all-in player. Correct strategy for you will now sometimes be dramatically different as compared to the situation where there is no side pot[*].

Obviously, if there is no side pot, or it is very small, you should essentially never bluff or semi-bluff. I have seen players do something silly like bet when holding 5-4s on a flop of K-3-2 into a dry side pot. Clearly, even if the short stack player was bluffing when they moved in, they are going to be ahead of 5-high. So there is not much point in getting the other player to fold, when you will have to improve in order to beat the all-in player for the main pot. Contrarily, if there is a significant side pot, semi-bluffing this draw might be

---

[*] This is also called a "dry side pot", in analogy to a dry lake, a lakebed that currently holds no water. You might also hear somebody say there is a dry side pot in a situation where there is an actual side pot with chips in it, but it is extremely small in comparison to the main pot.

a correct decision, as when it succeeds you will immediately win the side pot, and still be drawing live for the main pot. And if the semi-bluff fails, you might still improve to the best hand, and win even more chips as a result. But the value of bluffing and semi-bluffing always goes down significantly when there is an all-in player, as it is impossible to get them to fold, and therefore you cannot win the chips in the main pot without having the best hand at showdown.

The fact that you can't win the main pot immediately if you do get the other active players to fold does not mean you should never bet unless you have a very strong hand. For example, imagine a situation where a first player raised to 3xBB preflop, and you reraised to 8xBB in late position with A♥-Q♥. The player in the small blind called all-in for 5xBB, and the first player also called your reraise. You now have a main pot of about 23xBB (8x from you and the first player, 5x from the small blind, 1x from the big blind, and about 1x from the antes) and a side pot of only 6xBB. Obviously, you are much less likely to bluff or semi-bluff than if neither opponent were all-in.

Having said that, when the flop now comes J♥-10♠-3♦, and the first player checks, you should probably make your normal continuation bet here. There is a significant chance that you still currently hold the best hand. The fact that the first player just called preflop means they probably are not holding A-K or a large pair. As such, unless they hit this flop, they will often fold to your continuation bet. Of course, the all-in player certainly has a pretty good chance of having you beat right now, as most of their reasonable hands to play here either had you beat preflop, or took the lead from you on this flop. I mean, you are no longer beating A-J or A-10, and you were never ahead of any pair or A-K. But clearly, getting rid of the first player will improve your equity in the main pot, and will win you the side pot immediately.

The main reason to not make this continuation bet would be if you expect the first player to fold only when they have worse than your A-Q, and never or rarely fold when they are ahead. So if the first player is not going to fold pocket pairs for this C-bet, nor hands such as A-K or 10-x, then there is no value in betting, as you seldom get them to fold the best hand, but only get them to fold when behind. The only value in such a bet is when you are ahead on the flop, you are denying them a free card that might beat you.

There have been occasions where I have bet into a dry/small side pot with a hand that is not necessarily ahead of the range of the all-in player. However,

when I have done so, it is with the knowledge that I am playing against opponents who believe that you should never bet in this situation without the
nuts or something close to it. As such, I made the bet knowing that these
opponents were extremely likely to fold. And I did so knowing that while doing
this was creating huge equity for the all-in player, and greatly increasing their
chances of survival, I deemed it profitable for myself as well. As such, I did not
care that I was only getting some of the equity from the player(s) who folded,
with much of it going to the all-in player. What mattered is that I determined
betting was a more profitable play for me as compared to checking along with
the other live players.

As an example, imagine there are four of us, one player all-in, no side pot,
and the main pot is 20xBB. The two other active players check to me, and I believe that if I bet 10xBB, they will both fold more than 90% of the time. Getting
them to fold only needs to increases my equity in the main pot by just 6% to
be a profitable bet. When they don't fold, I usually lose 10xBB. When they do
fold, my extra 6% equity in the main pot is 1.2xBB. 90% of 1.2xBB is more than
10% of 10xBB, so this is a slightly profitable bet. In most cases, getting two
players to fold will increase your equity in the main pot by much more than 6%.

The guiding principle when playing against an all-in opponent, just as it is in
every other poker situation, is which decision will, on average, yield the highest
equity for you. What that decision does for anyone else's equity is, and should
be, of no concern to you.

23

SPECIAL SITUATIONS

There are many situations that occur repeatedly, but not frequently, in poker tournaments. And there is sometimes a lot of equity available to the alert, thinking player in these situations, so we will discuss a few.

Every hour or two you will be given a short break in a tournament, for 5-20 minutes, to use the restroom, smoke a cigarette, grab some food, and just relax a little. As the time for these breaks approaches, many players are in a hurry to get to break, and as a result, they may be much less likely to play the last hand. They know that as soon as they fold, they can leave the table, and are often in a rush to do so. Whether they're desperately craving nicotine, have a very full bladder, or whatever else, because of this impatience they are much less likely to play that last hand, and may only do so if it is clearly a strong starting hand with a very high EV.

This offers you a much better than average opportunity to steal the blinds, and to win the pot postflop with a continuation bet. Because of their rush, these players don't mind folding anytime the situation is not clearly profitable, and will therefore be much more likely to do so. Contrarily, if somebody doesn't fold, especially if they had seemed eager to go on break, you need to adjust your evaluation of their hand range. They are much more likely to have a very strong hand, and much less likely to have something of marginal value.

What about not just a bathroom break, but an extended break? Some tournaments have 30-90 minute dinner breaks, and if it's a major multiday event, there is the overnight break at the end of the day. Will players tend to be much tighter in their starting hand selection in these situations? Not necessarily, but many of them will be making huge adjustments to their starting hand ranges. Players with average to above-average stacks may tend to play much tighter as the extended break is approaching. They are happy with their stack size, and may not want to take any undue risk. They may be concerned with losing a big pot right before the break that either makes dinner less pleasurable, or makes sleeping less peaceful. It is not uncommon to see such players go into almost complete shutdown as they get close to one of these breaks, especially those with slightly above average stacks.

On the other side, players with short stacks, especially dangerously short stacks, may be looking for any reasonable opportunity to get all-in, so they can either rebuild to a good stack size, or be eliminated and not have to come back after dinner or the next day. It can be very annoying to come back after the extended break when you have a stack that is going to be all-in the first hand you play, as you know that you will frequently fail to advance significantly farther in the tournament. And in some cases you may be driving from your home hours away for this purpose, or having to reschedule your flight home. And even if it is just the dinner break, who wants to rush through something fast at the food court in 45 minutes, then get eliminated right after the break? Now you know you could've taken the time for a much better dinner instead.

This is one more reason that it can be such a great idea to chat with your opponents, and not just about poker. By learning that the player in seat 3 drove in from two hours away to enter this event, and that they have no hotel room tonight, you know they probably aren't going to want to crawl into day 2 as a short stack, needing to drive two hours tonight to go home, and then awaken in time for a two hour drive back the next day. So while they didn't give away their strategy directly, knowing where they live just gave you a big clue as to how you might want to adjust when playing against them late in the day.

You can also make some reasonable assumptions about players as you approach the end of the time for rebuys or re-entry (obviously assuming you're

24

in a tournament that allows them). If the re-entry will provide you with a fresh starting stack of T20,000, it is quite possible that as this deadlines approaches some of the players with very short stacks might start looking for any reasonable opportunity to get all-in. They would rather go broke with their short stack, and re-enter to have T20,000, as compared to playing on with only T5,000 or T10,000. Again, keep this in mind when this deadline nears, as you may want to make some big adjustments to the hand range you are assigning to a player.

Most players have a style that is fairly rigid, an approach to starting hand selection and postflop play that they don't adjust sufficiently for the situation. But nobody is static, with an approach to the game that is unchanging. One time when you will see the greatest variation in a player's style is on the bubble*. It is completely sensible that this should be the case, as this is a situation where ICM considerations are of the greatest importance, and thus there are the largest differences between correct play based upon a cash-game type analysis, and the correct play given the true money value (the ICM analysis) of each possible decision.

Most players fall into one of two camps on the bubble; those who play extremely tight in order to guarantee they are not eliminated, and those who play extremely loose and aggressive in order to steal the blinds and antes from the players in the first camp. Neither camp is inherently right, or wrong, and the best players will decide which approach is correct for them from tournament-to-tournament and hand-to-hand.

If you are at a table full of mostly players from camp 1, then you should probably try to steal more, to take fullest advantage of their tight play. But if your table has a lot of players from camp 2, then you shouldn't get involved unless you have a hand strong enough where it is correct to possibly play a huge pot for all or most of your chips. If everybody else is trying to steal on the bubble, then you're better off playing extra tight and letting them beat up one another.

Most importantly, you should be paying attention to who is in each camp.

---

* The bubble refers to the time when there is only one more player to be eliminated, and then everybody will be in the money. However, the term is sometimes also used to describe the period of time when there are still a few players to be eliminated, not just one, before reaching the money.

Sometimes the player who has been very tight all day will now loosen up, because they have heard that is the correct way to play on the bubble. Alternatively, the opponent who has been playing half their hands up until now might start playing only the nuts, as they don't want to waste all of those earlier gambles that worked out just to bust now on the bubble. Just like every other time in a poker game, you need to be accurately determining what your opponents are thinking, what range of hands they are likely to be holding, and then make the most profitable decision.

Once you're in the money, there are going to be some pay jumps along the way. It is possible that some players will start tightening up as a pay jump approaches. At least, this used to be the case reasonably often. In the modern poker world, most players do not seem to pay any attention to this at all, at least not until they are at the final table, and there is a pay increase for each player eliminated. Then you will find some players who are extra tight, hoping to move their short-to-medium stack up the pay ladder a few rungs before they take any chances. Look for this, and take advantage of it, but don't expect to find it very often.

Another intermediate bubble that exists, and which will cause some players to make huge adjustments, is the final table bubble. This is especially true if the final table is being filmed for television. At this time, just like on the money bubble for getting paid, some players will become unduly tight and cautious, to ensure that they reach the final/TV table.

In 2004, when we were 10-handed at the unofficial final table of the WSOP Main Event, I had a little over 5 million in chips. It quickly became clear that most of the table was only going to play premium hands, and did not want to take any significant risks, even profitable risks, that would reduce their chances of making the official final table the next day. And this was true even though we were already on the TV table and being filmed. The only players who seemed willing to mix it up and play marginal spots were Josh Arieh, Marcel Luske, and myself. Because of this, and obviously because of some run-good as well, I was able to grow my stack to over 8 million by the time Marcel was eliminated in 10th place. This clearly made my job the next day a lot easier, as I now had about 31% of the chips, compared to just under 20% of the chips when we started 10-handed play.

I have seen the same thing happen in other tournaments as we were on or near the bubble for making the final televised table the next day. Look for this, and take advantage of the tight players, while watching out for those who are trying to take advantage of you.

Last longer bets are somewhat common in the tournament world. This is simply a side bet between two or more players, who agree to wager a certain amount of money, to be won by whomever amongst them survives the longest in the event. If you know somebody at your table has a significant last longer bet, and they are close to winning it, for them it is like being on the bubble. All they have to do is last a little while longer, and they get to win some money. This means that they might be playing much tighter than they have been, and avoiding more risk. And that means they are going to be easier to steal from, and have a much stronger hand than average (for them) when they do continue in a pot.

Of course, in many instances these last longer bets are relatively small compared to the cost of the tournament, and therefore will likely not have much impact on their play. But keep your eyes and ears open, as you will sometimes find an opponent who has a considerable last longer bet, and will tighten up their game if they're getting close to winning it.

One area where you will commonly see significant last longer bets is in one table satellites, especially those during the WSOP. For example, if you enter a $525 single table satellite at the WSOP, it is very common for the majority of the table to each put up an extra $100-300 in cash, with the winner of the last-longer group getting all of this money. I have often seen tables where every player at the table participates (except for me). Because of this secondary bet, the players in the last longer group have an incentive to avoid risk and survive longer, just as is sometimes correct in a regular multi-table tournament (for ICM reasons). If you find situations like these, it can be hugely beneficial for you to take advantage of them, just as you would a bubble situation in a regular tournament.

Recently, I played in just such a one-table satellite at the WSOP, and all nine of my opponents joined in a last longer bet for $200 each. The normal structure of this satellite was winner-take-all for $5,120 (10 lammers worth $500 each, plus $120 in cash). But for each of them, this event was winner-take-all for $5,120, plus $1,800 winner-take-all amongst the nine of them. Thus, if I had been eliminated in the early or middle stages, this satellite would have become winner-take-all for $6,920, but as long as I was still in, each of them had an incentive to outlast one another, even if it meant playing differently against me.

As it happened, by the time we were down to four players, I had about half of the chips, and my opponents had about 20%, 20% and 10%. This created a dynamic where I could steal frequently preflop, and each of my opponents was correct to play extra tight, as they could hope that I would eliminate the other two, thus letting them win the $1,800. By the time we were down to heads-up, I had almost 90% of the chips, and won the satellite. The fact that I wasn't part of the last longer made me more than 50% likely to win at the time I had half the chips, because my opponents were trying to simultaneously maximize their equity in both prizes, while I was able to focus on just the satellite prize itself.

It may be true that if you are one of the better players, it will be profitable for you to participate in such last longer bets. However, it may be more profitable for you to not participate, as this will increase your equity in the main prize. Keep this in mind when deciding whether or not to participate in the last longer, and also when making your playing decisions later in the satellite.

And while all of this will be very different in a multi-table tournament, it is still important to pay attention, and know if some of the players at your MTT table are involved in such last longer bets, either against one other player, or a group of players, and look for situations where they might be correct to play tighter than usual in order to increase their chances of winning the last longer bet. This can only work out to your advantage.

Clearly I could write an entire book, even a library of books, just discussing special situations. But the point isn't that I tell you about every such possibility, but that you take these more common examples, and look for other special situations every time you play. Every bit of information you can gather might help you make a better decision, and it is better decisions that make you the better player.

SPECIAL PLAYS

This chapter will describe and discuss some special plays you should keep in mind and consider using in your game. Some of these plays have become quite well known, others not so much. This chapter exists because these plays are valuable enough, and come up often enough, that you should be aware of them, but they don't fit that well into any other chapter. The important thing to remember for all of these plays is to be sure the conditions are right, or using the play will backfire, and hurt rather than help your equity.

One of my favorite special plays is the stop-and-go. This play can be used to maximize your equity in certain specific circumstances that tend to occur occasionally in tournaments (though rarely in cash games). The proper situation for the stop-and-go play almost always occurs preflop, and mostly when you are the big blind. The first and most important criteria to properly using the stop-and-go play is that you must be in a situation where somebody has raised, and it is clearly wrong to fold. So, as you consider your options, while it may be unclear which choice has the highest EV, you are certain that folding is not that choice. The second criteria is that if you were to raise, the only reasonable option (given stack sizes) would be to raise all-in. However, you are certain that if you do so, there is little or no chance your opponent will fold. The third criteria is that if you just call now, and then bet all-in on the next street, this bet will be large enough that there is some chance your opponent will fold. Finally, you must be out of position, that is, first to act on the next street, so that you can bet all-in, rather than wait to see if your opponent checks or bets first. And while not mandatory, it is almost always the case that you are facing only a single opponent.

One of the most important aspects of the stop-and-go play is that no matter what cards are dealt next, you should always follow through with the all-in bet. Even if you are holding 6♦-6♥, and the flop comes as ugly as possible, such as A♣-K♣-Q♠, you should still go all-in. While it is true that your opponent is not going to fold many (if any) hands that hit this flop, they certainly might fold their pocket pairs 77-JJ, as well as bottom pair (e.g., a hand like Q-9). When this happens, it is a huge coup for you, as not only did you avoid going all-in preflop when it appears you were going to lose, you actually got an opponent to fold when they were an overwhelming favorite to beat you!

The result of the stop-and-go play is never worse than shoving all-in preflop (when you expected to get called), but it sometimes gets the opponent to fold postflop. Sometimes, they will be folding the best hand, and other times they will be folding a hand that still has many outs to beat you. The downside to the stop-and-go play is when the opponent folds, and your hand would have won at showdown. In this case, you fail to win those extra chips. But if used when the conditions are right, the stop-and-go play will increase your EV over the alternate play of shoving preflop and always getting called.

Let's examine a typical situation where the stop-and-go play would likely be the best choice. You are in the big blind, and a player raises preflop to 3xBB, and everybody else folds. Your entire stack, including the big blind you have posted, is only 8xBB, so you can reasonably assume that if you shove all-in now, you will always get called. Your opponent would only need to call 5xBB more to win about 12.5xBB, and it would be a mistake for them to fold anything, even hands that are clearly behind at the moment, such as low suited connectors. However, if you were to just call preflop, and then bet your last 5xBB on the flop, your opponent might now fold many hands that have missed the flop. If your opponent were convinced you hit the flop, then they could even fold hands consisting of two overcards to the board, as such a hand would be about a 3:1 underdog to beat your presumed pair, and they would be getting pot odds of only about 2.5:1 for the call.

If your hand is extremely strong, you will likely be correct to shove preflop, and not give your opponent a chance to fold when they miss the flop, as you would prefer to take on this greater risk of losing, in exchange for the greater profit of winning those extra chips they save when folding. And if you hit the flop extremely hard, such as top pair or better, this might be the only time to not automatically shove all-in on the flop. If your hand is now that strong, checking and giving them a chance to put you all-in, may be the higher EV choice.

Closely related to the stop-and-go play is the go-and-go. It is a similar idea, but now you have a stack size that is large enough that if you were to reraise all-in now, the opponent might fold. To correctly apply the go-and-go play, your hand is not only so strong that folding is clearly incorrect, but so strong that you don't want to shove all-in now and get your opponent to fold. Instead, you raise now, and then bet the rest of your chips all-in on the next street. This way, if your opponent is very weak, you force them to fold preflop. Yet if they are strong enough to call preflop, you deny them the chance to see the last two cards without paying up again when you shove the flop.

If your hand is stronger still, such as a premium pair, you might not want to apply the go-and-go play, as it might be more profitable, on average, to play the hand in a way that does not give the opponent as much opportunity to fold.

The go-and-go play is also going to make a lot of sense when your hand is strong enough that folding now would be incorrect, but there are other players yet to act whom you would rather raise out of the pot, or force them to pay a higher price to beat you. Specifically, the go-and-go play is going to most commonly be correct when you are in the small blind position, and if you don't reraise now, it is too likely that the big blind will also call, and you would then have two opponents who might outflop you, instead of just one.

Looking at a specific example, the opponent raises preflop to 3xBB, and it is folded to you in the small blind. Your stack size is 25xBB, which is on the large side for going all-in now, especially if you have a very strong hand that doesn't really want everybody to fold. Clearly, if you do shove now, there is a very high chance that both the big blind and the original raiser will fold. But you might gain more value in this situation with the go-and-go play. By reraising to 9xBB preflop, the big blind is very likely to fold, but the original raiser will be getting immediate pot odds of over 2:1, and will probably not fold most of their hands. If they reraise you all-in, you gladly call, because you should never make this play if your hand is not strong enough for this to be true. So, when they do just call, you then go all-in on every flop, except maybe on some flops where you now have a very strong hand, and don't want them to fold.

Good hands for this play include A-K, A-Q, and medium pairs. If the original raiser is especially loose, and also especially sticky*, then the strength of your starting hand for this play would go down accordingly. Just like the stop-and-go, if this play fails, and they call your shove postflop, it is no worse than if all of the chips had gone in preflop, as you are just as likely to win or lose at showdown. But when they fold on the flop, you are denying them the chance to catch a card on the turn or river to beat you, and you sometimes are getting them to fold the best hand. If you do the go-and-go play with A-K, they call with 8-8, and then fold to your shove on the J-10-5 flop, not only did your preflop reraise win those extra chips, you got them to fold after they had gone from a 54% to a 73% favorite to win the pot. The downside to the play is that when you would have won at showdown, you fail to win those extra chips. This is why the play is not recommended when you have a premium hand, or whenever you are likely to be a big favorite preflop against your opponent's range of hands.

The go-and-go play will also sometimes be correct for a very specific opponent type, the kind of player who is just way too loose preflop, but who is capable of folding postflop when they miss. Against this type of player, you reraise preflop because you probably have the best hand, and because it makes your hand look stronger than just calling. You do this knowing they are likely to call with a lot of marginal hands, even though they are not getting the proper combination of pot odds and implied odds, because they are simply too sticky preflop. These are often players who like to gamble it up a lot. You then bet

---

* The term "sticky" refers to a player who is very hesitant to fold, and is much less likely to do so in a given situation, as compared to most other players. While calling stations are by definition sticky, the terms are not identical. Calling stations call too much, whereas sticky players are more likely to call or raise, rather than fold, when compared to a more typical opponent. The term is also situational, and tends to be applied to the player who is sticky under the circumstances, and not just in some broader sense. Somebody might be sticky in one situation, and not sticky in another. There are some world class players who are known to be very sticky, so earning a reputation as sticky is not automatically a bad thing.

again on the flop, even when you miss, because they are now capable of folding. This way, you win more when they miss, and don't lose any more when the play fails, because your hand was so strong that you were never planning on folding preflop anyway.

Something that comes up moderately often (maybe 1-3 times in a full day of tournament action) is the squeeze play. The squeeze play is when a first player has raised, a second player (and sometimes a third player, a fourth player, etc.) has called, and you now reraise. By reraising in this spot, you are putting tremendous pressure on the original raiser. Not only do they need to be concerned that you have the superior hand, but also that the caller(s) might have been trapping with a better hand than either of you. Of course, players who just call a raise have a marginal hand most of the time, but not always. This means that if you successfully squeeze the original raiser out of the pot, most of the time the caller(s) will also choose to fold.

This play works best if the original raiser is known to be very loose and aggressive, and will often be raising with marginal hands, such as small pairs and suited connectors, not just premium hands. Knowing this, the player who called might be trapping, but most of the time would have reraised with their premium hands, rather than just call and have to play a guessing game as to whether or not this loose aggressive player hit the flop. The caller is also less likely to just call if doing so is often going to induce others to call, thereby putting their premium hand at even greater risk of getting beat. Therefore, the greater the chance that the original raiser is weak or marginal, the more correct it is going to be to attempt the squeeze play. Similarly, the less likely it is that the caller(s) might be trapping with a premium hand, the more correct the play becomes. Finally, the more sticky either player tends to be, the less the less correct it becomes to try the squeeze play against them.

If the circumstances are good enough, you should make this play even when your hand is absolute trash. But the stronger your hand is, the more often you will be correct to attempt the squeeze play, as you will have more of a fallback position when it fails to win the pot immediately. While you can make a squeeze play with an all-in shove, this is not generally recommended unless you also have what might be the best hand, even when called[*]. This play

---

[*] For more on this, see Ch. 12 on Stack Size Strategy.

is going to work more often when not only are the opponents facing the threat of the current raise, but also the threat that they will possibly have to commit even more chips postflop when you (presumably) bet again.

Another play that is sometimes useful but not typically recommended is commonly called the "weak lead" or "donkbet". This refers to a player, who is first to act on the flop, betting into the preflop aggressor. It does not mean the bet is weak in the sense of being small relative to the size of the pot. Simply put, it is an unexpected bet, and is a bet that is a mistake most of the time you see it. If you were not the aggressor preflop, and the pot is heads-up or 3-way, the most common pattern is for the callers to check to the preflop raiser, who is expected to bet most of the time, if not all of the time*. Therefore, when a player bets into the aggressor like this, it is referred to as a weak lead or donkbet.

When done by typical players of medium or lessor skill, the rationale for their donkbet tends to fall into one of two categories. In the most common case, the donk-bettor has hit the flop, but not that strongly. They are betting because they are afraid to give a free card, and they want to test the preflop aggressor, and see if they can get a fold. They also know that if they check, the preflop aggressor will likely bet, and if they call, they won't know where they are in the hand, and the preflop aggressor is going to see the turn card. If they check-raise, that is going to require investing a lot more chips. So instead they donkbet as they believe this will provide them with the information they want at the cheapest price, and also might get a fold from their opponent. The next most common reason for the donkbet is simply that the bettor wants to bluff at a flop they have completely missed, but would rather bluff with a bet instead of a check-raise, primarily because they wish to bluff at the lower price of a bet, rather than the more costly check-raise.

Hopefully you can already see why the weak lead is headlined by the term "weak". In both instances, the bettor is either marginal (for example, has hit a small or medium pair on the flop) or very weak (bluffing). As such, when you see a weak lead coming from a player of marginal or below average skill, you will know that this pot is quite likely yours for the taking. The only question is whether you should raise now and take it down immediately, or if you would be better off calling now and taking it down with a bet or raise on the turn.

---

* As we discussed in Ch. 17, it is frequently correct for the preflop aggressor to make this continuation bet.

Almost as important, I hope you can already see how you can use the weak lead as an occasional weapon yourself. If you believe that your opponent is aware of this general perception of the weak lead and what it usually means, you can make the occasional weak lead into this opponent when you have a strong enough hand. In many cases, if you flop a set or other extremely strong hand, the weak lead should be considered as possibly the best way to get a lot of chips into the pot.

What do I mean when I say "a lot of chips"? This will depend upon how deep the stacks are compared to the pot size. If the effective stack size between you and your opponent is something like 4-10x the current pot size, and you have a very strong hand that is happy to be all-in against this opponent, a weak lead might be the best play. If you bet first, and bet something like 50-100% of the pot, then your opponent might raise all-in whether they have a hand or not. However, if instead the effective stack was only 1-2x the size of the pot, you would prefer to check and let your opponent bet, as they will either go all-in, or bet so much of their stack that they will probably be pot-committed to calling the rest when you check-raise. If the effective stack is more than 10x the pot size, then the best way to play the hand for maximum value will depend upon a more nuanced analysis of the particular opponent, including not just how you expect them to respond to a weak lead, but how you expect them to respond to a check-raise, or a flat call, on the flop.

Another interesting use of the weak lead occurs when your opponent is very unsophisticated, and will simply fold if they missed the flop, even though they were the preflop aggressor. In this case, you can use the weak lead for the same reason that a weak player does, you are bluffing cheap with a bet, rather than with a more expensive check-raise. Just make sure you expect this opponent to never raise with a weak hand, as a response to your donkbet. You don't want to make and lose a donkbet (that will induce the opponent to successfully bluff you), rather than make a check-raise bluff that would have won the pot.

Finally, if you are facing a very strong and knowledgeable opponent, who knows that you are also knowledgeable, then once again the weak lead can become an effective tool. You can sometimes make the weak lead as a total bluff, and sometimes make this bet when you have hit the flop extremely hard. Because this tough opponent will know you know all of this, they will be mostly guessing whether you are bluffing or strong on this occasion, and therefore they will probably choose to fold many of their marginal hands. For example, let's say you are the tough opponent, you raise preflop with A♠-J♠, and get called by another tough player in the blinds. The flop is 9♣-7♠-3♥, and they come out with a donkbet. If they're bluffing, you have the best hand, and they have 3-6 outs, putting you way ahead. If they're not bluffing, they have at least a pair, and maybe a lot more. Given the difficulty of this situation, folding is probably your best choice. And thus the weak lead actually becomes a strong play when properly used by a smart player.

MAKING THE BEST DEAL

One area of tournament poker that is seriously overlooked by many players, and where a lot of money can be made, or lost, is the art of deal-making. There is never a requirement that a deal get made, but it is somewhat common, as you near the end of the tournament, for players to agree among themselves to split the remaining prize money in some manner that is not identical to the official payouts.

There are some very good reasons to consider making a deal when you are down to heads-up, or the last handful of players, chief among them reducing variance. Imagine you are down to heads-up in the WSOP Main Event, and the difference between 1st and 2nd prizes is $3M. Even though this tournament has the deepest structure of any tournament in the world, unless your opponent is basically incompetent, your edge won't be that big. And since this heads-up play is going to last anywhere from one hand to a few hours, short term variance (you can also call this "luck") is going to have a huge impact on who emerges the victor. Thus, if the chip counts are close to even, it would be perfectly reasonable for each of you to take something like $1.3M each, and play it out for the title, the bracelet, and the remaining $400K.

First things first. Before you even bring up the subject of making a deal, be sure that you are allowed to do so. Many tournaments forbid deal-making, and if you try to make a deal with your opponent, you might be subject to some sort of penalty. If you're not sure, ask the tournament director, preferably in a way that nobody else can overhear, if deals are allowed. If not, I highly recommend you do not try to circumvent this rule by making any "secret" deals.

If deals are permitted, ask if the casino will enforce the deal. By this I mean, if you and I had agreed to the deal as outlined above, and your opponent ends up winning the tournament, will they be paid the entire first prize (and then you must collect your $1.3M from them), or will the casino deduct the $1.3M from their prize, and pay it to you on their behalf? If the casino will not enforce the deal, now you must depend upon the honesty of your opponent to pay you as agreed. If you do not trust the opponent(s) completely to live up to the deal, then again it is highly recommended that you simply do not make the deal. There have been numerous instances where a player agreed to a deal, "won" the tournament, was paid the entire first prize, and walked off without paying the agreed amounts to the other players. And since many, maybe even a majority, of poker rooms will not get involved in enforcing the deal, caution is important.

Another concern is reporting issues and tax implications. Many tournament results are published, and if the prizes are large enough, you will likely need to complete paperwork (typically a w2-g or 1099-misc form) whereby your win is reported to the IRS[*] for tax purposes. In some locations, state income taxes are withheld by the casino and paid to the host state. And if the player is not a U.S. citizen, the casino may be required to not only report the win to the IRS, but also to withhold 30% and give it to the IRS on the winner's behalf. Even if you completely trust the player with whom you are dealing, if they were unaware when making the deal that some of the prize would be withheld, they might feel that the deal needs to be modified now to take this into account. And that means you will be getting screwed.

Moreover, even if everything is handled properly at the time, you might

---

* This discussion is presuming the tournament is occurring within the U.S. Obviously, if you are outside the U.S. playing a tournament, similar issues might arise with respect to the tax burden in that country. Be sure you know the full implications of any tax reporting or withholdings before you make a deal, wherever you are playing.

suffer problems down the road when you are claiming a win that is smaller than what was in the IRS paperwork, or reported publicly. The deal you made 4-handed might have been a good one, but when you end up later with tax problems, you might wish no deal had been made.

Now that we've figured all of that out, and we are still interested in making a deal, what is the best way to go about it? Clearly there is some fair number, a number that is identical to what you would win, on average, if you were to play this tournament out an infinite number of times from this point forward. But how do we determine this fair amount?

The simplest method of chopping a tournament is to just divide up the remaining prize money equally amongst all remaining players. If there are four of us left, and the prizes are 40, 30, 20, and 10, we can just add that up to $100 and take $25 each. While this seems fair on the surface, it completely ignores an extremely important factor, stack sizes. If the four of us all had stack sizes that were very close, this deal would make sense. But what if one of us has half the chips? Why would the chip leader accept a deal where they get paid the same money as their three opponents, even though they have 3x as many chips as their average opponent? As we know, the more chips you have, the more likely it is that you will win the tournament, so it makes a lot of sense to take stack size into account when making a deal.

This leads to the next method, which is to add up the prizes ($100 in this case), and give an amount to each player based upon their stack size. Thus, the chip leader with half the chips would get half of the $100. If the other three players had 25%, 15%, and 10% of the chips, they would respectively get paid $25, $15, and $10. The failure of this method to accurately pay each player is also now obvious. In this method, the chip leader just got more than first prize money, and the short stack just got paid exactly what they would have made if they were the next one eliminated. As such, it is unlikely the players would all agree to such a deal.

By making a small improvement to the method, you arrive at what is commonly referred to as the "chip-chop method", or "chip-chop model", which is probably the most popular method of deal-making. The small improvement is to first deduct the next prize to be paid, multiplied by the number of remaining players, from the total prize pool remaining, and then use the chip count percentages to divide the remaining prize money. At this point, all of the remaining four players are going to win at least $10. 4 x $10 = $40, which means that these players aren't really competing anymore for this $40 (they've already won it), but are only competing for the other $60 in the prize pool. Thus, the four players will get paid $10 each, plus $60 multiplied by their percentage of the chips in play.

50% of chips -> $10 + (50% x $60) = $40
25% of chips -> $10 + (25% x $60) = $25
15% of chips -> $10 + (15% x $60) = $19
10% of chips -> $10 + (10% x $60) = $16

While this is clearly a more fair distribution than the overly simplistic method that did not award $10 to each player before dividing the rest, it still is not fully fair. As we can see, even though they are only going to win the tournament about 50% of the time, the chip leader is being given the exact amount of first prize.

Since this is absolutely the best they can ever do, their average result must be lower, and they are being overpaid in this deal. In fact, with the chip-chop method, every player who has a chip count that is above average will be overpaid, while every player who has a below average chip count will be underpaid. Therefore, if your stack size is above average, you should usually be happy to accept a deal that is calculated by the chip-chop method. Contrarily, even if the deal sounds fair to you, if it was calculated using this method, and your stack is below average, you actually deserve more.

So what is the best way to calculate a fair deal based upon chip counts? Quite simply, it is ICM*. This method will calculate with complete fairness the prize money each player will win, on average, assuming all players are equally skilled. When I first learned about ICM in the mid to late 90s, there were no websites that would do ICM calculations for you, and certainly no apps you could download onto your phone. But now there are dozens of websites and apps, some completely free, that do ICM calculations. The free app on my phone does ICM calculations for up to 10 players. With this, I can input the stack sizes and remaining prizes, press the button, and be told exactly what

_____

* See Chapters 3 and 10.

a fair deal would be for each of us. With this starting point, I can then try to make the best possible deal, and know when it is either fair, or more than fair, for me to accept.

After determining the amount that would be mathematically fair, you should then take into account the relative skill levels of yourself and your opponents. Be sure you are being realistic here also. Most of us seriously over-rate our own skill level, and seriously underrate our opponents. Remember this when considering the relative skill levels. But if you are certain you are significantly better than your opponents, then you should hold out for more than a mathematically fair deal. If the ICM model says you deserve $20 in the deal, but you are much better than your opponents (especially factoring in skill at short-handed and heads-up play), you might want to hold out for 5-25% more money (i.e., $21-25).

Just be sure that when you are negotiating the deal, and the opponent is asking why you want more, don't say it's because you are that much better of a player. All that will do is piss them off, and make any deal unlikely. Even if your skill edge is apparent to everybody, it doesn't mean this player wants to have that fact shoved in their face. You don't need to have a reason, just say something like "Unless I get $23, I'd rather just play it out.", or even more specifically, just say "I know $20 is fair, but I don't get to play heads-up very often. So if I'm only getting the fair amount, I'd rather have the fun of playing it out." Also, if it is the opponent who is saying no to a deal, even a deal that is generous to them, there is no need to get upset or emotional. It is their right to make a deal or not, and getting mad about it just means you're the one acting like a child.

There are some well-known tournament pros who have publicly stated that they never make deals, and as soon as the subject comes up, they quickly quash the discussion. That is their prerogative, and if you choose to do likewise, it is yours. However, over the years I have been offered some deals that were so lopsided in my favor that I believe it is a tremendous mistake to just automatically reject all deals without even hearing them out.

For example, in a super-satellite tournament at Foxwoods in about 2001, the prizes were being paid out as a $5,160 main event seat to 1st, $1,000 in lammers to 2nd-6th, and $140 in cash to 7th. We were down to seven players, and on a 10 minute bathroom break. I had about 75% of the chips, and was thus a solid favorite to win, but would still fail to do so almost 1/4 of the time.

When I walked back to the table, the other six players informed me that they had made a deal, to which I replied, "How could you make a deal without me? We all have to agree before you can make a deal." They then explained the deal was 1st prize for me, and they would split the $5,140 in cash and lammers amongst themselves. When I heard that, I said "You're right, we have a deal."

With this and dozens of other such incidents during my 25+ years of playing poker, I am always willing to listen to an offer. And that is the next point, whenever possible, let the other guy bring up the idea of making a deal, and let them make the first offer. If their offer is favorable enough to you, you can take it (or push for even more). If their offer is not enough, just politely say no thanks, or counter with an offer of your own.

My only goal when I play poker is to maximize my equity, and my goal in deal-making is the same. If the deal is less than I estimate is fair to me, I will always refuse it, even if it is only slightly unfair and the variance is high. However, that doesn't mean you are mistaken if you take a slightly bad deal in order to reduce variance, just make sure you understand exactly what you are doing. For me, once I calculate the fair deal, and then factor in the relative skill levels, I will accept any deal that pays more than my estimated equity, and say no to anything less.

26

IMAGE IS EVERYTHING

Obviously math is by far the most important component of optimal poker strategy. Once you gather all the available data, it is simply a mathematical exercise to determine which decision is the most profitable. But part of the data you should gather is completely non-mathematical in nature, specifically tells and image. Tells will be discussed in Chapters 29-30. Here we are going to discuss image, both your image, and that of your opponents.

The title of this chapter is a bit over-the-top, as image is clearly not everything. But it is a huge factor when determining your best play. If we knew the game theory optimal solution to poker, it would usually consist of a random selection amongst weighted choices. For example, when facing a river bet in a heads-up pot, given the cards on the board, the cards you are holding, the bet size, stack sizes, and action up to this point in the hand, it will likely be that the game theory optimal play will not be to fold 100% of the time, or call 100%, or raise 100%. Instead, it will usually be a mix of all three, sometimes a mix of just two of these choices, and only rarely just a single correct choice. But the GTO strategy will also rarely be to do each 1/3 of the time, but instead will favor some choices more than others. For example, if your hand is a busted draw, and would almost never win at a showdown, then the GTO play might be call 0%, fold 80%, and raise (bluff) 20%. And the decision as to whether to fold or bluff would be chosen randomly. It would be the equivalent of rolling a 100-sided die, where you fold when the number 1-80 comes up, and raise if the number is 81-100.

But what if you had been caught bluffing a few times recently? What if your image were such that most opponents would assume any raise by you on the river here was highly likely to be just that, a bluff? GTO does not take into account such non-mathematical data, and therefore it would still tell you to randomly bluff 20% of the time. But if your hand is never going to win when you get called, and you think you are getting called every (or almost every) time you raise, then raising is clearly a mistake in this situation. This is an example of ignoring the GTO math, and using non-mathematical information to make a GTE decision. In this spot, even if it is technically correct for you to bluff-raise some of the time, now is not the time, due to your current image.

Contrarily, what if your current image is that of a super tight player who never bluffs? What if your opponents expect you to only bet or raise with a strong hand? With that image, you should probably be bluffing a lot more than 20% of the time in this scenario, and instead you should be bluff-raising this river 30%, 40%, maybe even 100% of the time. If your raise on the river is going to be 40xBB, the pot at the moment is also 40xBB (maybe the opponent bet 15x into a pot of 25x), and you think that with your image the opponent is going to fold more than half the time, it is clearly profitable to raise every time. The only reason you wouldn't always raise is if the ICM math indicates you need this bluff to work much more than half the time.

There are a lot more nuances to image than just that of being a frequent bluffer, or being someone who never bluffs. Every aspect of the game, and how each person plays that aspect, is a part of their image. Does the player have a very tight starting hand range? Do they only play high cards and big pairs? Do they play lots of speculative hands (suited connectors and such)? How do they play each class of hand? Do they ever just open-call preflop, rather than raise, when holding a premium starting hand? Do they ever raise or 3-bet preflop with speculative hands? Do they tend to semi-bluff or otherwise play their draws aggressively, or do they tend towards a lot of calling and passive play until they make a strong hand? Do they make lots of thin value

27

bets on the river, or do they try to get to showdown cheaply with such hands? We can go on with such questions, as there are thousands of them, but the point is that image is not just tight vs. loose, and passive vs. aggressive, but all of these nuanced little details about the player's tendencies.

When it comes to image, the most important thing is to know your own image, as it is perceived by your opponents. Obviously, you will also gauge your opponent's playing style and tendencies as best you can, but you should always closely monitor the image you are presenting, as this is the area where you will most often see a player make a huge mistake.

For example, a player might know they are generally a tight player. And they might find themselves in a perfect spot to make a squeeze play. But much of the value of the squeeze play is having a lot of fold equity. Even if you're a tight player, if you've been dealt a large number of premium hands lately, and it happens that none of those hands went to showdown, your current image might be loose and aggressive. As such, maybe this isn't such a good spot for a squeeze play by YOU, as your current image does not lend itself to getting opponents to fold semi-strong hands. To put it more succinctly, it doesn't matter what your style of play actually is, your image is going to be determined by what these opponents have seen from you recently. So remember that your image is dynamic, not static, even if you always play the same style.

But also keep in mind the concept of first impressions. If you get moved to a new table, and aggressively play the first few hands you are dealt, you are going to start off with a loose image. Even if you then play very tight for an extended period, some opponents are still going to think of you as a loose player. Similarly, it may be that you join this table, fold every hand for an hour, and develop a tight image. But one player at the table has played with you before, and their experience came at a time when you were the chip leader in an event, and you were (correctly) bullying that table. They might still be labeling you with a loose image, even though everyone else considers you tight.

While it is never a simple thing to do, you need to be constantly monitoring your image. And not just thinking of it as one thing, but also keeping in mind that your image is multi-dimensional, and varies from one opponent to another, and also varies through time.

Some players profess a strategy wherein they purposefully play in an extreme style when they join a new table in order to create the image that goes with it. For example, they might play super loose and aggressive, and try to bluff every hand until they get caught. Their thinking is that they will have this loose, bluffy image, and that once they create this image, they will then sit back, play tight, and expect to get paid off in full when they later make the best hand. I have also heard the idea that you should play super tight at the beginning of a tournament, when the blinds are small and there are no antes, as you will thereby develop a tight image as somebody who only bets/raises with the nuts. Their thought is to then start stealing a lot of pots later in the tournament once the blinds get large and the antes kick in.

Whatever type of image you think you would like to create, my strong advice is "Don't do it". By definition, when you look at these ideas, these people are playing their hands in a manner they consider less than optimal, in order to create an image. This means they are paying for their image. They are intentionally playing their cards in a sub-optimal fashion. They are giving up some amount of equity to create the desired image. Don't buy an image, because in my experience, you always pay too much.

First off, some players just don't pay that much attention. With them, you never have a strongly set image, as they just don't notice how tight or loose you have been, how passive or aggressive, or anything else about how you have been playing. Your efforts are wasted on such players[*].

Even if they are paying attention, this is a tournament, and you might get moved to a new table at any time. You could be moved to fill a nearby table that is short-handed, or your entire table might break and be sent off to other tables. This means you've spent equity buying an image, and now that image is useless at your new table, as they didn't see your image-creating plays. And even if you know your table is not going to break anytime soon, many of the players will be eliminated and replaced. If you are eliminated, it might have been the equity you paid earlier that helped cause your elimination. Even if you're still there, many of the players who saw your "image plays" will lose their chips, and be replaced by new players who didn't see, and won't know, what

---

* This is especially true when playing online. Most opponents are either multi-tabling and/or multi-tasking. In either case, they simply haven't seen what's been going on at this table, especially for the hands in which they were not involved. And if they're using a HUD to track your play, your image will be based upon the entire history they have on you, not just what you've done recently.

your image is supposed to be. In the end, if you buy an image, you will always overpay.

At least one image play that I will pursue is to pretend to be on tilt. If I take a bad beat, or otherwise lose a hand in a fashion where players would not be surprised for me to be upset, I will behave as if I am on tilt. If the next hand or two is junk, I'll just fold, and give up on the act. But if I get a strong hand soon enough, I will act as if I'm overplaying something marginal due to my tilt, and often receive too much action from somebody at the table who believes the act. For this to work, you have to behave like you're tilted before that next hand is even dealt, and then follow-up with the expected "tilty" behaviors. This might include a larger-than-average preflop raise or reraise, physically demon-strative betting (e.g., slamming your chips into the pot, rather than moving them gently), and loud verbalizations of your actions.

The best example of this I ever saw came during a one-table satellite at the Orleans Open in about 1999. I was sitting next to Chris Bigler, who would later become known in the poker world after making a couple of televised final tables in the first season of the WPT. Chris had been chip leader, but lost a big pot where his opponent was way behind and hit a longshot on the river to win. The next hand, it folded to Chris, who loudly said "Raise!" He grabbed at some chips in his stack, but fumbled a few of them, and knocked over some others. He then tried again, and knocked over some more. He then said "Fuck it, I'm all-in!", and shoved the entire jumble of chips into the pot. One or two people folded, and then the next guy quickly said call, and pushed his smaller stack into the pot. You could tell by the look on his face that he was so happy to have caught Chris bluffing and on tilt from the previous beat. That is, until the rest of the players folded, and Chris turned over two Aces. The caller had A-8o, lost, and the pot was pushed to Chris. While this was happening, Chris leaned over to me, and quietly said "Maybe I should become an actor, eh?"

HOW DO I BET?

In this chapter, we're not talking about the decision to bet. That decision has already been made, and you've decided to bet or raise. Of course, the decision as to whether or not to bet or check, or whether to fold, call, or raise, is not a simple one. You must take into account your cards, your image (as you believe it is perceived by the opponent(s), the cards on board, the history of the hand up to now, the image you have of your opponent(s), stack sizes, the stage of the tournament, and a host of other factors. But once you decide you are going to put chips into the pot, HOW you do so can make a difference.

Again, we're not talking how much you are going to bet or raise, but precisely how you are going to accomplish the physical act of moving chips into the pot. Watch a table playing poker sometime, and just notice the physical nature of chip movement by each player. Often players casually toss in a handful of chips. Sometimes the toss is low, sometimes high, sometimes faster, or slower. Some players will often take a handful of chips, and then cut out the ones they are putting into the pot, returning the leftovers to their stack. You may see a player slide the chips forward gently after carefully counting and assembling them. You may see a player grab the chips and slam them down hard on the felt as they make their play.

If you pay attention, you will also see that the same player does not always move their chips into the pot in the same manner. Obviously, if the bet or raise is a single chip, it will be moved differently than if it consists of several stacks of chips. Aside from this difference, you will see a given player put the same number of chips into the pot with a casual toss one time, with a gentle slide the next, and maybe a slam the time after that.

If you track these differences, you will find that some players tend to make certain physical moves with their chips when bluffing, and a different move when confident they have the best hand. And this means that YOU are probably also exhibiting a pattern, unless you are conscientiously ensuring you do not. Using a consistent betting move is the key. If you always follow the same routine, and always use the same movement when putting one chip into the pot, you will not fall into a subconscious pattern that observant opponents will notice. Likewise, once you need to move more than a small number of chips into the pot, you will now adopt a different move that meets the physical needs of this larger number of chips, but is the same every time you move this number.

Thus, you might have one move when you are betting or raising a total of 1-4 chips, a second move when it is 5-10 chips, a third move when it is 10-20 chips, and another move when it is more than 20. The point is that once the number of chips you are moving is determined, you will move them into the pot the exact same way every time, whether you are value-betting the nuts, bluffing with air, or anything in-between.

In addition to adopting these consistent movements, you also need to ensure that you are actually betting or raising exactly the amount you desire. It is quite common, especially if you travel the tournament circuit, to find different casinos using different colors of chips for the same denomination. You might find the T1K chip is yellow at one casino, while the T5K chip is orange, and then at the next casino these colors will be reversed. It is therefore quite easy to accidentally grab the wrong chips, and make the wrong bet.

One time, about the middle of day 1 at the EPT London High Roller, I was playing a pot against Ashton Griffin. We had built a pot of about T4,500 with a couple of raises preflop. His entire remaining stack was under T20,000, and consisted of three T5K chips, three T1K chips, and a number of smaller denomination chips. After the dealer spread the flop of 9-7-7, Ashton grabbed his three T5K chips, and tossed them into the pot. I was confused for a moment, wondering why he would bet more than 3x the pot, and over 3/4th of his stack. For a second, I thought, maybe he was essentially just going all-in, but only moving these big chips, as they effectively communicated that intent. I then realized that he had meant to bet T3,000, but had simply grabbed the wrong chips. Unfortunately for him, I had 9-9, and his mistake was costly.

The best way to avoid such mistakes is to verbalize your action before making any physical movement. Verbal is binding, so if you say "Three-thousand", and then toss three T5K chips into the pot, the dealer is going to correct your mistake. By verbalizing, you will avoid any such mistakes. Same idea if you are calling; by saying "Call" before putting out any chips, you will not accidentally raise when you put out too much, either because you grabbed the wrong chips, or because you misread the bet you were facing. It is true that many players prefer not to verbalize their action, as they are concerned that the tone of their voice might convey a tell. That is, they are concerned that their voice will give away whether they are weak or strong. If this is your concern, and you don't want to verbalize, you must be extra careful to put the correct amount into the pot, as you will be held to what you do, not what you intended to do.

One thing I've started doing in the last few years, whenever I am calling a bet or raise, is to put one chip into the pot first, then the rest. Thus, if you raise preflop to T600, and I want to call, I don't put T600 into the pot in one motion. If I did it all at once, but had accidentally grabbed a T1,000 chip instead of a T500 chip, by putting T1,100 into the pot, in one motion, I would be reraising, instead of making the call I intended. To avoid this mistake, I now put just the single T100 chip into the pot first, then the T500. That way, if I grab a wrong chip, I'm not raising by accident.

As an extra benefit, I've often found that I can elicit a tell with this method. I always try to accumulate a physically large stack, with lots of small denomination chips. Thus, if I'm calling a bet of T600, I might often put T1,100 into the pot, consisting of a T1,000 chip, and a T100 chip. That way, I get a T500 chip as change. If I use this string-calling method, and toss out first the T100 chip, then the T1,000 chip, I occasionally find an opponent who says I have to raise, as I put out too many chips for this to just be a call. Of course, it is a raise in a sense, but it's a string-raise, as I put the chips out in two separate motions. And we all know that a string-raise is just a call. So now I've done nothing wrong, nothing that should ever be considered an angle, and yet I've learned that my opponent wants me to have raised. And this knowledge might help me achieve a better result in this pot going forward.

28

TELLS

At its core, poker is a game of math. As we discussed in Chapter 5, once you've gathered the available information, all that remains is to do the math and calculate, from your current options, which decision has the highest equity. But before we get to the math, we have to gather all that information. And just like everything else in life, the more information we can accurately gather and process, the better we can determine the best decision. In live poker, one of the richest areas of information is tells.

Before I discuss anything else, let me define the term "tells", at least as I use it. Many players will use the term tells to include things like betting patterns. That is, they will say that a player's betting pattern is a tell indicating the strength of their hand. For example, if a player is one who will seldom bet or raise with a draw, then the fact that they have bet or raised is a strong indicator that they do not hold a draw. Similarly, some players consider bet-sizing to be a tell. Especially before the poker boom, it was not uncommon to find players who would make larger bets when bluffing, and smaller bets when confident they had the best hand. Therefore, based upon the size of the bet, you could deduce the likely strength of their hand. However, when I use the term "tells", I do not include these things. For purposes of this chapter in particular, I will only discuss physical mannerisms and body language. Of course, betting patterns and bet sizing are hugely important factors, and should not be ignored. I just do not include them within the definition of the term "tells".

While it is quite difficult to parse through this information accurately, most of your opponents will be providing you with a surplus of such information to consider. The best and most reliable tells are subconscious; that is, the player is not aware of the movement or body positioning that comprises the tell. Because the player is unaware of what they are doing, the tell is completely honest. The difficulty is interpreting the tell correctly, but at least you do not have to guess what the opponent is trying to say, as you would with an "acting" or conscious tell. But it is often the case that a given physical mannerism might signal weakness when seen in one opponent, and yet be an indicator of strength in another. As such, you must determine for each individual which tells they exhibit, and for each tell the type of information it conveys.

There are also "acting tells", things that a player does or says consciously, that are designed to throw you off or steer you into making a decision they prefer. Because these tells are consciously controlled by the player, it is usually obvious that they are providing the tell.

The difficulty lies in determining at what level the player is thinking. If they are providing an acting tell of strength, is it because they think you will interpret it as strength, or because they think you will interpret it as weakness? That is, when you spot the tell that is purportedly selling strength, will you think it is a subconscious tell, and thus an honest indication of strength, or will you, knowing it is an acting tell, decide that since they are acting strong, they must actually be weak, and are just pretending to be strong. Or, since they know that you know they are acting, will this act of strength be expected to not be believed, and that you will interpret it as weakness, in which case they are acting strong when they are strong, as a sort of double-reverse. As you can see, this can go level after level, an entire series of "they know that I know that they know that I know ...". In these cases, the tell itself is very easy to read, but the thought process behind the tell is difficult to accurately interpret.

The most important and first thing you should learn about tells is to hide your own tells. As I play poker, and especially when I teach seminars, it is amazing the amount of tells that players exhibit. Even after I coach a student to sit still, they seldom can do so. And sitting still is the secret. If you are moving, no matter how innocuously, your subconscious will affect your movements, and you will exhibit tells. If you sit absolutely still, there is nothing for your subconscious to affect, and you will give off no tells, or at least a lot less than before.

When you watch me play, you will see that when I am not involved in a hand, I am very animated, engaged, and talkative. I am enjoying myself, as well as talking to my opponents to learn information about their mindset and level of experience and skill. But once it is my turn on the first round of betting, I shut up, quiet my face and body, do a final scan of my opponents and their chip stacks, make sure I know what the action is (for example, has it folded to me, been raised, and the like), and then look at my cards. If I am folding, all is fine, I fold, and continue to stay observant and engaged at the table. If I am playing this hand, I put out the desired number of chips, place my fossil on my cards, put on my glasses, and get into my pose.

What do I mean by "pose"? Quite simply, I get into a position where I will be able to sit comfortably for the duration of the hand without moving. For me, this means leaning my head on one hand, and placing the other hand flat on the table near my cards. Which arm I lean on depends upon the location of my opponent, or likely opponent, for this hand. If the opponent is to my right, I lean on my left hand so my head is tilted to the right, easier to stare at this opponent. For opponents on my left, I do the opposite. If I have multiple opponents that are not all on the same side, I have to pick which hand to lean on based upon which angle will best permit me to look at all my opponents without having to move my head to do so.

Now that I am involved in the hand, and settled into my pose, I do not move until it is once again my turn. If I am going to fold, I can quit the pose, and toss in my cards. If I'm going to check, I make exactly the same checking motion each time, two taps of the index finger of the hand on the table. If I'm going to bet/call/raise, I remove that hand from the table, take the appropriate chips from my stack, and move them forward. Other than that, I do not move at all. If you are watching me, live or on television, and you see me do something else, I am acting. It means I have decided I can influence an opponent to do what I want, and I am purposefully moving, talking, or whatever, in an attempt to get them to make the decision I prefer.

Some subconscious tells might happen even if you don't move. If you see a flop that is especially exciting or interesting, your pupils might dilate. If you make a very strong hand, you might get a rush of adrenalin that will cause your pulse and breathing rate to increase, and this might be visible in a neck-vein or the heaving of your chest. In order to deal with these potential tells, you can simply cover up those parts of your body. Wearing hats, hoodies, and glasses can help to cover these body parts, and help to hide some subconscious tells that you might be exhibiting.

While you do not want to make yourself physically uncomfortable, if you are content wearing these items, then there is no reason not to do so. The only reason I don't wear hoodies and hats is because I tend to get hot if I do. But most players seem more likely to be cold inside a typical poker room, and as such, there is no reason for them not to bring a hat and hoodie, or other such clothing, that will both hide their tells, and keep them warm.

You may also notice that if you watch me play now, I tend to lean on one hand, and place that hand over my mouth. In the past, I leaned my cheek onto the supporting hand. However, when watching myself compete at the tele-vised final table of the $40K buyin 40th Anniversary tournament at the WSOP in 2009, I saw myself exhibit a micro-expression tell. That is, when watching the television show months later, I saw in a hand against Ike Haxton that you could see a micro-expression frown on my face at one point. Fortunately for me, Ike was not looking my way at that moment, but if he had been looking, had noticed the tell, and known what it meant, he would have known he could bluff me. After that, I started leaning my head in such a way that I covered my mouth. Obviously it is best if you never give off a tell, but the next best thing is hiding the tell by covering it up.

Adrenalin tells are my favorite, and the most reliable tells that occur more than occasionally. These tells can be faked, but it is not easy to do so convinc-ingly. Essentially, an adrenalin tell is a physical reaction caused by the release of adrenalin in the player's body. Adrenalin is associated with the fight-or-flight instinct, so feelings of fear and/or excitement cause the adrenal gland to acti-vate and release adrenalin into the blood stream. Since the biological purpose of adrenalin is to prepare the body to fight or run, it increases strength and heart rate (pulse), as well as the need for oxygen, thus causing the person to breathe heavily.

In poker terms, if something causes great emotional excitement or fear in a player, their brain may interpret this in a manner similar to fear or excitement caused by the presence of a predator or prey. In evolutionary terms, the presence of predator or prey means the person will soon need to fight or flee, and do so at their maximum ability in order to escape death or catch a meal. The fear or excitement a player may feel at the poker table is analogous, and will likewise cause a release of adrenalin.

The result of the adrenalin rush is most easily observed by noting how fast and heavy a player is breathing, or by observing a change in their pulse rate in a visible vein, such as those in the neck. The infamous "shaking hands" tell is also an indication of an adrenalin rush, as adrenalin makes your muscles twitchy. Just make sure to notice if the player has shaking hands all the time, as this is not uncommon amongst elderly players, as well as players with certain physical and neurological conditions.

If a player is experiencing an adrenalin rush, there is nothing they can do to prevent it. The only cure is to get so used to the situation that you no longer react in an emotional manner. During a televised poker event called the British Poker Open in 2005, we played 6-handed matches on live television, and the producers put pulse monitors on some of us. When watching the show the previous evening, I observed Gus Hansen, and noted that not only was his heart rate very low (a sign of his excellent athleticism), but that whatever was happening in a hand, it barely changed. The next evening when I competed, and was wearing the monitor, I asked friends afterward how my heart rate reacted, and was pleasantly surprised when informed that it almost never changed, and then only a little. Contrarily, one of the amateurs invited to compete the night Gus was playing showed massive variability in his heart rate. When uninvolved and resting, he had a normal pulse; but when he made a huge hand, his heart rate would more than double. The commentators were even saying, and only half-jokingly, that maybe they should have an ambulance at the ready, as it appeared he might have a heart attack any second.

Most players do not experience an adrenalin rush when they are weak and/or bluffing. Even with all of the tension of putting most or all of their chips at risk, they will probably not release adrenalin. However, when a player is dealt a premium starting hand, and even more so when a player has made a huge hand (nut flush, full house, etc.), they will tend to experience an adrenalin rush. If they make a huge hand and do not have this happen, they are probably experienced enough that they no longer react emotionally to such things. But even some very experienced players will exhibit this tell, when they make a big hand, if they are doing so in a situation that is new to them, or when they are competing for more money than they have before. As such, even though they are highly experienced, they are not highly experienced when it comes to playing for this much, or when playing on a televised table, or something else that is new and stressful to them.

The most common category of tells you will see at the poker table, and in life, are referred to as pacifying tells. These are things we all do every day to soothe ourselves, such as rubbing our chin, tugging on an ear, rubbing our hands together, and a million other small actions that can be summarized crudely as touching or stroking any part of the body. Just as a mother will stroke her baby's skin to calm it down when upset, we stroke and touch ourselves throughout each day to self-soothe and relax ourselves from all of the minor and major stresses of life. The more stress you are feeling, the more likely you will engage in a pacifying behavior.

Thus, the key to reading this category of tells is determining, for each opponent, whether they feel more stress and engage in more pacifying behavior when they have a strong hand, or when they are weak and/or bluffing. If you observe a player lightly stroking the back of one hand with another, and then at showdown has the nuts, it is less likely they are bluffing later when stroking their chin after making a bet. The fact that they engaged in pacifying behavior previously when holding a strong hand indicates they are more likely to exhibit such behavior whenever holding a strong hand.

Pacifying tells are not anywhere near as reliable as adrenalin tells, but to the extent they are being done subconsciously, they are very reliable indicators of stress. However, since pacifying tells are non-specific, the key to using them successfully is to learn what they mean for each player, based upon careful observation.

Distancing tells are an excellent indicator of hand strength. Simply put, distancing tells involve moving yourself, or at least part of your body, or your cards, closer to the board. This happens subconsciously when you like what you see. Of course, if you don't like what you see, the opposite can happen, and you can subconsciously move away from the board.

In case you're thinking this is silly, imagine a non-poker scenario. You hear somebody close behind you say your name. You turn around. If you see somebody you find attractive, you will probably move closer; but if you see somebody unattractive, you will probably back up a little. It won't just be based upon appearance, either. If it turns out to be your attractive, but hated, ex-spouse, you will likely distance yourself, even if it is only an inch or two.

When this happens at the poker table, you will find yourself shifting in your seat to get a little closer, or further, from the cards the dealer just revealed, depending upon whether you like them. Even if your body doesn't move, if you tend to shuffle chips, you might start gradually moving the hand shuffling the chips a bit closer, or further, from the cards on the board. Anytime your body, or a body part, is a different distance from the board than before, this could be a distancing tell.

Another good category of tells to look for are protective tells. These are movements where a player is placing their hands closer to or somewhat covering or hiding their cards, or chips. Anything that would enable that person to more effectively guard their cards or chips could be a protective tell. The fact that a player is exhibiting a protective tell does not necessarily mean they are weak or strong, it means they are concerned, and therefore feeling a greater need to protect what is theirs.

For example, if you take a flop of J♠-10♠-8♦ in a heads-up pot, and observe your opponent make a movement that appears protective, they are probably concerned. However, they might not be weak at all. They could still have an overpair, or top pair, or other strong hand, but are more concerned now than they were preflop. On the other hand, if the opponent had air to begin with, and raised your big blind with 7-4o, then they are not likely to start exhibiting a protective tell after seeing this flop. Their chips were at risk as soon as you called, so they would have been more likely to exhibit a protective tell right after you called, rather than upon seeing the flop.

Micro-expressions fall into the category of subconscious tells, and are exceptionally reliable, as they are almost impossible to fake. A true micro-expression is essentially a facial expression that occurs for a fraction of a second, so quick that the muscles do not even have time to fully move, but just twitch in a barely noticeable manner.

Imagine you are a disciplined poker pro, playing in a big event, and you flop top set. Clearly this is a happy thing, but being experienced and disciplined, you do not move. However, your brain knows that a great thing just happened, and you are a huge favorite to win this pot. Rather than focusing on if you will win, you are now figuring out how to win the most chips possible. Even though you are not moving, the strength of your happy feelings can be so great that a tiny fraction of a nerve signal leaks out from your brain, and causes the muscles in your face, the muscles that would be used if you actually were to smile in happiness, to twitch ever so slightly. If I'm watching you carefully at that moment, and your face/mouth is not covered, I might see that slight muscle twitch that lasts for only a tiny fraction of a second. And I'll now know that you're secretly happy. As previously discussed, seeing myself exhibit such a micro-expression on national TV is why I started to cover my mouth with my hand.

Whereas most tells are non-specific, and must be catalogued as to their meaning for each individual opponent, some tells are very specific, and will usually be associated with either high or low confidence feelings in the player exhibiting the tell. For example, pacifying tells indicate the player is under stress that is higher than normal, but until you know more about that player, it is impossible to know if they feel more stress when they have a monster hand, or when they are attempting a bluff. In contrast, specific tells will tend to have the same meaning from one opponent to the next.

High confidence tells indicate a player is feeling confident, and thus has a hand they believe is the likely winner. These tells are universal, and almost always indicate confidence (and thus strength) whenever they occur. If you see such a tell, and the opponent does not have a strong hand, then the likely explanation is either they are good enough actors that they exhibited this behavior as a false tell, and you did not realize they were acting, or they honestly thought they had a strong hand, and the tell was accurate in reflecting how they felt, but not accurate in reflecting the reality of their hand. Following are some of the most common and easier to spot examples of high confidence tells.

Territorial displays are behaviors in which a player is making use of more physical space than they were previously, or more than they usually do. When we feel confident, we "spread out" our bodies. Not only are such positions likely to feel more comfortable, but they exhibit confidence that we are in control of our surroundings. We are confident enough to stretch out our arms and legs, with no concern of impending danger.

For example, if a player is typically sitting at the table with their arms resting in their lap, or at their sides, and now they put their hands on their hips with their elbows sticking out to the sides, this is a territorial display. They are likely to have higher than average confidence in their situation, and as such they are willing to take more space at the table. Similarly, if a player has had their hands resting on the rail or felt straight in front of them, but now they move their hands outward, away from their body, farther apart on the rail or felt, they are using more territory than normal, and are likely to be feeling more confident. There are thousands of examples of this you can look for, but anytime your opponent changes position, notice if their new position uses more space than before, as this may indicate an increase in confidence.

Closely related to the territorial displays is the classic pose of the CEO or other leader, sitting with their feet up on their desk, fingers interlaced behind their head, and elbows extended out to the sides. This pose takes up a lot of territory, and is very much an indicator of strength and superiority. Imagine any movie scene where one character goes into the office of the other. You will not be surprised to see the leader of the two in this pose, no matter whose office they are in. But it would be surprising to see the non-leader of the two strike this pose. In fact, it is a common scene where one character is in their own office in this pose, but when their boss comes in they quickly exit this pose and sit up straight and attentive at their desk. And you might even see the boss sit down in a chair and assume the same pose their subordinate just quit. By doing so, they are claiming territory, and displaying superiority.

While you probably won't see your opponent put their feet up on the table in a poker game, you will occasionally see an opponent interlace their fingers behind their head and lean back, an extremely high confidence display. It will be very rare to see an opponent make a bet or raise, assume this position, and turn out to be bluffing.

Another classic power pose is called steepling. This involves bringing the fingers of your hands together, with the tips of each finger and thumb touching their opposite on the other hand. Think of the classic hand position for prayer in the Catholic Church, except when steepling the palms don't touch one another, just the fingertips. You will often see the hands held this way in political speeches, as this pose conveys strength and confidence. When an opponent does this with their hands at the poker table, they are almost always strong, or at least believe themselves to have a strong hand.

Thumb displays are another great subconscious tell. In evolutionary and survival terms, thumbs are critical body parts. Lose a finger, and you can still perform any task, and usually at a level almost as high as before. But lose your thumb, and that hand loses most of its ability. When we are confident, our thumbs are much more likely to be exposed and visible, whereas at times of low confidence we will tend to hide our thumbs. If a player has a hand on the poker table, thumb out and away from the rest of the hand, and then pulls that thumb under their palm, something has probably caused them to lose confidence. Look at each of your opponents as they sit in their typical poses, and see where their thumbs are. Then look again when they are in a hand, and see if there is a difference in their thumb display. It is very possible the amount of thumb display will correlate with their perceived strength.

Imagine you're watching a performance, and one of the characters is a person of power, such as a nobleman. Imagine a scene where they are interacting with somebody they consider of lower status. How do you expect them to look at this lower person? One thing that wouldn't surprise you is to see them looking down their nose. They stand with their nose held high, looking down, even if the other person is taller. While this trait is much less universal, and tends to be seen more in certain cultures (e.g., European), it is another good tell to look for. If your opponent raises their nose high, there is a greater chance they perceive themselves to be in a position of superiority; which will frequently mean they perceive themselves to be holding the stronger hand.

In a somewhat related manner, any gravity defying behavior will tend to correlate with strength. By gravity defying behavior, I mean any position where part of the person's body is higher than it would typically be, either temporarily or fixedly. Imagine a child getting Christmas gifts. What do they do? They will often jump up-and-down with excitement. What if instead it is an adult at work who gets some good news? They aren't likely to jump around, given social constraints, but they might often raise themselves up on their toes slightly and briefly. At the poker table, a player will likely be much more subtle than even that.

For example, if a player normally rests a hand on the table, palm flat and touching the felt, but now has just their fingertips touching the felt, the rest of the hand being slightly elevated, that is a gravity defying behavior. Look for any body part that has become elevated compared to before, or lowered, and this will be a clue that the player has gained or lost confidence.

In a somewhat related tell, when a player raises their eyebrows and opens the orbit of their eyes, that is often correlated with perceived strength. How do cartoonists draw sweet, gentle, little animals or children? They draw them with large, wide-open eyes; eyes that take up a lot of real estate on the face. And how do they draw the villains, thinking evil thoughts? It is often with closed, squinted eyes. Imagine a Wild West movie, and the hero, as he greets a friend. His orbits are wide open, eyebrows raised, as there is no tension or reason to worry. But now as he approaches a bad-guy, his eyebrows lower, his orbits become closed, as he squints at this potential enemy. He is concerned, you can see it in his eyes. Since players with strong hands are not usually going to feel concerned, they are more likely to exhibit raised eyebrows and large orbits.

Low confidence tells indicate the player is lacking in confidence, which almost always means they do not believe they are holding the winning hand. In many cases, these tells are merely the opposite of the high confidence tells.

Somewhat opposite to the strength tell of steepled fingers, when a player interlaces their fingers, they are probably feeling a lack of confidence. Think of somebody who is praying with interlaced fingers, that is this tell. Just be careful, if somebody is resting their interlaced hands in front of them, but with their thumbs up and exposed, they are likely feeling confident, not the opposite. In this case, the positive thumb display usually outweighs the interlacing of the fingers.

Turtling is when a player adjusts their head, neck, and shoulders in a manner that resembles a turtle pulling its head into its shell. The player will tuck in their chin, moving it closer to their chest, pull their head lower and/or raise their shoulders. This is a subconscious protective move when we feel threatened, as we are trying to protect our most valuable body part, our head, from the danger we perceive. Obviously turtling and other such behaviors will not protect us from the dangers involved in a hand of poker, but these are ingrained behaviors whenever we feel threatened.

Venting is something we do to cool ourselves, and again is linked to feelings of discomfort and lack of confidence. The clear visual here is to think of the comedian Rodney Dangerfield tugging on his collar. By loosening our collar, we allow air to flow, cooling us off. If a player suddenly feels the need to vent, it is more likely they are uncomfortable with their cards, rather than the room suddenly getting warmer. Any activity that might cool somebody physically will fall into this category, so also look for a player taking off or adjusting their hat,

29

or even fanning themselves.

Licking or pursing of lips is also a sign of discomfort and can be a tell of weakness, as is squinting or covering of your eyes, or using one hand to grasp the wrist of the other hand. If a player is holding their breath or takes a hard swallow, these are also signs of weakness.

A great tell of weakness is placing your hands palms up (especially checking with palm up). Placing your palms up is a universal signal of surrender, and those who feel they are in a position of strength, such as holding a strong hand, do not surrender. One reason I adopt a uniform manner of movement, for checking and betting, is to avoid just such tells. When you find an opponent who is always doing things differently, look carefully for this tell, as it is extremely reliable when you do find it.

The main key to reading tells is simply to remain observant. Many players mentally check-out of the game as soon as they fold, and don't pay attention again until the next hand is dealt. But this is the most valuable time for you to observe and learn your opponents' tells and patterns. Because you have folded, you have no vested interest in this pot, and will probably be more objective, and accurate, at reading tells. Then, in future hands, you will have this newly gathered information which you can use to "soul-read" your victims.

29

USING TELLS

Being able to read an opponent's tells only does so much good unless you can properly use that information to guide your decisions. For example, the fact that you are sure your opponent is bluffing when they raise all-in preflop doesn't really help much when your hand is 7-high. Even though you know they are bluffing, you still have to fold (unless you're getting great pot odds to call anyway, in which case the fact that they are bluffing still doesn't matter much). The key is to use tells to narrow the range of hands your opponent is holding, and use that information to possibly change your playing decision.

The first step in using tells properly is to assign them a confidence level. For example, let's say your opponent raised preflop, you called, they make a continuation bet on the flop, and then you see them hide their thumbs, a sign of weakness. How confident are you they missed the flop? How reliable is this tell? Are you 100% sure they are weak? Most likely, you are not 100% sure, but you believe there is a greater than average chance they are weak after this flop. Maybe this opponent would always C-bet in position with only one caller. And from previous experience you know that their range missed this flop about half the time. If you were 100% sure of this tell, instead of facing a situation where it is 50% likely that this opponent is weak, you are 100% sure of their weakness. In this case, you will play your strong hands differently to maximize value, and never fold your weaker hands.

But what if you are not 100% sure of this tell? Let's say you have 50% confidence in this tell. Normally, we would believe that this flop has missed their range about 50% of the time. But now we have spotted a marginal tell that is 50% reliable. This means that half the time they are definitely weak, and half the time the tell is meaningless. Thus, 50% of the time the tell is spot on, they are weak, and can probably be easily bluffed off this pot. The other half of the time the tell is meaningless, which means that half of those times they are weak and missed the flop (as their range misses this flop half the time in the absence of tells), and half of the time they are not weak given this flop. Overall, this equates to:

50% - tell is reliable, they are weak
25% - tell is meaningless, but they are weak anyway
25% - tell is meaningless, and they are strong

As you can see, this tell, in which we are only 50% confident, has still made a dramatic change in what we believe this opponent is holding. And this information should have a large impact on how we proceed. Of course, there are hundreds of potential tells out there, and just because you see one tell does not mean you should focus completely upon it. If they leaned forward at the same time they hid their thumbs, you have competing tells. Hiding of the thumbs tends to mean weak, but moving closer to the board tends to mean they like what they see, and have hit the flop.

You need to consider all of the tells you notice in the moment, and combine them into a read of how this opponent feels about the strength of their hand. If you are not relatively confident in your read, then you should rely more upon your normal basic strategy for the situation, and mostly ignore the tells. But do not be shy about using any tells you do spot.

One of the best ways to practice reading tells is to pay attention after you fold. Watch the remaining players compete for the pot. Watch them carefully for tells, and decide what range of hands you put them on absent all tells, and what range after considering their tells. Then, see the cards they reveal at showdown, and gauge the accuracy of your reads. Since you are no longer in the hand, and have no emotional connection to the outcome, you will find that it is much easier to spot tells, and to interpret them correctly. This practice will improve your confidence in reading tells later when you are competing for the pot, and are emotionally connected to the outcome.

Try this training exercise that will greatly improve your ability to read tells. Enter a cheap tournament, and for the duration of the tournament, do not look at your cards. You should pretend to look at your cards, so your opponents believe you know what you're holding. But instead of actually looking and using that information to make your decisions, instead focus entirely upon your opponents, and the cards you think they are holding. If you think they hit the flop or for other reasons won't fold, don't try to bluff them, but fold yourself. If you think they missed the flop or for other reasons can be bluffed, then bet and/or raise to make them do so. Obviously this is not the best way for you to play all of your tournaments, but by doing this in a cheap event, you will be paying a small price for a lot of practice in reading tells.

30

MANIPULATING OPPONENTS

Many years ago, I heard something really smart from a poker player named Steve Badger. He said, if you give no information to your opponent, they have at most two or three choices as to what to do (check/bet or fold/call/raise). If they have to guess, they are going to guess right either one-half or one-third of the time. If you can, you want to not just make them guess (because they might guess right), but actually steer them towards the worst of their possible choices (that is, the choice that is worst for them but best for you). Only if you can manipulate them like this will they get it right even less often than the random one-half or one-third of the time.

This is a really simple idea, and once you hear it, it seems pretty obvious. Yet I do not recall anyone else ever talking about this. With the dominance of math in developing correct poker strategy, there is very little writing or work being done with respect to these non-math aspects of poker. Moreover, even though this is a powerful idea, it is a two-edged sword, and it will cut you deeper than it cuts your opponent, if not used carefully.

Why is this such a two-edged sword? Simply put, the way you actively manipulate your opponent into choosing incorrectly is by providing false information. For example, if you're a good enough actor, you can provide the opponent with false tells. If you are certain enough that a given tell will make them think you're weak when you're strong, or vice versa, then exhibiting that tell will tend to manipulate them into making the wrong decision.

Just mixing up your game is not enough to qualify as manipulating your opponent. A Game Theory Optimal bot will mix it up, and do it so perfectly, you will be left guessing as to the strength of its hand, and the exact nature of the cards it is holding. But this means you essentially have no information, and must guess. To manipulate your opponent, you must do more than make them guess, you must also steer them towards the worst of their possible choices. But if you are going to do something, to provide this extra information, to steer the opponent, there is always a chance they will see through your attempted manipulation. And this will make it easier for them to choose the option you were trying to steer them away from.

For example, let's say I have the nuts on the river, and am going to bet into my opponent. Obviously, their best decision is to fold. But if they call, while that is worse (for them), it is nowhere near as bad for them as raising. Maybe you believe this opponent is a decent, but not great, player. You are pretty sure they know that a player who is practically holding their breath is more likely to be bluffing than somebody who is breathing heavily. So, in order to sell your bet as a bluff, and try to induce them to at least call (and hopefully raise), you act like a bluffer holding your breath. If this works, you will ensure that they don't fold, and maybe choose to raise, especially if their hand is so weak they can't beat some of your bluffs.

But what if instead this player is alert enough that they remember an earlier hand where you got caught bluffing? And on that occasion you were not "practically holding your breath"? This player is too skillful to fall for this trick, because they will realize this is not how you acted earlier when bluffing. As such, they will deduce you are not bluffing now, and might be more likely to fold than if you had not tried to use a reverse tell.

Therefore, in order to manipulate the opponent, you must not only be a good enough actor that they see what you want them to see, but you must know exactly where they are at in terms of skill level, so you know what behaviors, mannerisms, bet sizing, and reverse tells will elicit the desired result.

Similarly, you can also engage in "table talk" in order to manipulate your opponent. What is table talk? Simply put, it is conversation designed not just to chat, not just to pass idle time while playing poker, but to have a specific effect on your opponents. At a basic level, it is part of your image at the table. If you talk strategy all the time, you are creating the image of a serious, thoughtful player (usually an image you do not want to have, by the way). If you use a lot of "home game" expressions*, you are creating the image of the home game hero, the amateur who has stepped up to play this big event at the casino or poker room.

If you are not known to the players in the game, you can use such table talk to foster the desired image for yourself, whatever you want that to be. At a stronger level, you can use table talk during a hand to throw off the opponent, and talk them into folding, calling, checking, betting, or raising, as you desire. If you have made a value bet, and believe the opponent is about to fold, there really isn't much to lose if you say something to try to get them to change their mind. Similarly, if you see they are about to call, when you want a fold, there isn't much to lose by saying something.

Just be careful that you are not breaking the rules where you are playing. In many rooms, you will be penalized if you discuss the strength of your cards, or those of your opponent, during the hand itself. In some rooms, even something that seems pretty innocuous, such as betting the river and saying "It's the nuts or nothing", can get you a penalty after the hand.

31

---

* Certain poker terms, at least in my experience, seem to be strongly associated with home game regulars, and do not seem to be used often by players who frequent public poker rooms. The word that really stands out for me is "pockets", when referring to a pocket pair in holdem. Also, if the player refers to a full house as a "boat" or "full boat", that also seems to correlate strongly with a home game player. Of course, I'm not intending to put down or diminish home game players; that is where most of the great players started. I'm merely saying that, on average, the skill level of someone who primarily plays in home games is lower than that of a public poker room regular. Of course, the player who seldom plays at all, in public rooms or home games, has the lowest average skill level.

EMOTIONAL CONCERNS

As a general principle, emotions are a bad thing for a poker player. Too much negativity when things are not going your way can lead to tilt, and cause you to play horribly. Even if such emotions do not lead to tilt, they can still cloud your judgment, and lead to strategy errors. Also, it is emotions that tend to create tells. If you do not care, in an emotional sense, that the flop is A-K-7 when you are holding J-J, or that you just flopped the nut flush with your A-Qs, then you are much less likely to exhibit any tells that will clue in your opponent to the strength (or weakness) of your hand. Thus, to become a truly world class player, you must reach the point where you do not feel an emotional response to what happens at the table.

Clearly, this is easier said than done; so how do you learn to not react emotionally to the cards that are dealt and the short-term results that accompany them?

The most basic answer (and one that most players, especially beginners, do not want to hear) is experience. The more you play, the more bad luck you weather, the more often you flop a huge hand, the less you will react emotionally to these events. Humans have an amazing ability to adapt to anything. If I torture you every day, at first you will cringe in fear when you see me; but eventually you will stop reacting emotionally as you will have gotten used to

32

this horrible daily event. Similarly, if I show up at your door tomorrow at noon with $1 million and give it to you, you will (presumably) experience extreme joy. And when I come back the next day at noon with another $1 million, you will again be overwhelmed. But if I keep showing up every day, eventually when I knock on the door, you will not react emotionally at all. And if it's 1:00pm, you'll probably just wonder why I'm an hour late.

Short of putting in the years to gain this experience, what can you do? If I had a great answer, I would share it with you. Unfortunately, this is a very personal thing, and what works well for one person will be useless to another. For me, what hastened the process is my knowledge of math. I know intellectually that if I get all-in with A-A vs. K-K, I'm supposed to win about 80% of the time. And that means I'm supposed to lose about 20% of the time. So, when I lose, I can just say to myself "This was one of those 20%." By really understanding and believing in the math, you will know that however unlucky (or lucky) something seems, it really wasn't that big of a deal in the long run. When an opponent plays badly and gets lucky to beat you, you need to realize that this is supposed to happen some percentage of the time.

If you always make good decisions, then overall you will be putting your chips into the pot as a favorite, and you will win in the long run. The only thing that matters when you play poker is the quality of your decisions, as they determine your EV. If your EV is positive, you will win in the long run, and there is no need for emotion. If your decisions are creating -EV, then there is reason to worry.

Emotions are funny things. Even though I know better, I still find myself experiencing feelings that are backwards, so to speak. There have been many times where I have been stuck a lot of money in a cash game, and then I hit a rush, and win back most (but not all) of my loss. For example, I'll be playing 400-800 mixed games, be stuck $40,000, and then hit a rush to finish as a $5,000 loser for the night. As I'm leaving to go to bed, I will feel really good about this loss, as it could have been so much worse. On other nights, I have been up $40,000, then hit a streak of losers, and finished ahead only $5,000. When this happens, I tend to feel very negative about the result, wishing I had quit the game earlier or some such while I was ahead a lot more*. Obviously, I

---

* Phil Laak has been credited for coining a great term for this phenomenon, "upstuck". When you are winning in a game, but not as much as you were before, you are ahead or "up" for the game, but feel as if you were behind or "stuck". Pure genius.

did not know, in either case, that I was about to hit a streak of lucky or unlucky hands, and as such there was no logical reason for me to have quit sooner, or played longer, than I did.

And looking back at those nights, why would I be going to bed happy after losing $5,000 in the first instance, yet going to bed unhappy about winning $5,000 in the latter? The only thing that should matter, for all of those sessions, is how well did I play? If I played my best, then I should be happy, win or lose. And if I played poorly and made a lot of bad decisions, then I should be unhappy with myself even if I still won.

How about in the short run? How do you minimize the impact of emotions? If you are feeling overly emotional, you should consider quitting until you are done with those feelings, and ready to go back to playing your non-emotional "A" game. Obviously, if you are in a tournament, you can't just quit, but if things are severe enough, it may make more sense for you to step away for a little while, even though you will be getting blinded off, so you can calm your emotions, and return to the game when ready. But, if you are playing a cash game, you definitely should take a break, for a few minutes, a few hours, or a few days, whatever it takes, to regain your equilibrium.

What about in the middle of a hand? It is common for us all to make some of our decisions for emotional reasons rather than fully logical ones. Sometimes we cannot let go of a big starting hand, even though it is clear we are beat, because as soon as we saw those first two cards we were already expecting to win. Then, in the heat of the moment, we fail to admit we are beat, and instead rationalize why we should continue in the hand. Sometimes, you are sitting there trying to decide what to do, and you even realize that you are wanting to not fold for emotional reasons.

Here is a trick for you to use when you are facing a tough decision in a hand, and there is some chance that emotions are getting the best of you. Say to yourself "What would FossilMan do?" Seriously. And if not me, substitute somebody else. But take a few seconds, close your eyes, and imagine that you were talking to me, explaining this hand in full detail up to the present moment, and asking my advice what to do. Then, imagine the advice I would give you, and simply *follow that advice*. Or, imagine that a friend has asked for your help, and has described this hand to you. What advice would you give your friend, what would you tell them to do? Now, just follow your own advice!

32

Another trick I like to use when I have lost a big pot is to pretend that I just doubled up. For example, let's say I am a big stack in the middle stages of a tournament, the average stack is T40K, and I have T120K. Then, I lose T60K in a single hand. Whether I played the hand well and got unlucky, or screwed the hand up and can only blame myself for the loss, this is a situation where many players go on tilt. What I do is sit back and look at my new situation. I have T60K, which is well above average. How would I feel right now if I had started the last hand with T30K and doubled up to T60K? I would feel awesome. Well, however I got here, I have T60K right now, and I should feel awesome about that fact. Even if I lost T100K in that hand, and am now well below average with only T20K, I would still feel good if instead I had just doubled up to T20K. So, I can choose to feel good about my situation even though that is not what happened.

How you feel is always up to you. So choose to feel positive, and commit to making the best possible decision every time. If you do this, you will win more than you lose, and have every reason to feel good.

Also be careful to avoid what I call "happy tilt". Happy tilt is a lot like tilt, only instead of making poor decisions because you are upset about losing, you make poor decisions because you are on a rush, have won a lot of chips recently, and are feeling invincible. It is not at all uncommon to see a player win several pots in a short period of time, become one of the big stacks, and then blow it all off as they just won't fold a hand anymore. They have started to feel like they are "destined" to win, or "just can't miss", and therefore do not fold even when it is obviously the correct decision.

One of the best things you can do to avoid emotional reactions is simply to prepare for them. Expect that you are going to take bad beats, and their emotional impact will be reduced. Expect that you will make mistakes, misread an opponent, bet the wrong amount, or the like. And then when it happens, it won't hurt as much. Expect yourself to do your best to avoid these mistakes, but know that some mistakes are going to happen. In this game, everybody makes them. But it is up to you how you respond when those mistakes happen.

AVOID THE BIG MISTAKES

Poker and golf have a lot in common. In golf, being a really good player is not so much about making great shots as it is about avoiding bad shots. If you are unable to play a big swinging hook from out of the woods through a tiny gap in the trees to get on the green, that's really not a problem; just avoid hitting into the woods in the first place. While it is those great shots that get the press, just like you often see hero-calls and huge laydowns on the televised poker shows, the true path to becoming a strong winning player is simply avoiding big mistakes in the first place.

Thus, whenever you are spending a lot of time in the tank, trying to figure out what to do on a close decision, it really isn't all that important. If a player moves all-in where you are getting 3:2 pot odds on the call, then you need to have at least 40% equity in the pot in order to correctly call. However, if you are sitting there thinking for 10 minutes trying to figure out if you have slightly more or slightly less than 40% equity against their range, you are mostly wasting your time. If you call and it turns out you really only had 38% equity against their range, you only made a very small mistake. Likewise, if you fold and later determine that you had 43% equity, that mistake was not a disaster. The real

33

mistake is when you call and only had 25%, or even only 10%, equity against their range; or you fold when you were actually the favorite to win.

If you make a large number of small mistakes, these will only add up to a relatively small loss, whereas a single huge mistake can cost you much more.

33

CONTINUING POKER EDUCATION

When I was an active lawyer and member of the state bar, we were required to do CLE, continuing legal education. Every year we had to log a minimum number of hours of certified training to prove we were keeping up-to-date in our area of legal practice. Clearly, there is no such requirement for poker players. But if you don't continue to train and educate yourself to be better, you are going to fall behind, and your results will suffer. There is an old saying that has been applied to many things, and it is fully applicable to poker: "If you're not getting better, you're getting worse." I fully believe that you must continuously strive to learn and improve your game, or instead of standing still, you will get worse without even really noticing. Fortunately, there are numerous ways to improve your poker game. While some may not fit you and your preferred style of learning, you absolutely should make use of all of the tools that work well for you.

Since you're reading this, one venue of training is clearly already known to you, books. There are literally thousands of poker books out there for you to read. Unfortunately, there is no agency or organization in charge of auditing these books to make sure they only contain accurate, winning information.

As such, there are many poker books containing advice that will hurt, rather than help, your game, or at least make it harder for you to improve to a truly strong, winning player. Fortunately, the percentage of books coming out with really bad information is a lot lower than it used to be; some of the older books contain truly wrong information. And not just wrong in the sense that our knowledge has improved dramatically since the poker boom, and nobody knew better back then. I mean, some of these books were considered horrible when written, and are even worse now.

My favorite learning tool is live seminars. I taught for the WSOP Academy, and have been doing seminars under my FossilMan Poker Training brand since 2011. Live seminars tend to be 1-2 full days, and are typically taught by well-known poker pros such as myself. My seminars are typically a few hours of lecture and a few hours of live hand labs. In the live hand labs, the students sit at the poker table and play as if they were in a real game (cash or tournament) while I serve as the dealer. When the student folds, instead of mucking their cards they place them on the rail, and at the end of the hand, they show the cards so I can critique their decisions. For example, if you were at my seminar, called a raise preflop, checked behind on the flop, and then folded to a turn bet, I would critique each of those decisions, discussing why I thought you got it right or wrong, as well as discussing the benefits of other options you might have chosen. In many cases, I like to discuss the "why" of the decisions the students made, as usually the reason why they made a decision is more important than the decision itself.

Online training sites have been one of the most effective tools for turning beginners and losing players into winning players. In most cases, these sites charge a monthly membership fee, and offer the student unlimited access to their library of training videos. The videos have been prepared by the instructors at each site, and are often directed at a specific issue, or focused on a specific game/limit of online poker. While these sites do focus on training for winning at online poker, some of them provide videos tailored to live games, and even if they don't, most lessons that teach you to perform better at online poker will apply fully to live games as well.

While it is typically the most expensive option, private lessons can also be one of the fastest and most effective means for improving your game quickly, as well as improving your game to a higher level than you might ever achieve

FOSSILMAN'S WINNING TOURNAMENT STRATEGIES

using only the other tools. Of course, the trick here is to find the right instructor, somebody who has the knowledge you are trying to acquire, and who is capable of teaching that information to you effectively. The obvious and apt analogy here is to private tutors for high school students. With the one-on-one attention, the student can often quickly master subjects that were confusing and difficult when taught in a classroom setting and/or self-taught from a book. Plus, the private instructor can make sure your focus is on the right issues, and can spot your leaks and mistakes more effectively than you might see them yourself, and thus improve your game in areas where you didn't even know you needed help.

Online poker forums abound in today's poker world, and they are also a great source of both general information (details about games and tournaments at various poker rooms), as well as educational tools. Since almost the beginning of my poker career in 1992, I have been an active participant in one or more poker forums. These sites offer many of the advantages of private lessons, in that you can focus down on very narrow, specific issues where you want to improve your game. However, they also suffer from the fact that anybody can post and participate, and thus there is lots of clutter and bad information. I can't imagine how many hours I spent debating what were, to me, extremely basic and obvious poker concepts with people who refused to believe what I was telling them, and who would ramble on with their counter-theories in the thread. And of course, some people are reading these threads, and they don't know who to believe, and they might choose to model their game on the bad information. As a result they end up hurting their game rather than helping it. Of course, just because I posted something doesn't mean it was right, but that's the challenge, to wade through all sides of the debate, and figure out for yourself how to improve your game.

In a similar fashion, one of the best things you can do is simply talk with your poker friends. Nurture relationships with other players whom you believe know the game well, and discuss hands and issues with them. This offers all the benefits of online forums, but now you can pick-and-choose from whom to take advice.

In addition to other tools you will want to use, here are some training exercises that will help. My favorite is simply referred to as "no calling allowed". In this exercise, you should enter a very cheap poker game, preferably a tournament. If you have access to them, then really low limit online cash games will also serve. Now, clearly there are many times in a poker game where the best decision is to call. However, most players call much too often, and even worse, they play way too many starting hands.

In this exercise, even if you know for sure that calling is the smartest choice, you are not allowed to call, EVER. Preflop, you can fold, or raise the blinds. If somebody else has already raised, you can fold, or reraise. The only exception here would be if you are the big blind, and nobody else raises, in which case you can raise, but checking is also permitted. Postflop, if you are facing a bet/raise, your only choices are to fold or raise/reraise. If it is checked to you, then you may also check. The only time you are allowed to call is if raising is not an option. For example, if an opponent goes all-in in a heads-up pot, you obviously can't raise, and it would be silly to fold if you likely have the best hand, so calling is allowed. Similarly, if somebody bets more chips than you have, calling is permitted. But let's say that a short stack goes all-in on the flop, you have them covered, and there are one or more players behind you who also have the short stack covered. In this case, since raising is an option, you must raise or fold, and cannot just call.

This exercise will teach two hugely important lessons. First, because you cannot just call and see the flop, you will find yourself folding a lot more often. Since almost all of us play too many hands, this extra folding is likely improving your starting hand selection. Second, most players are too passive, do too much calling, and should be more aggressive. This exercise forces you to the extremes, as you must either fold or be aggressive. You are probably going to be surprised how often the other player(s) all fold when you raise, in a spot where you normally would have just called. If you had known just how often you could take down the pot immediately, you probably would have been raising a lot more often in these spots.

Another great training exercise, especially if you need to improve your ability to read your opponents, is "playing blind". We already discussed this exercise in Chapter 30, Using Tells, so refer back to that chapter as needed. When using this training exercise, you can do it one of two ways. You can play it pure, and if your read is to fold, then you just fold, and never look at your cards. Or, if you think that folding is best, you can then allow yourself to actually look at your cards, and if you have the nuts (or a hand so strong it is effectively the

34

nuts, insomuch as you would never consider folding it), then you don't fold. However, if you do this, and see you have this very strong hand, then you must play the rest of the hand very straightforwardly. You should bet/raise at all opportunities, and preferably make larger than normal bets and raises. Essentially, since you have the nuts, you won't fold, but you are going to make it pretty obvious how strong you are. The point here is to win the hand, move on, and continue the training exercise so you can improve your game.

SATELLITE TOURNAMENTS

Satellites are tournaments that pay out prizes of seats (entry fees) into bigger tournaments, rather than paying out cash prizes. Sometimes the payout is in the form of a non-transferable ticket or prepaid entry into the larger tournament, sometimes the entry is transferable, and other times paid out in lammers*. The advice in this chapter also applies to Survivor tournaments, events that work just like satellites, but pay cash to the winners. It is useful to know in advance how the winners are paid, as you don't want to win a non-transferable seat into a later tournament that you are, for whatever reason, unable to play. Also, even if you intend to sell the seat or lammers that you win, sometimes these are easily sold for full face value, and other times they are harder to sell, and/or only sell at a discount.

One-table satellites are the most basic. A full table of players each pays an entry fee, and plays down to one winner who gets the seat. A common example are the one-table satellites that run every day during the WSOP in Las

---

* Lammers are chips that have a cash value of sorts, but can only be used to buy into other tournaments. While you cannot exchange lammers for cash with the casino, they are often easily sold to other players for cash.

Vegas, where typically 10 players will pay a bit more than 1/10th of the cost of the prize, with the winner paid in lammers. Thus, if you are trying to win your way into the Main Event, 10 of you will pay $1,030, and the winner is awarded $10,000 in lammers (20 lammers, each worth $500), plus $120 in cash. Because these are winner-take-all, the correct strategy is very different than for a regular tournament, and more closely approximates that of a cash game. ICM does not apply in your decision-making for this format, and you can use your typical cash game math instead.

It is rather common for deals to be made in one-table satellites as you get near the end. By this time there will only be 2-4 players remaining, and the blinds will typically be very large compared to the stack sizes. It is not uncommon, if played to a conclusion, for the average stack to be only 5-15 blinds at the end. As such, there is a lot of variance at this point, and players are often interested in making a deal*. Because deal-making is so common, some players will try to survive until this late stage so they can make a deal and win at least a little bit.

However, if you get to this late stage with almost no chips, it is unlikely that you are going to get a deal for any significant amount of money. The more chips you have, the more you are going to get in a deal. Therefore, it is not a winning play to fold in a +EV situation just to survive to this later stage. In a regular tournament, once you get deep enough, you can ladder up the pay scale by mere survival, even with a very short stack. But in this format, it is not just how long you last, but how many chips you have, if and when a deal is struck.

There are also one-table satellites that pay multiple winners. Often these take the form of each player putting up a bit more than one-fifth of the cost of a seat (10 players to start in this example), and the final two players both win an equal prize of one seat. In this format, you are now playing something that is much more like a regular multi-table tournament or multi-table satellite, and mere survival does count, as long as you can survive to the final two spots. Therefore, just like in a regular MTT, ICM does apply to your decisions, and you must balance the need to accumulate chips with the need to survive, in order to maximize your equity.

Much more common are multi-table satellites, also sometimes called mega-satellites or super-satellites. These satellites play in the fashion of a normal MTT, but when you reach the money, the satellite is over, and everybody re-

---

* See Chapter 26.

maining wins an equal prize of one seat. The entry fee for multi-table satellites can be anywhere from 1/3rd the cost of a seat to as little as 1/100th the cost[*]. Typically you will see these at a price of about 1/5th to 1/10th of the cost, that is, where 1 in 5, or 1 in 10, of the entrants will win a seat. If 100 people enter such an event where 1 in 10 wins a seat, then the game will play until there are only 10 remaining contestants, and each of them wins the same prize regardless of how many chips they have at the end. This feature has a HUGE impact on correct strategy in these events.

Imagine a scenario where I am on the bubble of the Main Event, and have double the average stack. Because we are so close to the money, it would be a pretty big ICM mistake for me to get all my chips into the pot unless I was a significant favorite to win. But, if somebody who has me covered raises enough to put me all-in preflop, and I look down to find I've been dealt A-A, it is clearly correct for me to call and risk being eliminated on the bubble. Even though the times I am eliminated I will miss out on a payday of $15-20,000 that I could have won by just folding, I will on average make a lot more money by taking this risk, knowing that most of the time I will double my stack and greatly increase my chances of going very deep in the event, possibly winning millions of dollars.

Facing the same situation on the bubble of a multi-table satellite, it would be crazy for me to make this call. If I just fold this hand, and every hand after, it is probably 99% certain that somebody else will be eliminated before I get blinded down to a short stack. If I call and my A-A is a 95% favorite, then 95% of the time I win and increase my chances of getting a seat from 99% to 99.9%; whereas 5% of the time I lose, and am eliminated, getting nothing. Even if my A-A is this big of a favorite to win this pot, I have no real upside potential, as I can fold and still be virtually guaranteed to win a seat.

ICM truly rules the day in this format. It is often correct for you to fold no matter how strong your cards, and other times it is correct for you to raise, even all-in, no matter how weak your cards. For example, if it folds to you in the small blind, and you're a short stack on the bubble, and the big blind is a smart player who has plenty of chips, you should raise all-in with any two cards. As a smart player, the big blind will understand that they have nothing to gain by calling, and will fold everything, even A-A. And since you need to

---

[*] Or anything really, you could offer a satellite where 100 people pay 80% of a seat plus rake, and then 80 of the 100 win a seat, but who would want that?

win some chips or face being blinded out and bubbling, this is a perfect spot to get them. Of course, if the big stack is clueless, don't make this move unless you have a strong enough starting hand, as they might call despite it being an obvious mistake.

I have heard many otherwise smart players who cite some truly silly "rules" or guidelines when it comes to playing satellites. At a venue where the satellites typically cost about 1/10th of the full price, I have heard players spout things like "never play more than three satellites to try to win your seat into this, as by the time you are playing four or more, you might as well have just paid full price and bought in directly." This advice is just silly. When you enter a satellite, you are presumably doing so because you believe that this is the most profitable way to spend your time playing poker. If I enter a $550 mega-satellite at the WSOP, it is because I believe that my hourly win rate will be higher than if I enter a one-table satellite, or play a cash game, or whatever other options are available. And if I lose all my chips during the reentry period, and believe this is still my best option, I will reenter. And so on.

At least for me, I am playing satellites to make money. If I play eight satellites and fail to make money in any of them, then when the regular tournament starts, I will still enter it, if my bankroll permits. And the truth is, if you do not have an adequate bankroll to play a tournament, then you don't really have an adequate bankroll to play a satellite for that tournament (unless you can sell the seat/lammers that you win, and are planning on doing so).

Each game is an independent event, and should not be thought of as part of a series. The fact that you've already failed to cash in several satellites should not impact your decision to play another*. On the flip side, the fact that you've done well and won a lot of satellites does not mean you should now stop. Even though you've won your seat and/or lammers, if you're going to keep playing more poker, you still should just evaluate which of your options is the best place to spend your time and put your bankroll to work. If the satellites are still your best option, enter again, and hopefully win even more.

35

---

* Unless of course there are psychological factors at work, or your failure in previous satellites has led you to change your view of yourself and your profitability in them. If prior losses have put you in the wrong frame of mind, then you should avoid entering again until you have gotten past the negative attitude. Similarly, if you start to realize you have been playing poorly, then maybe you should skip these events until you can determine what you're doing wrong and fix it.

REENTRY AND REBUY TOURNAMENTS

Rebuy tournaments are becoming rather scarce nowadays, but reentry tournaments are becoming more and more common. So, what is the difference? In a typical rebuy tournament, you enter for a fixed price plus rake, and get a specific number of chips. Then, whenever you qualify for a rebuy, you may choose to purchase it, and get more chips. However, often the cost of a rebuy will not include any rake for the house, and the price may not be identical to the original entry price. Also, you may get a different amount of chips for your rebuy.

When I first moved to Connecticut in 1998, Foxwoods ran a Tuesday night NLH tournament that cost $25 (+$10 rake) for the original buyin, and you received T200. Then, anytime you had T200 or less in chips, you could purchase a rebuy, paying $20, and get another T200. This meant that you could take a rebuy before the first hand was dealt, as you then had exactly T200, and if you busted during the rebuy period, you could pay $20 for T200, or $40 for T400.

Typically, you either pay the rebuy price directly to the dealer at your table, who has chips in the rack to sell to you, or you call out for a rebuy, and the poker room has an employee(s) walking around selling rebuys. A key feature of this format is that you stay in your current seat, do not miss a hand, and are

36

still considered an active player in the game.

Many rebuy tournaments also offer an add-on, which is simply one more chance to buy extra chips. The add-on is usually only available at one exact time, and that is almost always at the end of the rebuy period. It is not uncommon for the add-on to offer chips at a much lower price per chip than the original entry or the rebuys.

In contrast, in the now much more common reentry format, when you get busted, you leave the table, go back to the cashier or wherever you originally bought in, and reenter the event at full price. As such, you pay rake again, and are treated the same as any other new player to the event. If there is a line and people are waiting to get in as alternates, you will (most likely) be at the end of that line, and will be treated the same as a player who just arrived and wants to enter for the first time.

The rebuy format offers several advantages to the player. First, you know what your table is like, and do not have to join a new table where you will have to learn the playing styles of a new set of opponents. Maybe more importantly, if you have drawn a tough starting table, you can simply choose to quit rather than rebuy, and thus avoid further play at a tough table. Most importantly of all, you do not pay extra rake*. There are many reentry tournaments out there where a typical pro will average 2-3 entries per event, and if they could participate while only paying rake once, this would add up to a LOT of money saved by the end of the year.

Most rebuy tournaments let you rebuy any time you have chips equal to or less than a starting stack, so you can rebuy any time you qualify, and never have to play a short stack during the rebuy period. In contrast, in most reentry events you cannot reenter unless you lose all your chips, meaning that if you have a short stack you must take the time to rebuild your stack, or risk it all at once.

One advantage of the reentry format is you will (most likely) end up at a different table when you reenter, meaning that if you started at a tough table, you can choose to play a higher variance game, knowing that it will either work

---

* This is not always the case. At the WSOP, they do not charge an amount of rake that is in addition to the buyin for their events, but instead take a percentage of the buyin as the rake and dealer tip. When the WSOP used to offer rebuy events, they took this same percentage out of both the original buyins as well as the rebuys.

out and you'll win a lot of chips, or it won't work out, you'll get busted, reenter, and hopefully draw a softer table.

There are a lot of misconceptions about both of these formats. In both cases, many players argue that these tournaments unfairly favor the players with deep pockets who can afford to rebuy/reenter as many times as they choose. The same people often complain that these deep-pocket players ruin the integrity of the game, because they play wild and crazy during the rebuy/ reentry period. The thinking is since these players can afford to rebuy/reenter, they play with a high variance style, hoping to get lucky and build a big stack, and can try again if they don't get lucky. There is also the argument that the players with the deep pockets tend to be primarily the most successful pros, and that therefore this format makes the average field tougher, as it is more likely to be these pros who rebuy/reenter, rather than the weaker amateur players. All of this is wrong, in my opinion.

As we discussed in Chapter 13, you should have an adequate bankroll before you enter a poker game, be it cash or tournament. If you have an adequate bankroll to enter the first time, then you also have an adequate bankroll to rebuy/reenter. Therefore, the only time you should ever be playing in an event like this if you don't have an adequate bankroll is if you are taking a shot. And any time you take a shot, you must realize there is a strong chance it will not work out well (that's part of why they call it taking a shot, rather than making a smart investment).

It is true that some players will choose to play wild and crazy during the rebuy/reentry period, but how is that a bad thing? Personally, I want my opponents to play worse than their best, preferably as poorly as possible. Especially if the player is a highly skilled pro, I would much rather they play wild and crazy as opposed to playing their "A" game. By definition, if their game is different during the rebuy/reentry period, it must be better or worse than their normal game. If it's better, you can be disappointed, but it's pretty harsh to be upset with somebody for playing better. If instead it's worse, then you should be happy that this person is playing less than their best game against you. Yes, your variance will go up, but so will your average profit, and overall that's a good thing.

The only complaint with any merit is that, on average, those who are most likely to rebuy/reenter are amongst the more highly skilled players. This may be true, but I doubt the impact is really that significant. If we could determine the average skill of the field for a given event that had no rebuys or reentries available, and compare that to the same event where they are available, I doubt the average skill level will increase by more than a little bit. And if many of those same pros are motivated to play wild and crazy during the rebuy/reentry period, it probably all evens out anyway.

It used to be that only the main event of a tournament series might have multiple starting days or starting flights, but now it is becoming more common to see multiple starting flights in many events. In almost all cases, these tournaments allow you to reenter. In some of them, such as the WSOP Main Event, you can choose which starting flight to enter, but you can only enter one time; if you are eliminated in the first flight, you cannot reenter that flight, or a later flight. In many tournaments, you can enter once per flight but not reenter the same flight, while still others allow you to reenter the same flight, but limit how many times per flight you may reenter. However, most reentry tournaments permit you to reenter anytime you run out of chips during the registration period of a flight, and reenter as many flights as you wish.

It is most commonly the rule that you cannot reenter a later flight if you made it through an earlier flight, and have bagged chips for day 2. In most cases, you may choose to surrender your stack and thus gain the ability to reenter. You are also often permitted to surrender your stack at the end of the registration period (which is typically well before the end of play for that flight), and thus be eligible to reenter that flight. In both cases, this means taking chips, chips that have equity, and giving them up. Essentially, you are taking the potential cash value of a stack and tossing it in the garbage. Should you ever do that?

The short answer is NO, but there might be some exceptions. And these exceptions will exist only when your stack is VERY small, and you are still quite far from reaching the money. If your small stack is still anywhere near 10xBB or more, or more than 20% of the starting stack, then do NOT surrender. Even if your stack is well below both of these parameters, think carefully before surrendering. Are you really gaining EV with this decision to surrender? Doing so means paying another entry fee, plus rake, and giving up chips that have real value. If you give up 10% of a starting stack, this means you are paying 10% more when you reenter, which is probably a mistake.

It is becoming more popular in tournaments with multiple day 1 flights to allow you to reenter a later flight even after bagging chips in an earlier flight, without making you first surrender those chips. Then, if you bag again, you keep whichever stack is larger and play that stack on day 2, but must surrender the smaller stack(s), and thus lose those chips. So, when should you reenter after bagging chips in an earlier flight? Again, it is going to be a -EV decision to reenter unless the stack you bagged is very small. It may not need to be as small as mentioned above when you had to first surrender your existing stack, but it should still be very small.

Again, if you have much more than about 10xBB, it is probably a mistake to reenter. While having a stack this short means you are likely to be all-in the first hand you choose to play, it is still a playable stack. If you manage to get that first double-up, you now have a stack large enough to play a hand or two, lose, and still be in action. Regardless of how many blinds are in the stack you bagged, if it is anywhere near as many chips as the starting stack, it is almost certainly a mistake to reenter. If you do make day 2 again, and now have a larger stack than the first one you bagged, you have to surrender the first one. If the chips you are now surrendering are half of a starting stack, you essentially paid 1.5x the buyin for the stack you are taking on to day 2. And no matter how soft the field, you are unlikely to be 50% better than average, and so you probably made a mistake to reenter.

So, now that you've entered a rebuy or reentry event, what strategy adjustments should you be making? On a theoretical level, you should mostly play exactly the same game as if there were no rebuys or reentries available. Realistically, from the viewpoint of your bankroll, is there any difference between buying more chips now if you bust, compared to spending the same money on a different event tomorrow? If I reenter now in an HPT main event, there really is no difference between this reentry and entering the next HPT main event a week or two later. Unless one field is softer, there is no reason I'm better off spending my bankroll on one versus the other. As such, there is no reason to play differently, or be willing to take on more risk, just because you are in an event with rebuys or reentries.

Having said all of that, you will make some serious adjustments in the real world. Not because you should in any theoretical sense, but because your opponents will often be playing differently when rebuys/reentries are available.

Some of them will be playing wild and crazy to build a stack, or go broke trying (to then reenter). Because of this, you might correctly judge that a player has a wider range of hands with which they will risk all of their chips, and therefore you will want to adjust your decisions accordingly.

There is one time when I will make some adjustments in my own play, not just because of what my opponents are doing, but because we are nearing the end of the time when I can rebuy or reenter. If my stack is very low, I might make these wild and crazy plays myself, especially in a reentry event. I just said above not to do that, and now I'm saying I will do that myself. Why the contradiction? Quite simply, the answer is I do it to make money, but can only correctly do it if I am much more highly skilled than average in this event.

Let's say I'm in an HPT main event, where it costs $1,500+150 for a T30K starting stack. I believe that because of my skill advantage, I will win twice as much as the average player. This means that while T30K are worth $1,500 in front of the average player, they are worth $3,000 in front of me. But what if it is near the end of the reentry period, and I only have T5K? For an average player, that stack is worth $250, but it is worth $500 for me. Now, I go all-in and lose. I just lost $500, but when I reenter, I'll pay another $1,650, and receive chips worth $3,000, or an expected profit of $1,350. This means that by losing the pot, I actually gain $850 in equity.

Plus, it's not like I'm trying to lose. For example, a player has raised, and I reraise all-in, despite believing it is a -EV play. But, if they fold, I now have T6K or T7K; if they call, some of the time I win and have over T10K, and when I lose, I reenter and gain $850 in equity. Even though this shove is a losing play in the general sense, because of my skill edge, it is better to take a risk like this than to "correctly" fold. However, if there were still plenty of time left in the reentry period, I would wait until later to do this, hoping that I could rebuild my stack without making losing plays. If my stack is much bigger than this, I don't make these plays even on the last hand of the reentry period, because now I'm not gaining enough equity from the reentry to make up for the -EV of the losing play.

In events with rebuys and add-ons, pay very close attention to the cost and number of chips you get for each. Some of these events offer a huge premium for the add-on chips, and therefore you should make some serious strategy adjustments. I have seen an online satellite with rebuys and add-ons

36

where each buyin and rebuy got you one stack of chips, and then the add-on cost twice as much but you received 10 stacks of chips. Since these add-on chips were bought at 1/5th the cost, it was a bad idea to ever rebuy unless you were busted, and then you should only take a single rebuy, not the double rebuy you were permitted. Making this event even more unique, it was a turbo, and by the time the rebuy period ended, the blinds were such that one stack of chips was only 2 big blinds.

Let's look at some numbers so you can see why I advise you to not rebuy any more than necessary if the add-on comes at a steep discount. A typical event might have 100 players enter, and make a total of 300 rebuys. But, because the blinds were so big, a lot of players would give up and not rebuy before the period ended, so there might be only 50 players left to take the add-on. And some of these players foolishly don't take the add-on. Apparently they feel that since they already have 30+ stacks from running good during the rebuy period they shouldn't spend money to just buy 10 more stacks. So, we might have 100 stacks from buyins, 300 stacks from rebuys, and 500 stacks from the add-ons, or 900 stacks in play. Players paid 400 for the buyins and rebuys, plus 100 for the add-ons, for a total of 500 buyins. This means that the average stack of chips cost 5/9th of a buyin, or about .55. Since every re-buy you take gets you one stack for one buyin, and since those stacks are only going to be worth, on average, about .55 buyins, you are losing money when you rebuy. However, you still should rebuy if you bust, because doing so let's you stay in the game long enough to purchase the add-on, where you will pay two buyins to buy 10 stacks, with a value of about 5.5 buyins. My main strategy in this event was to play super-tight during the rebuy period, minimize my rebuys, and spend the least amount possible to reach the point where I could purchase the lucrative add-on.

For all of these events, once the rebuy/reentry period is over, they play out the same as any other MTT. From that point on you can forget this chapter, and go back to your regular strategy.

SOME UNCOMMON TOURNAMENT FORMATS

Most tournaments are in the traditional format with multiple tables and about 10% of the field being paid, with the most money paid to the winner, less money for 2nd place, and so on. After this, the most commonly seen tournaments are satellite tournaments, as discussed in Chapter 35. However, there are numerous other formats that you will sometimes find, and many offer exceptional value. One of the major sources of this value is the fact that these formats are uncommon, and many of your opponents will not know how to properly adjust to the differences.

Bounty tournaments are growing in popularity. In a bounty event, instead of paying an entry fee (plus rake) where the entire entry fee goes into the prize pool, in these events part of the entry fee becomes a bounty on each player. Then, if you eliminate a player from the tournament, you win their bounty. For example, maybe an event is $235 to enter, with $35 going to rake. In addition, $50 of the $200 is not put into the prize pool. Instead, if you knock a player out, you win $50 immediately, regardless of where you finish in the tournament. You could potentially knock out a dozen short stacks, win $600, and then get eliminated yourself before reaching the money. Obviously this format

37

places a premium on eliminations, but many players enter these events and make little or no adjustments to their normal strategy. And some players make huge over-adjustments, taking on huge risks trying to knock somebody out.

So what is the smart way to approach bounty tournaments? Let me start by discussing a situation that exists for me regularly. I play in many smaller tournaments all over the country where I am a marketing attraction for the casino, and they advertise that you can play with me in the tournament. In these events, it is commonplace for there to be a bounty on my head only, and often the bounty is much larger than the buyin to the tournament. In a tournament where the entry fee is $50 + rake, there might be a $300 bounty for knocking me out. It is from playing in such events that I developed my method to calculate the value of bounties.

For these events, if I go all-in early in the tournament, even for 100xBB or more, my opponents are getting a huge overlay to call my shove, even with very weak hands. In essence, they are risking their stack of chips worth about $50 to win my $50 stack, plus $300 in cash. This gives them pot odds of about 7:1, meaning that they can correctly call with any two cards if they have to beat only me to win the pot (and the bounty). As such, when I play in these events, I make it very clear to everybody at my table that if I am dealt a premium starting hand, I am not going to play it as I normally would, but am just going to shove all-in. Because I've told them, they know I have a strong hand, but since they can call and get 7:1 pot odds, they should still be happy to call. If they call with any two cards, and I have a top 5% hand, then they are only about a 3:1 underdog to win. For every 3 times they lose one stack of chips, one time they will win seven stacks worth of chips and cash, which makes this a very profitable call.

In a typical bounty tournament where each player has a bounty on their head, the price of the bounty is not usually an amount larger than the value of their starting stack. But the analysis is the same and the simplest way to come close to optimizing your strategy adjustments is to convert the cash bounty into theoretical tournament chips when making your decisions. Let's look at an example. I enter a tournament that costs $500 + rake, with a $100 bounty on each player, and we start with T20,000. With regard to the prize pool, we paid $400 for T20,000, which means that $1 = T50*. If I eliminate a player, I

---

* At least until late in the tournament, before ICM math comes into play.

win $100. Doing the math, $100 = T5,000. So, if you go all-in, and I have you covered, instead of making my decisions based upon how many chips you have bet, plus how many chips are in the pot, I should pretend there is an additional T5,000 in the pot, and make my decision accordingly.

Going into more detail in this example, let's say you start the hand with T7,500. During the hand, you and I have each put T2,500 in the pot, and now you go all-in for your last T5,000. Normally I would look at the situation, realize it will cost me T5,000 to win T10,000, and call if I think I am going to win at least 33% of the time. But, since you are all-in and I have more chips than you, if I call and win here, I will get T10,000 in chips, plus cash equal in value to T5,000 chips. This means it is more like I am calling T5,000 to win T15,000, and only need to win 25% of the time to correctly call.

All of this means you should play differently in a bounty tournament. Sometimes you will pay $200 and $25 of it will be a bounty, while other times you might pay $150 and $50 of it will be the bounty. In the latter you will play much looser against an all-in whose bounty you can win. To some extent, you should also take the bounty into consideration even before anybody goes all-in. There are many close decisions in poker, and the bounty will often tip the balance and make one decision much more correct than the other. You will be much more likely to play speculative hands against somebody whom you have covered, as you can now win not just their chips, but also their bounty. On the other hand, you should be much less inclined to take a line that might often lead to you bluffing all-in, if the opponent has you covered, as it is probably going to be harder to get them to fold to your all-in bet.

Another tournament format preferred by many top players is a short-handed structure. Usually these events are 6-max, meaning instead of a full table consisting of 9 or 10 players, the table is full when 6-handed. Even more rarely you might find events that are played 8-max or 4-max. Obviously, as the game becomes short-handed, you must loosen your starting hand requirements. While it is correct to play only 10-20% of your starting hands at a table of 10, you should not generally play this tight at a 6-handed table. If you do, you will be folding so much that the pots you win will not make up for the all of the blinds you are paying.

Yet while it is true that you must loosen up, I find that most player significantly overadjust in short-handed tournaments. There are some very good players, whose game I know quite well, who will raise UTG in a 6-max game with a hand they would usually open-fold, even on the button, in a 10-handed game. The mindset seems to be "We are short-handed, the blinds are coming around fast, so I can't just wait for a good hand. I have to play anything that seems even slightly reasonable, or I'll get blinded out." But they are simply overreacting to the situation. Imagine you are at a 10-handed table, four players fold, and now it's on you. This is essentially the same situation as being UTG in a 6-max game. While this shortcut of reasoning is not 100% accurate in determining the correct starting hand adjustments, it is going to get you almost all of the way there. What becomes more important after making this adjustment is determining what your opponents are doing in this 6-max format, and how to best take advantage of their mistakes.

Since many of your opponents are overadjusting and playing too many hands, how do you counter this mistake? One of the main things you should do is defend your blinds more often, and more aggressively. If your opponent is coming in for a raise with weak A-high and K-high hands, you will want to be both more aggressive and stickier when you have a good A-high or K-high hand.

You will also have to significantly amend your judgment when estimating how likely it is that your opponent hit a flop. If a solid player raises UTG at a 10-handed table, and the highest card on the flop is an 8, you can usually assume that the flop did not improve their hand. Most of the time they either have an overpair, or two overcards, to any such flop. However, in the 6-max game, your opponent is quite a bit more likely to have a card that paired such a flop, and simultaneously that much less likely to have an overpair. In the 10-handed game, this opponent has a range that mostly consists of hands that will often be easy to bluff (overcards), and hands that will be very hard to bluff (overpairs); whereas in the 6-max game the same player will have a range that includes a lot more hands in the middle, i.e., they just made one small-to-medium pair using a card on the board.

Why is it that so many top players prefer short-handed games? The reason lies in the very reason they are top players. What makes one player better than another is their ability to make better decisions. And since you should play more hands when short-handed, you will be in action more often (rather than folding preflop and watching others play). Since you play more hands, you

37

make more decisions, and your edge increases against weaker opponents. Of course, this is only true if you correctly adjust while your opponents do not.

Turbo tournaments are another enjoyable variation, and are really no different than regular tournaments, except that they are structured to finish much quicker. If a regular tournament at your local poker room has 30 minute levels, then a turbo tournament might be the same structure in terms of blind sizes and starting chips, but each level will only last 10-20 minutes. The main impact of this turbo structure is that you spend relatively little time playing deep-stacked, and much of the tournament is spent with everyone short-stacked. In fact, it is common for a turbo tournament to get down to the point where the only correct play is to shove-or-fold preflop (that is, the average stack is only about 10xBB or less) even with as much as half the field remaining. Therefore, the player who is skilled at short-stack play will have a nice advantage in a turbo tournament.

Similar to short-handed tournaments, in my experience many players tend to overadjust in a turbo event, and play much looser than they should. Similar to a short-handed game, many players seem to take the attitude that "this is a turbo, blinds are going up fast, I don't have time to wait for a good hand; I have to win soon or get blinded out*." But the truth is each hand should theoretically be played the same regardless of how soon the blinds are going up, with only a few exceptions.

When you are playing any given hand, the dominant factors guiding your decision include the size of the blinds and antes, how many chips are in your stack, how many chips are in each opponent's stack, and how close you are to the money (or if already in the money, what are the payouts). The fact that the blinds are going to go up in five minutes rather than 50 minutes is of very little or no importance, the vast majority of the time.

If you look down at a mediocre hand UTG, one that is -EV to play in this spot, it does not become correct to play it just because each level is 15 minutes instead of 30. If you are going to lose EV, on average, by playing the hand,

---

* I was playing a turbo event at the WSOP-C at Harrah's Cherokee one time, and shoved UTG for 9xBB with A-J. A guy I know called from the cutoff seat with Q-3s, and busted me. I later asked him why he called, mostly wondering if he thought he had spotted a tell or something. He said "Well, I hadn't played in hand in like 2 orbits, and this is a turbo, so I couldn't just wait around forever. I had to play something." This is a common (and mistaken) mindset in turbo tournaments.

then you fold, regardless of the structure. As such, there really are no significant adjustments you should make to your strategy because you are in a turbo tournament. You still play each hand for itself, in whatever fashion you believe will maximize your equity in the tournament, given the blinds and stack sizes right now, ignoring how soon they will increase.

The only exceptions basically boil down to scenarios where the blinds are going to increase before your next turn in the blinds, and you are short-stacked enough that you are going to fold or shove each hand you play. It might be better to shove now with a mediocre hand where you still have 6xBB, rather than wait for a better hand but now the blinds have gone up and you can only be shove for 4xBB (and are much more likely to get called). This same situation can occur in a regular tournament, so this is not something unique to turbo events. It is simply going to come up more frequently in a turbo event.

Why would you want to play a turbo tournament? First, they are fun. Players don't seem to take them as seriously, so the atmosphere is usually a lot more loose and carefree, which is more pleasant. And, if players are less serious, they might not be playing their very best, which gives you an edge. Second, if you are better at short-stacked play than your opponents, this gives you a big edge as well. Finally, if you can avoid the trap described above, of thinking you have to play a lot looser in a turbo, you will gain another big edge. Overall, many very good players prefer turbo tournaments because their edge can be as large or almost as large as a slow-structured event, but the tournament finishes in much less time. If you win almost as much on average, in less time, your win rate per hour will increase, which is a very good thing.

Shootout tournaments are another fun but uncommon format, but are very much worth your time. In a shootout, you do not merge tables. In a regular event, as players are eliminated, the tournament staff will "break" tables, and send the players from that table to the empty seats at other tables. In a shootout, they never break a table. Instead, you stay at your same starting table until only one player remains with all the chips. Then, when all of the tables have finished, the winners are placed together at new tables, and the process continues. If 100 players started, then 10 tables of 10 will play down to 10 winners, and then those 10 winners will play the final table. If 1,000 players started, 100 winners from the first round will play at 10 tables of 10, and the 10 winners from round 2 will play the final table. Typically, you only make money if you win your first table. Then, you only win more money if you go on to win your second table, and so on, until the final table, at which point there are usually increasing payouts as each player is eliminated.

In a standard tournament, there is always some value in surviving a hand to play another. Chapter 3 taught us how ICM math demonstrates this fact. But correct strategy in a shootout is very much like the correct strategy for a one-table, winner-take-all satellite. Unless you win your first table, and you must win all the chips to do so, you get no money at all. Therefore, there is no need for ICM math, as the value of chips is always linear. If an opponent bets enough to put you all-in, and you think that it would be a correct call in a cash game, then it is pretty much always going to be a correct call in a shootout. One of the biggest edges you can find in this format is to play against opponents who do not understand this, and who avoid big risks as if this were a standard tournament format.

Another very fun format that I have only seen online and at the WSOP is the ante-up or ante-only tournament. In this event, you either never have blinds at all, or the blinds are always as small as possible, while it is the antes that increase each level. Online, the most common format is called ante-up, with blinds of T5 and T5 throughout the tournament, with antes starting at T5 in level 1, and going up until the conclusion of the event. Thus, at the final table you might have 5- or even 6-figure antes, yet blinds are still T5 and T5. In the ante-only format, there are never blinds, and the antes start relatively small and increase throughout. In the ante-up events, you can limp in for just T5, even when the antes are huge. In the ante-only format, the player to the immediate left of the button is first to act preflop, and can fold, raise, or call for one of whatever is the smallest chip in play. The strategy adjustments for these events are quite dramatic.

In the ante-up format, after the first level or two, the blinds are ridiculously small compared to the antes. As such, you can call the big blind with any two cards, as you are getting a huge price to see the flop if nobody raises. Even if somebody is raising almost every hand (and that is usually going to be the case), if you call the T5 blind and have to fold most of the time, that is not significant when the antes have become T25, T200, T1,000, or more. By limping in every hand (that you don't raise), you will be able to frequently limp-reraise with your really strong hands in early position.

If you have A-A, or some other premium hand, in early position, you certainly are going to play the hand, and you obviously want to win. However, it would be advantageous if you could win more than just the antes. If the blinds are T5, and the antes T100, your normal opening raise might be anything from T300-T1,000, depending upon your style of play and how your table has been playing. Whatever amount you are using as your standard opening raise, if you win the antes for T900, you were hoping for more. Instead, if you always call in early position, even with junk hands, but also just call when dealt a premium hand, now maybe somebody else raises, possibly they get a caller or two, or even a reraise, and now you can put in your own reraise, and either take down the pot now (which will be much more than just the antes), or play a very big pot with what is usually going to be the best hand.

You do not even need to be in early position to make this play. Any time you can limp in, and are likely to get raised, that is how you would like to play your premium starting hands. However, if you are often folding as your first decision preflop, then your opponents will learn you never have a junk hand when you do call, only cards that have some value as a starting hand. This should make them less likely to raise, as they know you are not as likely to fold. But when you never fold when you can limp in for the minimum, then your limps are more likely to be raised, which sets up this play.

In the ante-only format, there are no blinds, and to limp in you must call the smallest chip in play. This means that the size of the antes is never massively larger than the minimum to call. In the ante-up format, you might be at the final table limping in for T5, when the antes are T20,000. Even earlier when the antes were T100, you were getting something like 200:1 pot odds to limp in and see a flop. In the ante-only format, if the antes are T100, then T100 will typically be the smallest chip in play, the T25 chips having been removed. This means it costs you a full ante to just call preflop, and that is pricey enough that you will be better off open-folding your worst hands. The more often that somebody raises preflop, that is, the less often you will be able to see the flop for the minimum, the more hands you should be folding preflop, even before anybody has raised. However, as the size of the antes goes up compared to the minimum to call, you should fold fewer and fewer hands. Overall, you will find that you are getting involved preflop much more often in these events than in a traditional tournament format.

And of course, there are many other strategy changes that should be made for these formats. This is just the tip of the iceberg, and as these formats become more and more popular, there will eventually be the need for books devoted to just the new format. When that happens, we can more fully explore the proper strategy adjustments for each of these unique formats.

HEADS-UP TOURNAMENTS

Although heads-up tournaments are also relatively uncommon, and not likely to become much more common in the future, I still felt that this format deserved a chapter of its own. Plus, more so than any other format, heads-up poker just has a cachet all its own, and seems to attract the best players. As such, from a purely EV point of view, heads-up tournaments might be best avoided, as the fields will often be much tougher than regular format tournaments. But, these events are certainly the most fun, as this is the only format where you truly are involved every single hand, and never sit out and have to wait for others to finish a hand before you get another chance to play.

Also, if you're ever going to win a tournament, you are going to have to win heads-up. So knowing how to play well once heads-up is critical, and is something that most players just don't know how to do. In fact, over the years, I have done numerous livestream commentaries for tournaments, and so far I have only seen one or two players who were not basically incompetent at heads-up play. Therefore, if you become a strong heads-up player, you will enjoy a large advantage once you get to that stage of a regular tournament. While there is certainly some luck involved, it is not just due to luck that I've

38

never lost when heads-up at the end of a regular NLH tournament.*

Unlike most tournaments, heads-up poker has absolutely zero use for the concept of ICM, nor any of the strategy changes that ICM math dictates. Survival has zero value in this format, as you must beat your single opponent in order to advance and make money. There is no other way to win.

However, that does not necessarily mean that you will take a pure cash-game approach either. In a heads-up cash game, your equity calculations are about making the most money you can, and doing so in less time. Since you can reload if you lose all your chips in a cash game, you would never fold in a spot where doing so would cost you equity. No matter how risky the play, it would always be correct to pursue it if it was a higher equity decision than folding. If you ever were in a spot where it was correct to fold to reduce variance, then you are playing in too large of a game for your bankroll, and should just quit that game anyway. But in a tournament, your goal is to play in the manner that gives you the greatest chance of winning the match, regardless of time. Thus, there could be situations where you would fold in order to reduce variance, if this decision will increase your overall chance of beating this opponent.

Here is an example of sorts. While this was not a heads-up tournament, it was a regular tournament where we were down to just the two of us, effectively the same thing as a single round of a heads-up tournament. On this occasion, my opponent had the most glaring tell I've ever witnessed in all my decades of playing poker. He was seated directly across from the dealer, and as the dealer would spread the flop, he would stare at the cards as they were revealed. Then, if he liked the flop, you could just barely see a slight nodding of his head up-and-down. Contrarily, if he didn't like the flop, you could again barely see his head moving, this time in a tiny side-to-side motion, as if shaking his head "no". These movements were extremely tiny, but easily seen if you were looking for them.

At first I thought he can't be doing this accidentally, and he must be trying

---

* Through the end of 2017, my Hendon Mob record (www.TheHendonMob.com) shows that of every time I made the final 9 in a no-limit or pot-limit tournament, holdem or otherwise, my record is 9 wins, 0 seconds, 3 thirds, and 16 finishes of 4th-9th. This does not include team tournaments or invitation-only tournaments. If my results were average, out of 28 times in the final 9, I would expect about 3 wins, 3 seconds, and 3 thirds. My record in limit tournaments is not as strong, with 5 wins, 3 seconds, 2 thirds, and 8 finishes of 4th-9th. I credit most of this to my relative strength at heads-up and short-handed play.

to set me up. But after a while, it became clear that this tell was real, and not an acting job. As such, it became rudimentary to beat this opponent. All I had to do was bet every time he shook his head "no", and take the pot. And since you will miss the flop about 2 out of 3 times, this meant I could grind him down with almost 100% certainty.

Against this opponent, why would I want to risk all my chips preflop, or on the flop, even if I knew I was a huge favorite? Since I was almost 100% certain to win by grinding him down slowly, why risk a large pot, even if I knew I was a 90% favorite to win? The only hand where I was ready to play a big pot was the time he showed his tiny "yes" nod, the flop was K-7-3 rainbow, and I held K-K.

Of course, you will likely never see an opponent who is this obvious, and this easy to grind down. But you will find opponents who are not familiar with heads-up play, and who play too tight for this format. Even if you are raising your button almost 100% of the time preflop, they might still be folding 30% of the time, even 50% of the time, or more. Then, when they do play, if they tend to just call preflop, and often check-and-fold when they miss the flop, you have found the perfect heads-up opponent. While nowhere near 100%, this is still a player you can grind down with a high degree of certainty. And as such, you should usually avoid building large pots preflop, and avoid playing large pots anytime you do not believe you are a huge favorite to win.

But most players who choose to enter a heads-up tournament are not of this sort. Most will be much more aggressive than average, and understand how to loosen up and correctly play more hands. If anything, there are some players who are rather bad in most tournaments, because they play way too many hands, and are overly aggressive. But when they enter a heads-up event, suddenly this weakness becomes a great strength, and they are often quite successful in these tournaments.

As we discussed in Chapter 4, there is your basic strategy, or starting strategy, or GTO strategy, whichever you prefer to call it, and then there is the strategy you adopt to take advantage of the opponents you are facing. At a full table, you should be somewhat hesitant to diverge from your basic strategy, as doing so opens you up to being taken advantage of by good opponents. Even if there are a few terrible players in your game, if you adjust to take advantage of them, the good players at the table can now adjust to this, and take advantage of you. However, once the hand gets down to just you and one or two opponents, then you will often start making the adjustments you deem correct, given the nature of these opponents.

But in a heads-up game, you obviously are not concerned with adjusting to one opponent only to get blind-sided by another. As you learn more about the given player, you absolutely should be adjusting. This can lead to you making plays that are extremely different than your basic strategy plays. Therefore, keep in mind that any advice I give you in this chapter is only about basic strategy for your heads-up game. You should feel free, even obligated, to make massive strategy changes in your real life matches.

One of the most common mistakes I see in heads-up play is the big blind defending a preflop raise a bit too loosely. Since the small blind has the button, and will act last on all future betting rounds, you should have a hand with some value before defending against this raise. Calling the raise with hands like J-4, 9-2, 8-3, and the like is probably going to be a mistake. These hands seldom flop top pair, they always have kicker problems, and cannot flop straight draws (that is, straight draws requiring the use of both cards). As it is, you miss the flop about 2 times out of 3 with any hand. With these hands, even when you hit the flop, you will usually have to play defensively, as your opponent is likely to have you beat anytime they are willing to put many chips into the pot.

While a hand like 7-5 may not seem that much better, or any better, than a hand like 10-6, the 7-5 can flop many more possibilities than pure junk like 10-6. I often refer to hands like 7-5 as "playable junk". If suited, these hands are even better. Just how weak of a hand you should play when defending your big blind depends almost entirely upon your opponent, and how often they are raising their button. If your opponent is only raising with really strong hands, say 15% of the time or less, then you can just fold most hands, and especially hands that are likely to be dominated. Against an opponent this tight, I'd rather call with 7-5 than A-7, as flopping one pair with A-7 could easily cost me a lot, as my opponent will often have me outkicked or be holding an overpair. If I flop one pair while holding playable junk, against this opponent, I will know there is a good chance I'm behind, and am unlikely to lose too many chips. If the opponent is rarely attacking, let them win most of the times they do. You're going to make your money off this opponent elsewhere.

What about an opponent who is raising a lot more often preflop? My personal starting point is to raise my button about 85% of the time, maybe a bit more, and then adjust as I learn my opponent. You will find some players who raise 100% of their buttons. How often do you defend against these players who are never letting you see free flops, and rarely folding preflop? Obviously here you must be much looser when choosing hands to play, or they will simply run you over, grind you down, and guarantee themselves a slow but sure victory. Therefore, you must fight back a lot more than against the tight and/or passive opponent. This is where I see a lot of mistakes from players who are inexperienced at heads-up play. Some decide that if the other guy is raising 100%, then they should defend with 100%. But this is a big mistake. The opponent has position on you, and with this, they are going to be able to outplay you more often than you can outplay them. They can bet when you check because you are weak. They can check behind when you were intending to check-raise, and instead give themselves a free card. Of course, they will not always get these decisions right, but with position, they will get it right more often than you will from out of position.

Primarily for this reason, even when they are raising 100%, you need to fold your worst hands. I am recommending you fold about 15-30% of the time, depending upon how well the specific opponent plays postflop. The better they play, the more you should just fold preflop. Only if they play very poorly postflop, and are easy to read, should you even start to approach defending 100% of the time. If they play really well postflop, you might be correct to fold as much as 40% of your hands to their first raise.

When you defend, should you call and see the flop, or should you 3-bet? While determining the answer to this question depends mostly upon the opponent, the depth of your stack is also a huge factor. If stacks are shallow, and your 3-bet is going to be all-in, then you 3-bet whenever you feel there is a large enough chance the opponent will fold, or when your cards are strong enough that you don't mind getting called. If the stack sizes are such that if you 3-bet, the opponent is likely to either fold or 4-bet all-in, the answer is actually somewhat similar. In that case, you only 3-bet when you feel there is a large enough chance the opponent will fold, or when your cards are strong enough that you don't mind calling if they go all-in.

This is another spot where I see lots of mistakes. The loose, aggressive opponent raises the button, and is doing so frequently. Our hero looks down at a hand like A-6, knows they are likely ahead of the villain's range, and decides to 3-bet; but then elects to fold (often after a long period of agonizing) when the villain 4-bets all-in. The mistake here wasn't the 3-bet, or the fold, but the fact that our hero didn't know what they were going to do in response to the shove, BEFORE they made this 3-bet. If our hero thought the villain would often fold to the 3-bet, and would only shove with hands stronger than A-6, then 3-betting and folding is fine. However, if these facts are true, then why not just call with a hand like A-6, and 3-bet with weaker hands? Essentially this play has turned the A-6 into a bluff, but why turn a hand that is likely to be ahead into a bluff?

Against this opponent, my basic strategy when defending my big blind is to 3-bet-call (or 3-bet-5-bet) with my stronger hands, fold my weakest hands, 3-bet-fold some of my weaker hands, and just call with my moderately strong and playable junk hands. The exact ratio of each group would depend upon how many blinds are in the effective stack.

Let's explore this more. My standard button raise is 2xBB, and this is true of many good heads-up players. There is a trend towards larger preflop raises again, but for our analysis, let's use a villain whose standard raise is also 2xBB. Against this size of raise, my standard 3-bet sizing is going to be 5xBB. If the effective stack is only 20-25xBB, then I really don't expect to see the villain ever call my 3-bet. I expect almost 100% of the time for them to fold or 4-bet shove. In this case, I am going to call their opening raise with my moderately strong and playable junk hands, and just see a flop. With my strongest hands, all of those where I expect to be a favorite if I call a 4-bet shove, I am going to 3-bet and call. With all other hands, I am going to fold if I think villain is 4-bet shoving more than 3 out of 7 times when I 3-bet.

Why 3 out of 7? When I 3-bet to 5xBB, I am putting in 4xBB more in order to win the 3xBB that is out there. I posted a big blind, and villain raised to 2xBB. For my 3-bet to 5xBB, I risked 4 more big blinds to win the 3 out there. If villain shoves, and I fold, I lose those extra 4xBB; whereas when villain folds, I win the 3xBB out there. If they shove 3 times out of 7, then the 3 times they shove, I lose 4 blinds, and the other 4 times they fold, I win 3 blinds, and thus break even. If they shove more than 3 times out of 7 when I 3-bet, then I am losing money by bluffing with these hands. Remember, I'm only talking about hands that are so weak that I will fold them if villain shoves.

What about those stronger hands? When should I call and see the flop, and

38

when should I 3-bet (intending to call if they shove)? It's harder to just do some simple math and answer that question. A lot depends upon how well I believe my opponent will play postflop. The easier they are to read, and the more often I believe I can outplay them, the more often I should just call and see a flop. The tougher they are to read, and the less often they are going to be making mistakes postflop, the more often I should 3-bet hands I'm not going to fold. You will also find opponents who are much too tight when responding to 3-bets preflop, even some of those who raise their button every, or almost every, time. Against this opponent you are 3-betting a lot more often, and only calling their original raise with very strong hands that you want to trap with, or hands with which you are going to try to hit a great flop, and usually give up on when you miss.

How loose and aggressive should you be when you are the button? If your opponent is letting you run them over (i.e., they are folding their big blind frequently), then you should raise pretty much 100% of the time. The only reason to ever fold against this opponent is that you don't want them to "wake up", realize they need to defend more, and start doing so. I often fold a bit more often at the beginning of the match, just to set the image that I fold at least some hands on my button, so my opponent will assume I am never playing garbage hands. Later on, if they are not defending frequently, I may start raising almost 100% of the time. My starting point is to open-raise about 85% of the time, and fold the other 15%. I will adjust depending upon the opponent and the stack sizes. But I will only rarely open-call the button, and I will never do so unless something about the opponent causes me to believe it is the correct play (i.e., I will never do it as a GTO strategy, only as a GTE strategy).

Since I always raise if I play, clearly postflop play will tend to fall into three categories. First, if the opponent folds, there is no postflop play, I win now. Second, if the opponent calls and we see a flop. And third, if the opponent 3-bets preflop.

On the flop, if I raised the button and the opponent just called, I will almost always C-bet if they check to me. There are just so many advantages to always C-betting that the downside isn't enough to get me to ever check, unless my current opponent has given me a GTE reason to do so. As we know, I'm going to have missed the flop about 2 out of 3 times, and want my opponent to fold, which they can only do if I bet. And since they also missed the flop about 2 out of 3 times, folding will often be a valid option for them.

Most importantly, I want to be consistent, and difficult to read. If I always C-bet, then the opponent cannot use my action to narrow my range, I am still at the same 85% of hands. No matter what the flop, the opponent won't know if I hit or missed. If they hit, they probably shouldn't fold, even if it's bottom pair. But all those times they miss, they'll just be guessing as to whether or not this is a good time to bluff. When they don't fold to the C-bet, now we're getting into a situation that is just too multi-variable for this book. Literally, an entire book could be written just about this situation. Now it's time to play poker, and decide when you are ahead, when you are beat, when you will get called, and when another bet will get them to fold.

What about when my opponent 3-bets preflop? Pay very close attention to stack sizes here, as that is going to be the primary factor in your basic strategy. If the 3-bet is all-in, you just do the math. What pot odds are you getting, what range of hands do you put them on, and how often will you win against that range? After this analysis, simply call or fold as you deem best. If the 3-bet is not all-in, but any reasonable 4-bet by you would be, then the stacks are not deep enough for you to correctly call trying to hit the flop, and you need to fold or 4-bet shove*. Again, it is time for math. If you shove, how much will you win when they fold, and how much are you risking? How often do you expect them to call, and with what range of hands? How well does your hand match up against that range? After estimating these answers, you use them to do the math, and decide if shoving is more profitable than folding.

Often, if you are facing an aggressive opponent, you will find yourself in a spot on the button where if you raise, you expect to often get 3-bet, your hand is not strong enough, and you would fold to this 3-bet. The correct response to this situation is to open-fold your button. But this is where I see inexperienced players start to call on their button instead. They hope the aggressive player will check and let them see a flop, and even if they get raised, they feel they can afford to call with this hand for the price of a single raise (though not for the price of a reraise).

The problem is, most of the time you miss the flop, the aggressive opponent C-bets, and you fold. Or, you finally decide you have had enough of this aggression, and you raise all-in, even though you missed the flop. It might work

---

* Given these stack sizes, if you were to just call, this might be a situation where the opponent is correctly using the go-and-go play, see Chapter 25.

out, the opponent might fold, but if they hit this flop, they will call, and now you are way behind, maybe even drawing dead. I've seen this happen over and over again. The solution to beating an aggressive opponent is not calling more often, until you snap and make an emotional shove. The solution is hitting back with aggression of your own, at the times of your choosing, when you have determined it to be the smart move.

Heads-up play is fun, especially when you are the last two players in a regular tournament. Instead of seeing action between the two or three best starting hands dealt to a table full of players, we see two almost random hands struggle to win the pot. This format places a premium on flexibility, adaptability, and observation. You must get to know this player as intimately as possible in order to give yourself the greatest chance to win. Start with a strong GTO strategy, but be ready to quickly make large adjustments as you proceed.

LIMIT AND POT–LIMIT TOURNAMENTS

In today's poker world, most events are contested as no limit holdem. However, there are still plenty of events that play other games, including limit holdem and pot limit holdem, as well as stud games, draw games, and Omaha games, any of which may be played with limit, pot limit, or no limit betting. Much of the discussion in this book about no limit holdem is readily transferable to other forms of poker when played with no limit betting. However, once you move to pot limit betting, and especially to limit betting, there are a lot of adjustments that need to be made.

One of the most important strategic changes that players have made in their no limit tournament strategy since the beginning of the poker boom was discussed in Chapter 12, stack size strategy. Before the poker boom, players did pay attention to stack sizes, but they frequently did not make proper use of that information. Now, we understand that stack size has almost as much impact on proper strategy as the cards you are dealt. While almost every decision depends a lot upon the cards, there are times when the stack sizes, either yours or your opponents, matter even more. And the stack sizes are always critical in guiding you to the best decision.

Once you move to a game with pot limit betting, much of these strategy considerations either go away or are significantly diminished. For example, I advise that if your stack is about 10xBB or less, you should almost always fold or shove as your first decision. But in a pot limit game, you are limited to betting the pot, and can only open-shove when you have 3.5xBB or less. And if you have 3.5xBB or less, you usually expect to get called. That is why in a no limit game, if I see a player shove for this small of an amount, I know that they either folded hands earlier that they should have shoved (when they still had enough chips to get everyone else to fold), or they just lost a big pot that left them in this situation.

How do you properly address this concern in a pot limit game, when if your stack is large enough to get people to fold, you have too many chips to immediately raise all-in, but if you are so short-stacked that you can go all-in, you don't really expect them all to fold? Even though you cannot go all-in when you are short, you can, in effect, threaten your opponent with your entire stack. If you have a total stack of 8xBB, and raise the maximum to 3.5xBB, your opponents cannot intelligently call unless they are willing to risk the 8xBB of your entire stack. If they have a strong enough hand to call your 3.5xBB raise here, then it should be strong enough to call when you bet your last 4.5xBB on the next round. Therefore, raising the pot when your total stack is about 8xBB or less is effectively the same as moving all-in, as nobody should (intelligently) call unless they intend to call again when you bet the rest of your chips. If they are intending to fold some of the time on the next round, then they are probably making a big mistake by calling now.

Thus, looking at this from your perspective, when you are this short-stacked, you should never (as a basic strategy decision) make a raise when your stack is this short unless you fully intend to put in the rest of your stack regardless of what comes on the flop. That is, whether you are reraised now, or bet into on the next round, you intend to never fold. It would require a very specific opponent with specific tendencies and/or tells for you to correctly put in so much of your stack, and then fold to save the rest.

The really difficult part is when your stack is in the range of 10-20xBB. Here, you might make the first raise, but you have so many chips left that you could often be correct to fold on a later betting round. Imagine you have been dealt a premium hand like K-K, raise to 3xBB with 10xBB left behind, get called, and the flop comes with an Ace? Now what? If your opponent checks, any reasonable bet you could make would essentially commit you to the pot. But if you check, and the opponent now bets on the next round, are they betting because they flopped a pair of Aces, or because you showed weakness by checking the flop? Maybe they're betting what they think is the best hand (e.g., they hold J-10 on the board of A-J-6-4), but are mistaken. As such, even if you are good at reading tells, and sense they are not bluffing, there is still a chance you have the best hand. The point is, this is a very awkward stack size, and you can find yourself in a lot of very tough spots, even if you make good decisions and do not put yourself into such situations unnecessarily. There is not much you can do about this, other than being fortunate enough to not run into these tough spots when it matters the most. You simply have to use your judgment to make the best decision you can in these situations.

Once the effective stack is more than 20xBB, and especially once it is more than 30xBB, you will be less concerned about stack sizes with respect to first round betting decisions, as it is going to take at least a 4-bet before you are all-in. Stack sizes are still a critical component in making the best decisions, but you are now much less likely to run into the horribly difficult spots that you will find when the effective stack size is 10-15xBB.

In limit poker, the effect of stack size drops drastically in importance. In most games, you can now call all the way to showdown by investing about 7-8xBB in the pot. This means that anytime you have about this much or more, being all-in is not really a big concern (though being crippled might be). As such, you will often not let stack sizes alter your normal strategy until you get down to such amounts, less than 10xBB at least. In a no limit game, you might choose to play some hands when you have 20xBB that you would fold if you had 30xBB, and vice versa. But at these stack sizes in a limit game, you should rarely make such differentiations. You still need to pay attention to stack sizes, but really only if you or your opponents are down to about 10xBB or less.

The most important difference in limit games is the fact that once you get past the early stages, almost everybody is somewhat short-stacked. In a no-limit WSOP event, the average stack will seldom get below 40xBB. However, in a limit event, even when the structure requires several days of play, it is quite common for the average stack to drop to 20xBB or less by the time half the field is gone. In events that only last one day, it is not uncommon for the average stack to drop below 15xBB, or even below 10xBB, for the last few tables. If the players are even moderately aggressive, there is probably going to be a bet on most streets, meaning the average pot will be about 10-20xBB in total. This means that just playing a standard pot, no bad beats or cold-decks involved, can cost you a huge portion of your stack. In the simplest terms, your variance is going to be much higher in limit games, whether you play tight and solid, or a loose aggressive style.

How do you deal with this extra variance, and still come out a winning player? The first thing to do is understand and accept the variance. Be emotionally prepared for the huge swings you will experience in these tournaments. Even though in no limit you can go from chip leader to broke in just a couple of hands, it is much more common to see a player quickly go from chip leader to broke in a limit event, or for a player to go from short stack to chip leader. When the average stack is only 20xBB or so, and players are winning 5-10xBB in ordinary pots, it doesn't take long to move your stack significantly. In no-limit events, the average stack in late stages will probably still be at least 30-50xBB, so huge moves up and down the leaderboard just don't happen as frequently. When players get to 10xBB or less in a no limit game, most of them shove or fold, and when they shove, their opponents often fold. In contrast, in a limit game, they can only raise one more blind, and often get called. Even though it is now popular to min-raise preflop in NLH tournaments, players are less likely to call those raises with weak or marginal hands, because they are not just thinking of the 2xBB they can lose now, but the fact that the rest of their stack is at risk on later rounds. In a limit game, the players know they can only lose so many blinds if they choose to call down an opponent, which makes them more likely to do so.

Compare two identical hands with one dealt in a limit game, and the other in a no limit game. Imagine it folds to the button, who raises the minimum pre-flop, and you are in the big blind with 7-6s. In both games, you probably defend your blind with a call. The flop comes J-9-6 rainbow, none of your suit. If you check, the button is likely to bet. In the no limit game, they are probably going to bet 2-3xBB. If you call, you know they might bet again on the turn and/or the river. If they do bet again, the next bet is probably going to be 5-7xBB, and if they bet a third time, it is likely to be about 10-15xBB. This means calling down is going to cost you something like 25xBB, such that you are risking

39

about 25 to win about 30. In contrast, if you call the flop bet in a limit game, and then call down all the way, it will cost you 1 + 2 + 2, or 5 to win 9.5. In other words, you are getting almost 2:1 odds to call down in limit, and only about 6:5 odds to call down in no limit. It is obviously more likely to be correct to call down in the limit game, everything else being equal.

The math shows how much harder it is to bluff in limit, and why so many decisions are more automatic. Unless you have an opponent who is rarely going to bet all three rounds postflop without being able to beat your medium-strength hand, it is almost mandatory that you not fold. But check-folding the same flop (or a later street) in a no limit game will be correct against many types of opponents. Because so many decisions are more automatic in limit, the expert player tends to have a much smaller edge. And since players tend to be priced in to the river more often in a limit game, the result is a lot more variance, despite the fixed bet sizes.

What does this mean for you as a player, and the strategies you choose to utilize? Primarily, it means you are going to experience more swings, and need to be emotionally prepared. When you expect something to happen, it typically will have a reduced emotional impact, as compared to unexpected happenings. When you're doing great in a limit event, have a large stack, and are playing well, know that it can turn against you fast, and you need to be prepared to deal with such situations.

Beyond emotional or psychological issues, you need a much different general strategy for limit games as well. Be prepared to do a LOT less bluffing. It is usually going to require a perfect situation for bluffing to be the correct choice. In a no-limit game, even if your opponent feels you are likely to be bluffing, they can still fold a weak-to-moderate hand, since not folding risks so many chips. Since they can call you down cheaply in a limit game, they are going to be harder to bluff. Likewise, you need to do a lot less folding yourself. If your hand has some showdown value, then folding is often going to be wrong, especially in a heads-up pot.

Do not take this advice as a license to become a calling station. In a multiway pot, weak-to-moderate hands are still just that, and you're not getting the correct pot odds and implied odds to try to hit a longshot. Even though this is an over-generalization, I endorse the idea of playing very tight when the pot is small (that is, preflop and to some extent on the flop), but playing very loose once the pot gets big. When somebody raises preflop, I become very tight in all positions (except defending my big blind), whereas I almost never make a big laydown after I get to the turn or river.

Which leads us to the next issue, implied odds. In no limit, you can sometimes call with hands that are drawing pretty thin (e.g., gutshot straight draws) if you are confident enough that you will get paid off when you make your draw. In a limit game, you cannot do this, as it is simply too unlikely that you will get enough chips in the pot after you hit your longshot draw to make up for the chips that went in before you made it. Effectively, implied odds are much less important in limit games, and they are really only useful in close decisions where just a little bit one way or the other can change which decision is best.

Semi-bluffing is another area where strategies change a lot from no limit to limit. When you semi-bluff in no limit, it is usually a mistake unless there is some reasonable chance the opponent will fold now. That is, if you knew the opponent was unlikely to fold, then you shouldn't have tried to semi-bluff. In a limit game, you will often run into spots where you are semi-bluffing for value, so to speak. Since there tend to be more multiway pots in a limit game, if your draw is strong enough, you will often be correct to raise even though you expect few or even none of the opponents to fold.

An example of this is you seeing the flop in a 4-way pot, in last position, with A♠-Q♠, and the flop is J♠-7♠-4♥. If the first player bets and the other two call, raising here for value would often be correct. Even though you might expect all three to call, you have anywhere from 8-15 outs to make the best hand, meaning you will win about 30-50% of the time, and are only putting 25% of the chips into the pot. Then, if you miss the turn, you can choose to continue the semi-bluff, or take a free card if they all check. And if you instead cause one or two of the opponents to fold, that's fine, as they might be folding hands that are taking away some of your outs (e.g., A♥-7♥, because if an Ace comes you are now beating the remaining player who had paired the jack, and not losing to the player with A-7 who would have made two pair).

In these situations, semi-bluffing is not really even the correct term anymore, as you are often not bluffing at all, in the sense that you are realistically hoping everybody will fold, but merely putting more chips in the pot when you have more than your fair share of the equity.

The best way to improve your tournament play in limit and pot-limit events will be to learn how to better play the underlying game, and then review the portions of this book that teach you how to adjust for tournament situations. A great limit holdem cash game player is going to automatically be a winning limit holdem tournament player. But they will be even better if they also understand concepts like ICM, and uses them to fine-tune their limit holdem tournament game.

BIG BLIND ANTE

The hottest trend in tournament poker, as I write this book, is the big blind ante (BBA). However, by the time this book is published, most tournaments will probably be using the BBA format. I even suspect that the BBA will become the format for almost all NLH tournaments by 2020. In a traditional NLH tournament, in any level where there are antes, each player must post an ante every hand. For example, if it is the 400/800/100 level, then the blinds are 400 and 800, and each player also antes 100. In the BBA format, when blinds are at 400/800, only the player who has posted the big blind also posts an ante. Most often, this ante is equal to the big blind. Thus, the player in the big blind posts an ante of 800, plus the big blind of 800. In both formats, the ante is dead money, and does not count towards any bets that this player makes preflop.

The genesis of the BBA was the idea that having one player post the ante for everybody would speed up play, by eliminating the need for the dealer to collect an ante from each player individually. And certainly, this is true. However, despite popular belief, this system does not result in a huge increase in the number of hands dealt, at least it does not do so because of the time saved collecting antes. It does result in an increase of up to 5% more hands due to time savings, which is not insignificant. The more interesting question is whether the structure itself is having a big impact on how people play, and thus results in significant changes for this reason.

Now that you are playing in a BBA tournament, how do you adjust? The simple answer is that if you do not adjust at all, you will be playing pretty much as well as you did in a traditional ante tournament. The fact that all the ante came from one player creates no inherent change in strategy. The main difference is that if you are at a full table, the pot will be slightly smaller than before, at least in most cases. At a 10-handed table, our 400/800 level has T2000 of dead money before the cards are dealt in the BBA structure; whereas it has T2200 of dead money in the traditional ante structure. With 10% less available to be won, you would theoretically play slightly tighter, defend your blinds slightly less often, and make raises that are slightly smaller than before. But these adjustments are very small, and if you open with the same range as before, or raise the same amount as before, it is not a difference that matters much. As such, you can mostly ignore this change in a typical hand that doesn't involve short-stack concerns or some of the other things we will discuss below.

One of the first changes you will likely notice in a BBA tournament is the lack of T25 chips. While most traditional ante tournaments that start with T10-30K would include some T25 chips, most of the BBA tournaments start with T100 as the smallest chip. If a traditional ante tournament started at the T50,T100 level, the same event might start at T100,T100 in the BBA structure. The next level might have been either T75,T150 or T100,T200 in the traditional ante structure, but it will likely be T100,T200 or T100,T100 with a T100 ante in the BBA structure. Whichever blinds are chosen for early levels in the BBA structure, you lose the ability to make preflop raises that are 2.5xBB or the like. Whereas before you might have open-raised the T100 big blind to T250, now you can only choose between T200 or T300 for that raise. I recommend the larger raise (3xBB), rather than the min-raise, at these early levels. As you go deeper in the tournament, this lack of granularity tends to go away. But when you're used to making it 2.5xBB, it is slightly annoying to lose that option. However, in the big picture, it is no big deal.

The real change to your strategy, the place you must make the biggest adjustment, is when you become very short-stacked. If you are UTG in a traditional ante tournament, with 8xBB, and are dealt a weak hand, it is correct to just fold. Now, if you find a good hand in the big blind the next hand, you still have almost 8xBB (maybe 7.9xBB after posting your individual ante), and if you win you will more than double up, as you will win 7.9xBB from the player you beat, plus at least all of the antes, and often the small blind. Thus, you will probably have a stack of about 17.5xBB after this win. In the BBA tournament, if you fold this hand UTG, you will post 1xBB for the table ante the next hand, and then if you go all-in and from the big blind, you can only win 7xBB from the player you beat, plus your ante back, plus maybe the small blind. This is a new stack of about 15.5xBB after you win. Since the result, when you choose to play your big blind, is so much less (about 10-13% less), this means that you should be going all-in the previous hand, when UTG, with a much wider range in the BBA tournament.

Frequently, when you become very short-stacked, you end up with nothing but losing options. For example, what if you have 1xBB in a no ante tournament, and you are dealt Q9o while positioned UTG? This is an above average hand, but going all-in here is a losing play, as you will likely get called by one or more better hands. But, if you fold, you will be all-in the next hand with two random cards, and this is also a losing situation. The question therefore is not which choice wins you the most, as there is no such option. The question is, of these two choices, which one will, on average, lose the least? Similarly, when you are UTG with 8xBB in the BBA tournament, there are now more hands where going all-in is the least bad choice, as compared to the same 8xBB stack UTG in a traditional ante tournament.

What if you fold both blinds? In the traditional ante tournament, you will be down to about 6.3xBB on the button. In the BBA tournament, you will be down to about 5.5xBB. Again, this shows why it is going to be correct to go all-in when UTG with a wider range of hands in the BBA tournament. And if all these reasons indicate you are correct to shove all-in with some weaker hands in the BBA tournament, then your opponents (if they are aware of this) will correctly call your all-in with a wider range of hands as well.

How big of an adjustment do you need to make when short-stacked in the BBA tournament? It is hard to say exactly, as it will also depend upon the depth of the other stacks at your table, and not just how short-stacked you are at the time. It will also depend upon how much less likely your opponents are to call your all-in now, when you can shove for 8xBB, compared to later, when

40

you have paid the blinds and ante, and can only shove for about 5.5xBB. If you believe that you have a lot more fold equity now with 8xBB, and a lot less fold equity with 5.5xBB (as will often be the case), then you should widen your range more while you still have 8xBB. If this is a fast-paced tournament, and the average stack for all players is only something like 10-15xBB, then you can probably fold more hands UTG with 8xBB, as you are likely to still have a decent amount of fold equity later with 5.5xBB.

Of course, how much you should widen your range with which to shove will vary with your exact stack size as well. We have been discussing 8xBB, since that is a number that probably leads to some of the greatest changes in strategy. But if you are in a traditional ante tourney, in a spot where you would shove 10% of your hands given your current stack size (whatever size that is), you are probably correct to shove with more than 10% of your hands, everything else being the same, in a BBA tournament. Similarly, if your current strategy would have you shoving with 25% of hands in a given spot, you are probably correct to shove more than 25% of hands in the BBA tournament.

So, how much more? As a rough estimate, about 10% more. That is, if you are in a spot where you would shove 10% of your hands in a traditional ante tournament, you should probably shove about 11% of your hands in the BBA tournament. If 20%, now move up to about 22%, and so on.

If you get extremely short, such as having only about 6xBB or less, then you absolutely prefer to shove all-in at some point before posting the ante and big blind, even if that means going all-in when UTG with the very worst hands. About the only exceptions here will occur if you are on the bubble, or very close to the bubble, and think you can fold your way into the money. Then, it will likely be correct to still fold all your weak hands, crawl into the money, and then hope to get lucky and rebuild your crippled stack.

There is another interesting situation that arises in BBA tournaments. What about when you get critically short-stacked? That is, when you have less than 1xBB? I witnessed a hand in one of my first BBA tournaments where two players with very large stacks ended up getting all-in on the river, and the losing player was left with T100 at the T800,T1600 level. The next hand, this player went all-in blind from UTG. Somebody else raised, and all the other players folded. This player won the pot, getting T100 from the raiser, another T100 from each of the blinds, and getting back his own T100. Plus, he won

40

all of the T1600 ante. Thus, he went from T100 to T2000 in a single hand at a 9-handed table! The point is, when you get this short, you absolutely want to go all-in before being in the blind/ante position. If he had folded UTG, the next hand he would have posted his T100 as the blind, and there would have been no ante. In that spot, he could never win T2000. At best, if nobody folded preflop, he could have won T900. The value of that dead money from the ante will outweigh the weakness of your two cards, no matter how bad they are.

This also leads to a very interesting strategy. If you are in a spot where you were going to bet all your chips, you might consider betting almost all your chips instead. In our story above, the hero just happened to have his opponent covered by T100. But what if his opponent had more chips than him? If it was the hero betting the river, he should consider not betting all-in, but instead betting all but the single T100 chip instead. That way, not only does he have some tiny chance to make a comeback, but that comeback will get a huge jump-start those times he wins the next hand he plays. And with no ante each hand, if you are not going to be UTG the very next hand, you can be selective, wait for the best hand you are likely to find before you reach the big blind position, and go all-in at that time.

PLAYING THE MAIN EVENT

More than any other tournament, maybe even more than every other tournament combined, I get asked for advice on playing the Main Event of the WSOP. And unless there just isn't time, I'm always happy to chat with fans, take pictures with them, autograph stuff, and answer such questions. In this case, there is the short and easy answer, and the detailed answer. For the short answer, it's just another tournament, so play your regular game, and hope you can run good at this, the perfect time!

But of course, that is not what people want to hear, nor is it a complete answer. Because it is the Main Event, many of your opponents are going to play very differently than they would in any other event, and so you will want to adjust to their changes, and thereby take maximum advantage of their mistakes. That is, there are some GTE changes you can make in this tournament before you even get to know the players at your table, as there are some changes you will probably see in this tournament, no matter which table you draw.

Most of the time, at the start, almost all of your opponents are going to be playing their A-game. Even if they are a pro or a skilled amateur, and compete in dozens, even hundreds of events every year, this is still the big one, the one that matters the most. It is tough enough when you get eliminated from the Main Event; it's even worse when you do it to yourself with bad play. Therefore, most of your opponents start off intending to play better than normal, whatever that means to them. They might know they play too many hands, and so will tighten up. They might think they are usually too passive, and come out betting and raising aggressively.

Whatever you see from a player at the start, do not let that image get too fixed in your mind. In most cases, the person who comes in with good intentions to play their best will revert back to their usual style of play before too long. It might just be an orbit or two, or it might take a few hours, but eventually they are going to be playing very much like they do the rest of the year. So be prepared to adjust your image of each player, possibly a lot, as the day progresses.

Another common pattern to see in the Main Event is for some players to tighten up drastically as you approach the end of day 1. For many people, it is extremely important to make day 2. In fact, some players find so much satisfaction in making day 2, they will do almost anything to achieve that goal.

In 2004, I had won my seat online on PokerStars, and had to go to their suite at Binion's to sign some paperwork and get my day 1 seat assignment. It was there that I met Terrence Chan in person for the first time. We knew each other online, and Terrence was one of the people who had a piece of all my action from the start of 2004 through the Main Event. As we chatted, he told me about two players who had been there earlier. They had gotten a structure sheet from Terrence, and asked him about how many hands per hour should they expect to see the next day. Doing some math, they estimated that by simply folding every hand, they would lose about 80% of their stack. And they decided to do just that, as they really wanted to tell their friends back home that they made day 2.*

---

* Recently, with about three hours to go in day 1b of the 2017 Main Event, the floorman moved a stack to an empty seat at my table. Normally, the assumption is that stack/player came from a table that broke, but the player was away from the table when it was time to move. I asked the floorman who it was, just so we would know who it should be, when somebody finally showed up. He said the name, but told us not to worry, as apparently the guy had started the day and played a while, but had not come back since the second break, 4.5 hours ago. Even after missing out on 3 hours of play (1.5 hours of the time was the dinner break), this stack still had over 20% more chips than a starting stack. The leading theory at the table was the player had won a big pot (or pots) early on, and chose to blind out the rest of the day, to make sure not to bust before day 2!

To me, this is totally insane. You aren't even going to make the money until at least day 3. With this plan, they are pissing away $8,000 in equity, just so they can say they made it to day 2. I'm sorry, but it's not even that impressive to make day 2, as about 70% of the field will do so. And if I find out this is how you made day 2, all I'm going to do is laugh, or cry, at your stupidity.

While you are unlikely to see anything this extreme, you will be very likely to have some players at your table who tighten up considerably as the end of day 1 approaches. Your job is to figure out who it is, and steal chips from them accordingly. Just be careful, because if such a player does voluntarily put chips into the pot, they are almost always going to have a premium starting hand. And you also need to be alert for other players who are also trying to take advantage of this, and who will likely notice what you are doing. If they think you are raising primarily because one of these tight players is in the big blind, they might 3-bet light, knowing your opening raise is often light itself. Be prepared to either give up right away when you are stealing, or be prepared to 4-bet light yourself, if that looks like the best play.

Where you are truly going to see some of the tightest play you have ever witnessed is when you get close to the bubble. Very few tournaments have such a big bubble, both in terms of the dollar amounts on the line, and the size of the field. In recent years, the WSOP has been paying 15% of the field, so about 1,000 players will make the money. The min-cash has been $15,000 lately, which is, to most players in the field, more than first prize in the tournaments they typically play. Even if you can ignore the importance of earning $15,000, there will be no pay jumps this large again until you are well within the final 100 players, which is several days away. So not only does the ICM math dictate large strategy changes, the psychological impact of $15,000 and getting to say "I cashed in the world championship" is going to lead to some extreme play.

In theory, you should play this bubble the same as any other. If your stack is extremely short, then folding your way into the money is often the correct strategy. And if your stack is very large, especially if it is a top stack at your table, you probably should be playing quite loose and aggressive to steal from the short- and medium-stacks. Of course, the best way to approach the bubble is to be fully aware of what's happening at your table. If your table is going to let you run them over, you do it. If they are not going to let you, but instead will fight back, then don't try to run them over. As always, you can only bully

41

players that let themselves be bullied. If you try to bully a player who won't let you, then you will just be spewing chips, and needing to get lucky to win.

Now, it is perfectly acceptable for you to play extra tight on this bubble, whether it is the money, the prestige of cashing in this event, whatever is driving your decision. Even if you have a very large stack, the largest at your table, you might prefer to just take no chances now that you are so close. This is fine. The only big mistake you can make is to try to have it both ways. By that, I mean do not try to steal pots, invest a big chunk of your stack doing so, and then "wimp out" and fold what you believe is the best hand, just to avoid further risk.

I have seen this many times. A player has a good stack, average or better, and understands that this is a good time to play aggressive and steal some pots. Then, they get played back at by somebody who also has a good-sized stack. It is one thing if you raise preflop, and then fold immediately to a reraise. The big mistake I see is they call the reraise, call the C-bet on the flop, and then agonize before folding their overpair to a turn bet. They invest a large portion of their stack into the pot, and then fold what they honestly believe is the best hand, because emotionally they can't stand the heat. If you're going to do this, then you should fold much earlier in the hand. The lesson is to either play su-per-tight on every street, or to ignore the risk, attack the bubble, and win a lot of chips when it works out.

One of the biggest issues when playing the Main Event is lack of sleep. As there are three day ones and two day twos, you will get some days off in the first week. But after that, you will play five or more consecutive days, from day 3 until you make the final table (at least, we sure hope you do). While these days are scheduled so there is plenty of time to get a full night's sleep, you may struggle to do so. When I won, I was so tired at the end of each day, I had no problem falling asleep. However, I found it impossible to stay asleep for a full night, and would generally awaken after 5-6 hours. After that, I just lay there for another hour or two, trying to fall back asleep, until I gave up and got out of bed. There are many ways you might choose to deal with this issue. I can't really advise you how to best deal with it, as this will vary too much from one person to another. All I can do is let you know this might be an issue, so be prepared with some options you think might be of help.

Before you start each new day, be sure to research your new table draw, and take advantage of online information. Typically, your table for the next day

41

will be posted within an hour or less after you bag your chips. www.TheHendonMob.com is a great resource, and you should research all of your opponents there. While their career results on Hendon won't tell you anything about their playing style, it is still useful to know who is more or less experienced, and what kind of track record they have. When I see an opponent with a short record of results, and none of them in big events, I can guess they are more likely to be risk averse on the bubble, and less likely to be making sophisticated plays. It is also a good idea to reach out to friends via facebook, twitter, and such, and ask if they know any of your opponents. Nothing is more useful than a thorough scouting report from a skilled friend.

Some touring pros travel alone, but many travel with friends, and many non-pros, when playing the Main Event, travel with a significant other or a friend(s). It is hugely beneficial to have a support system in place for the Main Event. Even though you usually get 90 minutes for dinner break, it is so much easier if your support person goes to a restaurant ahead of time, gets a table, and maybe even places your order. You can then go there and eat at a relaxed pace, not rushing to get done in time. Your support person can also bring you food from offsite, or have a car ready to drive you to your preferred place. If you need something throughout the day, they can get it for you, so you don't have to rush to a store to buy it on a short break, if it's even available at a store onsite. This is also somebody who is on your side, and who you can talk to on breaks or in-between hands, to help you stay calm, focused, and playing your best.

Whatever you do, do NOT let this person create more stress. If your spouse or friend is texting you about getting them comped tickets for a show across town, or arguing about where you want to eat on dinner break, or anything that is distracting you from the game, basically, tell them to "F**K OFF". You are here, competing in the most important tournament of the year, and trying to win millions of dollars. If they are not going to help you as much as they can, you need a better spouse or friend. Of course, some other time of year, when it is their big thing, you should likewise be doing all you can to support them. Even if it's something that seems silly or unimportant to you, it is a big deal to them. So, support them when it's their turn, and expect their support now, when it is yours. And if they aren't helping, get rid of them, fast. Maybe you make up with them later, but for now, good riddance.

FINAL REMARKS

Now that I've finally finished this book, more than a dozen years later than intended, I am both happy with the result, and disappointed. While I think I've been able to share a lot of great advice and insight into how to play a better game of poker, there is just so much I have had to leave out. I could take almost any chapter of this book, and expand it into a book of its own. That means there is much more to write, and hopefully I'll be much more diligent with future efforts.

I mention this as I would like to hear from all my readers. While it's great to hear about what you liked, I also want to hear about what was lacking, whether you believe more is needed, what I wrote was unclear, or there is wrong advice of some sort. The easiest way to provide feedback is through the contact page on my website, www.FossilManPoker.com. I look forward to your feedback. And thanks for reading my book!